Common Warfare

Leave your home behind, lad,
And reach your friends your hand,
And go, and luck go with you
While Ludlow tower shall stand.
—A. E. Housman, "The Recruit"

All wars are boyish, and are fought by boys.
—Herman Melville

Men love war because it allows them to look serious.
Because it is the one thing that stops women laughing at them.
—John Fowles

At ease, Attention!, A.W.O.L., C-Rations, "Dear John" letter,
Detached Service, Double-time, "Dug-out Doug," Fall in!, Firing
Range, First Sergeant, 4-F, Full-field pack, Furlough, Gigged,
Goldbrick, Guard Duty, Inspection, Khaki, "Kilroy was here,"
K.P., K-Rations, Latrine Orderly, Lights out, Mail Call, Mess
Call, Ninety-Day Wonder, ODs, Over-the-hill, Pass, PX,
Reveille, Roll Call, Section 8, Short-arm inspection, SNAFU,
S.O.P., S.O.S.
—A Soldier's Dictionary

COMMON WARFARE

Parallel Memoirs by Two
World War II GIs in the Pacific

by

Carl M. Becker *and*
Robert G. Thobaben

McFarland & Company, Inc., Publishers
Jefferson, North Carolina, and London

*To Marilou, who waited
and who has endured and loved me;
and to the memory of
my brother John, an infantryman*

—C.M.B.

———————

*To my wife, Janet Smith Thobaben,
with love;
and to the memory of
my parents, George and Edna Thobaben*

—R.G.T.

*All photographs are from the authors' personal collections except as noted in
the captions.*

British Library Cataloguing-in-Publication data are available

Library of Congress Cataloguing-in-Publication Data

Becker, Carl M.
 Common warfare : parallel memoirs by two World War II GIs in
the Pacific / by Carl M. Becker and Robert G. Thobaben
  p. cm.
 Includes bibliographical references and index.
 ISBN 0-89950-699-2 (lib. bdg. : 50# alk. paper) ∞
 1. Becker, Carl M. 2. Thobaben, Robert G. 3. World War,
1939–1945—Pacific Area. 4. World War, 1939–1945—Personal
narratives, American. 5. Soldiers—United States—Biography.
6. United States. Army—Biography. I. Thobaben, Robert G.
II. Title.
D767.9.B43 1992
940.54'8373—dc20   91-51003
                                                                    CIP

Manufactured in the United States of America

*McFarland & Company, Inc., Publishers
 Box 611, Jefferson, North Carolina 28640*

Contents

Part I.   Carl M. Becker: A Draftee

Part II.   Robert G. Thobaben: A Private

List of Illustrations

Part I. Carl M. Becker: A Draftee

Part II. Robert G. Thobaben: A Private

Preface

Looking back at their personal histories, millions of the Americans who entered the armed forces during World War II recall their service as the central event of their lives. Then and later they knew that they were caught up in a great maelstrom, a great struggle somehow affecting the destiny of their generation and many generations to come.

For those who had to meet the enemy in direct combat, the war, no matter its elemental meaning for freedom, was brutal and terrible. The infantrymen who fought in the hedgerows of Normandy, the Marines who clung to the bloody beaches of Iwo Jima, the pilots who flew a gauntlet of fire over Germany, the sailors who exchanged gunfire with the Japanese fleet—all suffered the psychological and physical wounds of battle. If any men wanted to embellish their days in uniform, to "remember with advantages" what feats they did, they had that right.

The vast majority of soldiers and sailors, though, engaged the enemy at a far remove and seldom were participants in the fighting for blood and ground. Rather, they were support troops—driving trucks laden with food and ammunition, securing a captured area, servicing the machines of war, and manning desks on the home front. Though theirs was not the blood of battle, they believed, or at least hoped, that they were instruments of success, that they had something to do with victory.

Whatever the role they played in the war, these men knew that they all shared to a lesser or greater degree in a flawed and frustrating crusade. For they could not escape the ironies, the incongruities, the absurdities inherent in the massing of men for gigantic ventures. Inevitably they developed irreverence, if not contempt, for the system that seemingly held them in the embrace of useless routine and jaded ritual. In retrospect, as the years passed and they searched for meaning in their lives, they might invest their experience in war with the sheen of nostalgia or excitement. But they might also place it in a realistic perspective, tinting it with the gentle cynicism of age and reducing it to its proper proportions.

We were two soldiers in the U.S. Army who lived at the fringe of battle nearly a half century ago and, probably like thousands of our comrades-in-arms, have abiding recollections of the days of our youth when we stood ready to drill and die for our nation. Measured by any one of several adjectives — *ordinary, typical, common, conventional, quotidian* — our interests and abilities seem to be of the millions, those of Everyman in uniform. And our memories spring out of the ordinary routines and relationships of an army of citizen-soldiers at war, not out of extraordinary exploits, not out of the habit of command assumed by men wearing stripes on sleeves or bars and stars on shoulder straps. Our recollections strike no grand chord of decision making by generals and admirals reviewing the numbers and strategic dispositions of soldiers and sailors. But we believe that there might be some worth in our setting forth the short and simple annals of the military poor, depicting along the way the quirkiness of life among ordinary men at war in the Pacific.

We come to our task having led, in a proximate way, parallel lives. We were born in 1924 in Ohio, one in Cleveland in the north-central part of the state, the other in Miamisburg in southwestern Ohio. Our families were middle-class families, really lower middle class, in occupations and outlook. We attended the public schools of our communities, graduating from high school in 1942, only a few months after the Japanese attack on Pearl Harbor. One by enlistment and the other by the draft, we entered the U.S. Army in 1943 and served long months in the Pacific. Then, with honorable discharges and veterans' benefits in hand, we attended colleges and universities in and out of Ohio. After flailing around in various kinds of employment for more than a decade, through a train of similar circumstances we became faculty members in 1964, one in political science and one in history, at a new state university in Ohio. As we sweated over our doctoral studies and harangued young men and women in the classroom, we became good friends, often sharing accounts of the "good war" that we had fought against the "Japs" (yes, we called them Japs). Now we are both retired, and we are both returning to the war by the pleasantest and safest way possible — by re-creation in words of the way it really was for two soldiers in the Pacific, and probably for millions more.

Carl M. Becker
Robert G. Thobaben

Acknowledgments

Like all men and women laboring in the vineyard of research and writing, we did not create our manuscript solely out of our own means. Indeed, ours has been an interdependent effort. Two colleagues at Wright State University gave us invaluable encouragement in the conception and execution of our venture. Charles Berry, a historian who could have easily grown weary of our accounts of "our" war and dismissed us as garrulous old soldiers, urged us to preserve our reminiscences in written word. Matt Melko, a sociologist who can discover meaning in seeming triviality, gave us wise counsel in our search for a publisher. Though our work did not require intensive research, at several points we did depend on archivists and librarians at Wright State and at governmental agencies, especially at the Naval Historical Center, for direction to pertinent sources. Several comrades-in-arms, notable Don Flamboe and Rae Lalley, provided us with clarifying detail on what our outfits did in the Pacific.

Two persons sharpened our remembrance of the military environment in which we moved decades ago. At Schofield Barracks in the Hawaiian Islands, Herbert E. Garcia, curator of the Tropic Lightning Museum, led us on a nostalgic tour that cleared away some of our misconceptions about that installation as it existed during the war. Closer to home, at Wright State University, Captain Michael L. Mundell, a member of the military science department, refreshed our recall of traditional military language.

We owe a great debt to several people who gave physical shape to our manuscript: Joanne Ballmann and Joan Mullins were dutiful, patient typists who deciphered our handwritten and poorly typed copy and translated it into a finished manuscript. Our cartographer, Philip Nolan, turned our memories of journeys in the Pacific into useful maps. Kathleen Bidne, of Media Services at Wright State University, saw to the transformation of our amateurish snapshots into usuable photographs. And Bill Rickert, associate dean of the college of liberal arts at Wright State, shepherded our requests for financial support into grants from the college facilitating production of the manuscript.

We must note, finally, the men with whom we served and the women who waited. To them we owe the shared experiences often described in our pages. In most instances, scattered as they are by time, distance, and death, we have been unable to locate these men and women, either to secure permission for use of their names or to reminisce about the old days. Thus, we have employed pseudonyms for nearly all of them. But we have not deliberately magnified or understated their behavior for the sake of a good story. Warts and all, they were like us, contemplating and acting out the fears and hopes, the despair and optimism, the boredom and exhilaration felt by millions of American soldiers and civilians. Those few persons whose real names we can record here by permission are C. Robert Good, John H. Foley, Barbara Harper Handke, Betty Shimogawa Ihara, and John J. Survill.

Though many people extended their support to us, only we can claim responsibility for factual or interpretive errors in our manuscript.

Timeline: Major U.S. Military Action in the Pacific

1941

December 7	At 8:00 A.M. (Hawaiian time), Japan launches a surprise attack on Pearl Harbor.
December 8	United States declares war on Japan. Japanese forces invade Malaya, Thailand, and the Philippines.
December 11	United States declares war on Germany and Italy.
December 25	Hong Kong falls to Japanese troops.

1942

January 2	Japanese forces occupy Manila; MacArthur retreats to Bataan.
February 15	Singapore falls to Japan.
April 9	U.S. forces on Bataan surrender.
April 18	U.S. B-25 airplanes, led by Col. James Doolittle, bomb Tokyo.
May 4–8	Battle of the Coral Sea.
May 6	General Wainwright surrenders U.S. forces to Japanese on Corregidor.
June 3–6	Battle of Midway. U.S. Navy wins *major* victory.
August 7	U.S. Marines land on Guadalcanal (six-month battle begins).
November 8	*U.S. forces land in North Africa.

1943

February 2	*Russian troops defeat Germans at Battle of Stalingrad.
February 7	Japanese troops evacuate Guadalcanal.
March 2–4	Japanese naval forces lose Battle of the Bismarck Sea.
May 11	U.S. forces land on the Aleutian island of Attu.
September 3	*Allied forces invade Italy. Italy surrenders.
November 20	U.S. Marines invade Tarawa while Army troops invade Makin in the Gilbert Islands.

*Indicates an important event in Europe

1944

February 2–7	U.S. Army and Marines capture Kwajalein and Roi-Namur in the Marshall Islands.
April 22	MacArthur leads American landings at Hollandia.
June 6	*D-Day in Europe. Allied forces land in Normandy, France.
June 15	American forces invade Saipan in the Mariana Islands.
June 19	Battle of the Philippine Sea ("The Great Marianas Turkey Shoot").
July 21, 23	Marines and infantry land on Guam and Tinian in the Mariana Islands.
August 10	American forces secure all Mariana Islands.
August 25	*Paris liberated.
September 15	American forces invade Peleliu in the Palau Islands.
October 20	U.S. forces land in Leyte in central Philippines.
October 23–26	Battle of Leyte Gulf.
December 16	*Battle of the Bulge launched by Germans.

1945

January 9	MacArthur's American forces land on Luzon.
February 19	U.S. Marines invade Iwo Jima.
April 1	American forces invade Okinawa.
April 12	FDR dies. Truman becomes president.
April 25	*American and Russian troops meet on Elbe River.
April 28–30	*Mussolini killed near Lake Como. Hitler commits suicide.
May 7–8	*Germany surrenders unconditionally: VE-Day.
June 21	U.S. victory over Japanese in Okinawa.
July 4	MacArthur announces liberation of the Philippines.
August 6	U.S. atom bomb dropped on Hiroshima, Japan.
August 8	Soviet Union declares war on Japan.
August 9	Second U.S. atom bomb dropped on Nagasaki, Japan.
August 14	Japan surrenders unconditionally.
September 2	Japanese military and political leaders sign surrender terms on USS *Missouri* in Tokyo Bay.

Part I

CARL M. BECKER: A DRAFTEE

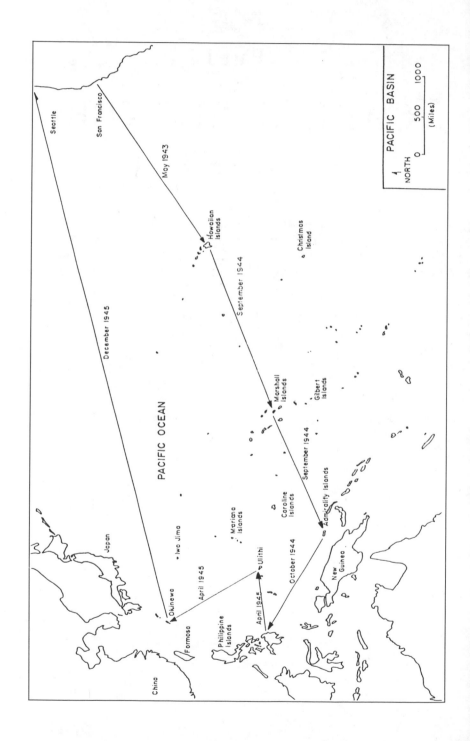

PACIFIC BASIN

Military Timeline

June 30, 1942	Registered for draft
December 9, 1942	Classified 1-A
January 18, 1943	Inducted U.S. Army
January 25, 1943	Entered active service
January 25, 1943–January 31, 1943	In transit
February 1, 1943–May 3, 1943	Basic training, Battery C, 30th Coast Artillery Training Battalion (Camp Wallace, Texas)
May 23, 1943–May 31, 1943	In transit
June 1, 1943–December 7, 1945	Headquarters Battery, 866 Anti-Aircraft Automatic Weapons Battalion
June 1, 1943–September 12, 1944	Oahu, Hawaiian Islands
October 20, 1944–c. April 10, 1945	Leyte, Philippine Islands
c. April 17, 1945–December 7, 1945	Okinawa, Ryukyu Islands
December 8, 1945–January 5, 1946	In transit
January 5, 1946	Honorable discharge

Length of Service: Continental service—four months, eight days; foreign service—two years, seven months, three days; total service—two years, eleven months, eleven days.

Opposite: **An Odyssey in the Pacific, 1943–1945.**

Carl M. Becker, the author, Honolulu, 1943.

"All You Little Boys"

1

The Call and the Departure, Training for Fighting (?),
The Way of the Flesh, Sojourn in California

There it was, falling and fluttering out of the manila folder crammed
with the personalia of a lifetime, a yellowing, frayed card measuring about
three by five inches. At the top, the words were there for me to read again,
forty-five years later—NOTICE OF CLASSIFICATION. Appearing immediately below in lowercase letters, signifying my petty role in the
business, was one word, Registrant, and typed to the right was my name,
my full name—Carl Monroe Becker, Jr. No mistake about it, the Jr. meant
that the card had been sent to me, not my father.

The next line told much and foretold more: Local Board Number 14
had classified me 1-A "until further notice." Underneath that prescient line,
I could see three little boxes in a vertical column, indicating the origination
of my classification. One was for the president—Franklin D. Roosevelt, I
supposed—to check. He hadn't. Another was for a board of appeal; no
check was in it. I hadn't even known that I had a right of appeal. A check
did appear in the box for the local board. It was close and democratic. My
neighbors on that board had decided that I was legally eligible for the draft,
that the nation could use my services in the war against the Japanese and
Germans.

My immediate recognition of the card summoned up, and summed up,
my years as a draftee (though by rank I was often called an enlisted man)
in the U.S. Army when the nation fought its second great and good war of
the century.

I knew that year of the inevitable arrival of the card. Mine was no un-
common situation. I had been a senior in high school in Miamisburg, Ohio,
when the Japanese attacked Pearl Harbor. Though my classmates and I had
heard rumors of war in the months after Hitler's armies swept into France
in 1940 and as the Japanese threatened to move farther into southeast Asia,
we were not ready for such an abrupt and terrible introduction to it. We
felt properly outraged by the attack; after all, Roosevelt declared it to be
"infamous." We knew too that it spelled an end to old routines; surely we

could not long continue to date our "steadies" and linger at Jimmy the Greek's. It threatened plans for the future. Boys who wished to become freshmen at college might instead become rookies in the Army. And for those who otherwise might flail around aimlessly, it could provide order and direction.

Like nearly every other boy in my class, I was fearful of going to war, for I was certain that it could not be a "pleasure to be short." Yet, like the other seniors, I was fearful of not going. Whatever my fears, I had to be true to our class motto, "Uncle Sam, Here We Come!" and to our class colors — red, white, and blue. Moreover, as A. E. Housman put it, it was better to "fight and see your slain / And take the bullet in your brain" than to die a coward's death at home. We had not read the poetry, but we lived its words in our bones.

O! We were patriotic, and we had no time for studying or for teachers who spoke irrelevancies about math and history. We wanted to be a part of real history. Teachers whom we had respected almost became our enemies standing in the way of our heroism. Besieged and beleaguered. they could hardly maintain discipline among the boys becoming men, who saw school as an unnecessary way station en route to manhood in a uniform.

Our parents were another problem for us. They were patriotic, all right, but they counseled patience. Besides, they could always point to families whose sons,older than we, had not yet gone into service. My father was a foundry worker who had not graduated from high school. He very much wanted me to go on to college, said that he would "bust a gut" to send me. He was reluctant to encourage me to take a decision at variance with his dreams for me. My mother, a housewife, was bewildered and frightened by the coming of war but was stoically courageous. She had no specific plans for me but knew that she had not intended me to become a soldier.

My parents feared that I would rush into service and then John, my younger brother by a year, would follow suit, unwilling to let the older brother become the sole standard-bearer of the family. He and I had long lived in tandem. We went to school together, played on the high school football team together, spent our summers on the golf course together, worked at odd jobs together. If he could not go with me, he would soon enlist, they were certain, in the Army or Navy. The parents would be alone at home with my sister, a vibrant fourteen-year-old whose carefree years would become anxious years.

Then there was my girlfriend, my "steady." Two years younger than I, sweet and innocent, she envisioned sharing a hearthside with me. But she could not openly object to my becoming a soldier or sailor. The girls in her circle could all talk of boyfriends who intended to fight the Nazis or Japs. It would not do for her to lament my leaving home. Secretly, each girl probably shed teenage tears at the demands of war; publicly each attempted to become a woman bravely enduring the departure and distancing of her man going to war.

If our patriotism had flagged, my classmates and I could have taken a cue from our hometown. Miamisburg, a small city of just over five thousand people about ten miles south of Dayton, was a blue-collar community shaped by a substantial ethnic and religious uniformity that did not readily accept minorities as equal members of society and did not tolerate dissent. Hundreds of men and a growing number of women were working on defense contracts at General Motors plants and the National Cash Register factory in Dayton. Many families in the city had seen their sons enlisting in the Army and Navy and answering draft calls. The weekly issues of the Miamisburg *News* ran numerous accounts of local boys in service going to the corners of the earth. Civil defense workers, undeterred by the realities of distance, kept everyone prepared for the imminent Japanese or German attack on Miamisburg. Saving their pennies and dollars, adults and children bought war bonds to defeat the enemy. There was no gainsaying it: The community was at war. And though we had spent our pennies and youth down "meandering lane and street and found it sweet, very sweet," we were prepared emotionally to leave the bosom of community—our hometown.

Of course, many of my friends had tried to enlist during the final months of their senior year, but usually parents and even recruiters persuaded them to remain in school for a few more months, noting that the enemy would wait for them. I made an abortive effort at enlistment only a month before graduation. Three or four friends and I hitched a ride to the naval recruitment office in Dayton and took a physical examination. The petty officer, his face long gone from my memory, told me in a summary tone that I was color-blind and could not enter the Navy. I was thunderstruck, speechless. The Navy did not want me! What I didn't realize, until later, was that the Navy had all the recruits it needed and turned me down because I was overweight.

Chagrined, I returned home to mark time, waiting for events to direct my course. After graduation in June 1942, I found employment as a punch-press operator in a small factory in Miamisburg. It was a wretched job, paying low wages for my long hard hours at a dirty and dangerous machine. I endured it only because I believed the product that I worked on—a steel rod for reinforcing concrete used in the construction of "Victory ships"— would win the war. After a few months of this torturous labor and a dispute with a foreman, I took a job as a tool-crib attendant in Inland, a General Motors factory in Dayton. My wages were higher, and the work was light and clean and still seemed patriotic; the tools that I dispensed were used in the production of carbines, helmet liners, clutch plates for trucks, and other articles of war that might confound the enemy.

Then in the fall of 1942, Congress enacted legislation lowering the draft age from twenty-one to eighteen. Now young patriots in work attire could become patriots in uniform. Now I knew that I could become a hero—or a coward. Already registered for the "muster," as Roosevelt defined the draft, I received the notice of my classification in December. And in a few weeks, along with about eighty other young men (or boys), all from Miamisburg and the surrounding area and all selected by Local Board 14, I boarded a bus that supposedly would take me to Fort Hayes in Columbus for a physical examination and induction into the U.S. Army.

Many of us had never been more than sixty or seventy miles from home; most of us had never seen an Army base. We had in our mind's eye gleaming white barracks surrounded by snappy soldiers drilling and marching as to war. We would hear ramrod generals exhorting us to fight and, yes, die for liberty if need be. But much to our disappointment, instead of going to an Army base, we found ourselves disgorged from the bus in downtown Columbus and driven like cattle down a busy sidewalk of High Street, then down an alley to a dingy three- or four-story building that appeared to have been long unoccupied. Pedestrians stared at us indifferently, apparently not realizing that we were on the path to glory. It was humiliating.

Hundreds of other young men, evidently from many other points in the state, also marched down the street. We all stood in long lines in the gray building, awaiting perfunctory but sometimes embarrassing examinations of our bodies. I still flinch in pain at the remembrance of the doctor's jamming his finger under my testicles and demanding that I cough. No one discovered that I was color-blind, and like nearly everyone else, I passed the physical examination. Only the lame and the halt, it seemed, failed to pass it. En masse, we took an oath of allegiance to the nation. I was now in the U.S. Army. Off we marched again through downtown Columbus. But now we quickened our pace, no doubt from anxiety and pride. Still the pedestrians vacantly stared at us. Why didn't they cheer?

On the return trip to Miamisburg, all of us were subdued, realizing, I suppose, that we were about to enter a strange new life, one that might take life from us. We had one week to await our departure for a reception center at Fort Thomas in Kentucky. Presumably, we could use the week to put our affairs in order. The hiatus was hardly necessary. Few of us were married, and few of us had any business to conclude. I know that I lolled around. We did kiss our girlfriends—and tried more. My mother, unaware that the Army supplied all undergarments for soldiers, insisted on buying new underwear for me.

At last, we gathered—seventy-three draftees—at the depot in Miamisburg to await a train on a brisk grayish day in January (appropriately, a hint of a bitter cold wave was in the air). For years passenger trains had routinely sped past the depot, but now it was seeing occasional use as a rendezvous for inductees. A large crowd of parents, close relatives, and friends—

especially girlfriends — assembled around us and a small wooden platform from which the mayor delivered a short patriotic address. Then we stood around in the cold, talking about nothing in particular as we waited for the train. Max Southern, a Mickey Rooney look-alike who would soon die in North Africa, and Danny Schmidt, who would meet his death in Italy, were horsing around as usual. Art Doty, Jack Christian, and many other sons of the town were joking and laughing in nervous anticipation of our departure. And then the train pulled alongside the depot. Waving at the crews, we boarded it. Our families and friends waved back in hope and anxiety. And we left, the scenes of our youth falling and fading from view.

Hardly any of us had been on a train before, and we expected to enjoy a speedy journey to Fort Thomas, which lay just across the Ohio River from Cincinnati, about fifty miles south of Miamisburg. The trip, though, was laborious as the train fitfully steamed through a dozen or so towns and cities and then stopped for an hour in Cincinnati before finally moving slowly over the railroad bridge at the river.

In midafternoon, we reached a siding at Fort Thomas. Immediately, cadremen herded us to a supply room where we received an issue of clothing — government issues for the GIs — and packed away our civilian attire. I remember little about the clothing piled up on our outstretched arms except for the overcoat. Olive-drab and woolen, it seemed incredibly coarse and heavy. I did not believe that one could walk burdened with such a weight, but against the rapidly falling temperature, no one hesitated to pull on his coat. We marched in a fashion, with only a slight semblance of order, to our quarters in an old red brick building. Now we saw the merit of the great heavy coats; the building was not heated. In the evening we wore the coats in our rooms, shed them quickly at bedtime, and leapt into beds covered with thick woolen blankets — overcoats without arms.

Early the next day, we marched, again in a jumble, to various buildings scattered around the base. At one building we went through a series of physical exercises that left many of us puffing. In another we took some kind of tests that, so we thought, would determine what branch of the Army awaited us. At still another we saw two movies. One detailed the perfidy of the Japanese. And then we saw the obligatory film about the transmission of social diseases; the sequence suggested that we were fighting the Japanese to preserve our right to suffer the pain of sex. Nearly all of us, I suspect, had lived only at the fringe of a sexual life and consequently tittered at the images of flesh gone wrong.

That night several of us ventured into the downtown of Fort Thomas and went to a real movie. Much to my surprise and embarrassment, in the middle of the film one of the Miamisburg boys came into the theater and noisily searched me out, announcing in a loud whisper that my parents and girlfriend had come to visit me and were waiting for me at the barracks. So I departed hastily and joined them. I really did not appreciate their visit. I was a big boy now and did not, I thought, need them to hold my hand.

Fortunately, our stay at Fort Thomas was brief. On the third day most of us took trains to our basic-training camps. We had felt little homesickness until this point; but now, as the cadremen began to push us into different cars stretched behind the locomotive, we sorrowed a moment over the loosening of ties to our common home. Only two of the Miamisburg boys were in my car, which, so we heard, was headed for Texas. As I would learn again and again, the Army did not ordinarily apprise the troops of its plans for them.

The trip was pleasant enough. We had ample space, played cards, had good food, and slept in Pullman berths. But we were all feeling some isolation and loneliness, even in a crowd. Few of us had traveled much and knew little about the states through which the train moved. So often, at least at first, we carefully scanned the countryside through which we moved, seeking to discover something there that characterized Kentucky or Tennessee — or wherever we were.

For nearly three days, the train lurched along, often running onto sidetracks and discharging cars that, we assumed, had either reached their final destination or were to be coupled to another train. Comfortable as we were, we easily endured the lengthy stay on the track. Finally we heard the uncoupling of two or three cars at our camp, Camp Wallace.

Located between Houston and Galveston near the Gulf of Mexico on a ragged, sandy coastal plain that had no redemptive use other than as a military installation — it proved the truth of the old folktale that had the devil dumping unused sand from hell in Texas — Camp Wallace trained soldiers for the antiaircraft artillery, particularly in the use of searchlights. A few of us, knowing that the infantry bore the brunt of battle, expressed relief at the prospect of manning searchlights, believing moreover that such duty was almost glamorous — we had seen movies depicting searchlight crews in action during the Battle of Britain.

We marched from the siding, several hundred strong, for a mile or so to an open space. There a sergeant read assignments. Like many others, I was assigned to Battery C, 30th Coast Artillery Training Battalion; but none of my friends, old or new, came with me. Now I was stripped of all familiar associations.

At the time, the lyrics of a popular song warned draftees: "This is the Army, Mr. Jones, soldiers no private rooms or telephones." I learned the accuracy of that song at my barracks. It was one of seemingly hundreds of identical buildings, a typical Army barracks, a dirty white two-story frame structure accommodating about thirty trainees on each floor. Sparse metal beds awaited our bodies there. Their sagging springs bespoke a constant motion of men in and out of sleep. The wooden walls were paper-thin, and the wooden floors creaked with every footstep; the latrines were permeated with the odor of encrusted urine, though every GI seemed to be on latrine duty every day. About fifteen or twenty of the barracks enclosed a large rectangular area around which ran a narrow crushed-rock path. Each morning we assembled on the path in front of our barracks for roll call, and as I learned later, there too selected rookies could do penance for all manner of sins.

But it was not the material conditions in the barracks or camp that gave shape to our lives; it was the men who led and trained us, except the captain or colonel (I forget his rank) commanding the battalion. Appropriately named Skinner, he was a wraithlike figure, thin as a pine from the top of his head to the tip of his toes. He was an anonymous man to us; seldom did we see or hear him.

Really commanding us was the first sergeant of the battalion. He met all our expectations of a first sergeant. Surely he was a Regular Army man. Small and foulmouthed, a Texan, he was a disciplinarian, a brooding presence always threatening to invade our lives. I forget his name, but not his face. Fixed in a fiery gaze and punctuated with gleaming white teeth, it gave him the aspect of a banty rooster ever ready to peck someone. I shuddered and stiffened at his sight. Every morning at 5:30 except Sunday— thank God for Christianity, I often thought—his voice, resonant yet screaming, came over the loudspeaker in our barracks: "All you little boys, wise to fuck up, all you little boys, wise to fuck up." Sometimes he would add "Drop your cocks and grab your socks." What he said was vulgarly eloquent and allowed no misinterpretation: Get moving!

For all his threatening appearance and rhetoric, he did not hold the immediate terror for us that we felt in the presence of the two cadremen in our barracks. Sergeant William Koth was aloof, uncaring, and indifferent to our problems. Twenty-three or twenty-four and a native of Wyoming, he exuded an air of phlegmatic authority implying no challenge. Besides, he was a big man standing well over six feet and weighing at least two hundred pounds. He was not, all the trainees agreed, a pleasant man. Still he was a prince viewed in the dark shadows cast by Sergeant Billy Ray Bass.

Bass was no more than twenty-one. He was blond, slender, and handsome, his finely chiseled features, especially his chin, giving him sharp definition. A Texan, he expressed nothing but contempt for every soldier in the barracks; every word he spoke dripped with sarcasm. Occasionally, he acknowledged that he was a tough man but always added that we would find people even tougher in combat. We wondered, uncharitably, how he knew since he had never fired a shot in battle, had never been overseas. He could have been a cowboy bulldogging and branding us. We resented his good looks and his meanness—and his ownership of an automobile enabling him to escape the barracks almost at will. Often, of course, we called him, behind his back, a son-of-a-bitch who was genetically Sergeant Bastard.

Early on, I incurred his wrath. In my barracks seven or eight bunks diagonally across from mine was one Arthur Rennler. A streetwise, brash, pimply diminutive squirt from Cincinnati, he tried to intimidate all of us one way or another. No doubt that accounted for my willingness to lend him my watch one day. He had failed to return it to me at day's end, and as lights went out in the barracks, I politely but firmly requested him to do so: "Rennler, I want my watch." He shouted back an obscenity suggesting that I demonstrate affection for his backside. I reiterated my request. "Go to hell," he replied. I responded in kind. Within a few seconds, the door to Bass's room swung open, the light from it shining out to the front of the barracks and revealing Bass stepping out like the Grand Inquisitor. "You two little boys! Get up!" We shot out of our bunks, wearing only our skivvies. Saying virtually nothing for a change, he directed us to the crushed-rock path and ordered us to run around it four or five times. The running was not terribly strenuous, but barefoot as we were, it became a painful experience. Never again did I utter a word in that barracks once the lights went out.

The training that we had come to Camp Wallace for was nothing if not rigorous — and sometimes irrelevant to the realities of modern war. Occasionally we spent an hour or so looking at a searchlight, learning something of its nomenclature, technology, and operation. More often we were drilling, running the obstacle course, firing on the rifle range, hiking, performing bayonet drill, walking guard duty, undergoing inspections, and so on.

Drilling was an exercise in subordination of individuality and exposed one to a train of abuse. Rooted in ancient military tradition, it had something to do with the development of discipline and the habit of obedience. Before the introduction of rifled weaponry to warfare, it also prepared men for mass deployment on the battlefield. What it directly had to do with fighting in the twentieth century we did not know. But certainly it was rewarding for the cadremen. Especially in the early days of our training, we were often out of step as we drilled, and Bass and Koth obviously relished singling out offenders. "You, you little boy, don't you know your left foot from your right foot?" "What do you have in your ears, wax or straw?" "Clean the crap out of your ears!" So went their trite and unimaginative litany. Anyone who was overweight, as I was, and fell out of step, as I often did, heard himself addressed as "Heavy" in scathing terms.

Bass took great delight in repeatedly giving the order "To the rear, march!" After about the fifth such command, he would shout "To the rear" but would not add the crucial word "march." We would anticipate the command and turn to the rear. The result was chaos as we bumped and fell into one another. Bass, with Koth seconding him, would scream at us, "Don't anticipate the command!" We could see behind the mask of their anger perverse delight in our frenzy.

The author, first month of training, Camp Wallace, 1943.

At the obstacle course, they had additional opportunities for derision. Some of us could not scale a wall, climb a rope, or jump a ditch. They declared our insufficiencies a personal affront and reviled us as traitors to the nation, as pantywaists and cream puffs. At least we saw purpose in an activity intended to prepare us physically for the demands of fighting.

We discerned meaning too in firing on the rifle range, but it was a messy and sometimes bloody experience. To prepare us for firing, the cadre expended volumes of verbiage in instructing us on the nurture of our rifles. Springfield '03s, they could be dangerous to everyone on the range. Much to the anger of the cadremen, some of us seemed bent on swinging our loaded rifles around in the direction of other soldiers. We endangered ourselves too once we began to fire at the targets. If we laid our thumb incorrectly on the butt of the rifle behind the bolt, at its firing the bolt recoiled and struck the thumb, bloodying or breaking it.

Firing from a standing, kneeling, or prone position, we imagined (at least I did) that we were shooting at a Jap or German framed in the target, a large heavy white paperboard nailed to a wooden frame. Had an enemy soldier seen my attempts at marksmanship, surely he would have felt safe. Time and again after I loaded and fired my rifle, the red flag—the infamous "Maggie's drawers"—rose above the target indicating that I had missed every last inch of the paperboard. Bass always drew a sigh of relief and disgust when I completed my firing.

Small wonder that I was quite happy to depart the firing range to mark the targets in the "butts," a long bank of earth protecting the trough housing the targets. Standing in the trough, the trainees raised and lowered the targets, numbering about fifty, by a rope. After pulling down a target at the conclusion of a round of firing, we hoisted it again, along with the appropriate scoring marker over the bullet hole. Lowering it once more, we dipped out fingers in a messy paste pot and pasted pieces of paper over the holes. It was tiresome and dirty work, but we were freed from the cadremen and the incessant noise on the firing range. Altogether, the day on the range was bearable, and it seemed to offer a threat to the enemy.

Though a harrowing experience, we also saw the need for crawling under rifle and machine-gun fire in a simulation of combat on the battlefield. Early in the morning in the fifth or sixth week of our training, the entire battalion climbed into trucks and headed in convoy for a beach near Galveston. Once there, we watched several machine-gun crews attempting with little success to hit a sleeve pulled by an airplane, a slow-moving one at that. We all thought, I suspect, that we could expect little protection from such crews and that an enemy would not require any.

Then came our testing. We had to crawl for a hundred yards through sand and around barbed wire while machine gunners fired over our heads. The cadre had warned us, though rather flippantly, not to raise our heads or bodies in any way. Trembling, I began my journey, burrowing in the sand halfway to China. About fifty yards through the course, I heard a scream, and then all was quiet for a moment. Cadremen rushed to an area near me. A bullet had ricocheted off something and struck someone in the arm, mangling it hideously. I expected that we would be called in and the exercise ended. Not so. We were getting ready for war, and the casualty made it all the more urgent that we train realistically and hard—now. So we crawled on, fearing that any moment would yield another accident. Finally I came to the end of the course. I would have preferred home.

The weekly hikes were another kind of playing at war, but one that ultimately held a reward for me. At the outset of training, the hike was not long, eight or ten miles, but gradually the cadremen lengthened it until as a final test of our endurance, we had to walk twenty-five miles with full field packs on our backs and rifles slung over our shoulders.

As much as in any other part of our training, we noted in the hiking the privilege of rank. As privates and trainees, we had to stuff all kinds of supplies into our packs—socks, shirts, and more—until they weighed twenty or thirty pounds. But as we packed, we could always catch a glimpse of Bass and Koth placing empty produce cans into their packs, which then appeared loaded but in fact were nearly empty and weightless—and too symmetrical for belief.

On the hikes we became real soldiers momentarily. At points, acting as though we were pursuing or escaping an enemy, we had to run about a hundred yards or, pretending that we were being strafed, jump into ditches along the road. Though it was late winter and early spring, the weather could become damnably hot on the flatlands around Wallace. Invariably, someone could not make it, his feet becoming blistered, his legs and testicles galled, or his entire body dehydrated. In a bad case, as a man fell behind his company, the "meat wagon," a medical vehicle, would pull up to rescue him; though thus spared more physical pain, he became the butt of the cadremen's derisive remarks. On one occasion, I fell behind, my chubby legs terribly chafed, but fearing the embarrassment of the meat wagon, I managed to catch up with my company.

In the last week of training, by which time I had lost about thirty pounds and was in fighting trim, we had to make a forced march of about twenty-five miles in full gear. To my surprise and pleasure, I was able to negotiate the mileage with little discomfort. It was kind of a benchmark for me. Perhaps, I thought, I could make my way in the U.S. Army.

I took little inspiration, though, from bayonet training. The cadremen sought to persuade us that our very lives depended on our ability to parry or deliver a thrust to a stuffed bag, indeed that the nation's existence might hang in the balance when we fixed our bayonets. Sergeant Bass seemed really to believe that thrusting a bayonet around somehow would instill in us a primeval barbarism and that in combat we would be engaged in one bayonet fight after another. No one took him and other cadremen or the drill very seriously. Perhaps they protested too much. At least I thought that later as I used my bayonet to open tin cans.

I also found little pleasure or worth in guard duty. Arriving at the

The author, final month of training, Camp Wallace, 1943.

guardhouse after a day of hard training, I had to recite the ten orders for walking my post and hear admonitions to be prepared to reiterate them at any time during the next twenty-four hours. I had to walk my post for four two-hour stints—two hours walking my post, four hours resting in the guardhouse, another two hours at my post, and so on. The post led me past a row of foreboding, jerry-built shacks that no rational or irrational man would have sought to enter. I had to give my full attention, nonetheless, to my duty, understanding as I did that courts-martial, stockades, dishonorable discharges, executions all lay ahead if I breached any rules. I walked like a robot, ever fearing a challenge that never came. Between each tour of my lonely road, I fitfully slept in the guardhouse. There was no disputing it: Guard duty was a pain in the ass.

Nor was kitchen police, the infamous KP, a pleasant duty. Joining elements of training and punishment, it was a day's descent into hell. Appropriately enough, it began in the dark of night, at about 4:30 in the morning when everyone whose name had appeared on the duty roster had to present himself at the mess hall. Then, under the benign direction of the mess sergeant, we began the labor of setting the tables, carrying the chow to them, scraping and washing pots and pans, emptying garbage, mopping the floors. We had no scheduled breaks, and if we dared take one, the cooks, a mean and nasty lot, were on our backs immediately, demanding that we return to work that would destroy Hitler, Mussolini, and Hirohito. We worked without surcease until late in the evening and then returned to our barracks bone-weary. Even though KP might give respite from a day's training, all viewed it as a curse. It was a doubly repugnant duty when one pulled it on a Sunday, ordinarily a day of rest. After my first stint in the kitchen, I anxiously scanned the duty roster each day praying that I would not find my name there. But alas, I seemed to have a dark angel on my side. Through about thirteen weeks of training, I was on KP at least five times, four on Sunday. Of course, I earned the assignment at least once as a punishment for my failure to pass inspection.

If I disliked guard duty and detested KP, I absolutely loathed inspections. They were, in preparation and execution, dreadful in the extreme. Usually held on Saturday mornings, the inspections threw us into frenzied activity on Friday evenings after the day's training. Like little armies of worker ants, with Bass and Koth as our leaders, we policed the area around the barracks. Bass and Koth, probably resenting the intrusion into the time they ordinarily had free, shouted at us as we picked up everything that did not move: "All you little boys, all we want to see is elbows and assholes." Inside the barracks lay the laborious work. Here we washed windows, scrubbed floors, shined plumbing in the latrine. It was never ending, and Bass always threatened to work us even longer. Hercules had it easier redding up the Augean stable.

Our labor on windows and floors completed, we turned to our beds and equipment. Though we would be sleeping in the beds (we hoped), we began preparing them for the next morning. We practiced tucking in the sheets carefully and drawing blankets taut. We had to make our footlockers immaculate, with everything—toothbrushes, combs, and so on—precisely and properly in place. Our rifles we had to make even cleaner. To that end, we took them apart, cleaning and recleaning every piece, then cleaning and recleaning the fully assembled rifle. Particularly we tried to give a shine to the stock. I could not believe that a speck of dust remained on my rifle, but the inspecting officers were Argus-eyed and always found one. We had to be concerned too about our personal appearance—our haircut properly in a burr, our faces shorn of all stubble, and above all our shoes shining sufficiently to serve as mirrors.

In the morning we were up early, feverishly preparing for the ordeal. We shaved carefully, bolted down our breakfasts, and returned to the barracks for a final use of brooms and mops. Then we marched to the parade ground and stood at attention to receive the battalion commander and his party as they walked down our line. The inspection was routine and ritualized. As the commander stepped in front of one of us, the soldier (the little boy) brought his rifle to "inspection arms" and pulled the bolt to present a clear view of the loading and firing mechanism. Uncoiling like a snake, the officer thrust his arms out, seized the rifle, looked at it for a second (it seemed like an eternity), and literally threw it back into the hands of the soldier. He might also give a cursory look at one's attire. Ready with pencil and paper to record any deficiencies was the first sergeant. It was all terrifying.

In one instance, as the inspection party neared me, I heard a voice behind me whisper, "Becker, Becker, your safety lock, your safety lock." I didn't understand the import of his words at first but finally furtively glanced down at the rifle at my side. Horrified, I saw immediately that I was facing disaster: The safety lock on the bolt was in the upright position, the position that would permit the bolt to fly free from the rifle when I brought it up for inspection. An enemy, a prankster, or Becker had done me in.

What could I do? If I raised the rifle and returned the lock to its proper position, no matter how stealthily I did it, surely the commander or the first sergeant or, worse yet, Bass would see me in the act; if I didn't, surely the bolt would come flying out at inspection, and I would discover new meaning in the phrase *direst of consequences*. In a flash, I chose the lesser of the two great evils. I quickly raised my rifle, snapped the offending safety lock back, and lowered my rifle. Apparently no one saw my maneuver; for a moment, I believed that there was a God in heaven. But my dexterity didn't help much. As usual, the commander found my rifle dirty, and as usual, I was gigged—another day on KP. Probably the failure with the rifle meant little. I still had to face inspection at my bunk, and invariably I fell short of the mark there also — my blanket not tight enough or my footlocker sloppy. It was one damn thing after another.

Probably the Army expected the ordinary routines of our communal life   roll call, mess, mail call, and so on — to play an ancillary role in the shaping of our obedience to command, subordination of individualism, loyalty to the group, and bonding one to another — presumably virtues that would make us readier for combat. But such desiderata were a will-o'-the-wisp. Our ordinary routines fostered instead an ethos of every man for himself and the devil take the hindmost. The trainee sleeping next to you, standing by you at roll call, sitting beside you at mess was always secondary to your concerns about your own security and comfort.

Our typical day in the ordinary routines began in a frantic atmosphere. As soon as the first sergeant delivered his notorious command to the little boys, always exactly at 5:30 A.M., to rise and drop our socks and everything else, we scurried for the latrine, shoving and elbowing for a place to perform our ablutions under the duress of the clock. Always there were those fastidious men who brushed the hell out of their teeth or shaved off their whiskers until kingdom come while others awaited their turn at the washbasin and worried about being ready for the order to "fall out."

When Koth bellowed that order, we ran and stumbled into the dark and onto the path in front of the barracks, formed the appearance of lines, and awaited the calling of our names. We might have fallen asleep during that perfunctory procedure but for two prospective incidences. Usually we heard our names called, followed by the response "here" intoned in various inflections and growls. Yet we listened attentively, especially on Mondays after weekend passes expired, awaiting the silence suggesting that someone had gone AWOL (absent without leave) or had somehow found his way into the stockade. When that happened, we all felt a vicarious fright. Eliciting our mirth was the age-old prank of "goosing" — as the dictionary defines it, the act of poking between the buttocks. Knowing that a man was particularly sensitive around his rear, some intrepid soldier would reach forward to the next line and goose him. The victim's involuntary shout or scream would pierce the morning air, and we would muffle our laughter. Then the cadremen would search in vain for the parties to the foul deed; in their eyes, the one who poked and the one who shouted were equally guilty. My guess is that they rather enjoyed the break with routine (though of course it became part of the routine) but could not outwardly join us in laughter.

From roll call we marched off to the mess hall, a long, one-story frame structure obviously concealing crimes against mankind. We had different standards as to what constituted good food and certainly were not gourmets, but nonetheless we felt obliged to complain about it, constantly taking in vain the names of the men who had the audacity to call themselves cooks. Yet we shrank not at all from the sight of the meat and vegetables on the mess tables; indeed, we attacked the viands and created a scene resembling feeding time at a zoo, devouring everything in great gulps with little effort at mastication. Knowing no decency, we also became adept at the art or practice of "shortstopping." Seeing that a dish a few feet down a table still contained a few morsels, one would ask a man near it to pass it. Inevitably, two or three men would interrupt its passage, help themselves, and send it along licked clean. We roundly condemned the resort to short-stopping and yet rather admired the brashness of the men who denied us a last bite.

Mail call was another routine that saw individualism and self-security manifested. After the noon meal — we seldom used such terms as "lunch," "dinner," or "supper" — several hundred of us gathered near the battalion office. There, standing on a small platform and attended by two or three trainees, the battalion clerk began calling the names, sending letters and packages to them through a route of outstretched arms. After only a few days, we all realized that certain men received a disproportionate number of letters. The clerk would repeat their names three or four times once or twice a week. They were the objects of some envy and enjoyed some status — to a degree. A few in the crowd were quick to suggest that the re-cipients of many letters — their names became legion — were momma's boys who could not cut the apron strings to home.

We developed no real comradeship or unity through the informal routines of life in the barracks. At the end of a day's training, we were all weary and had to use our free time, if it could be called that, for cleaning rifles, footlockers, and the barracks in anticipation of impending inspec-tions. We had little time for talk among ourselves, for cultivating friend-ships. I'd snatch a few minutes for writing letters home, and occasionally I helped a nearly illiterate man in the bed next to me write or read his let-ters. That was as close as I came to becoming concerned about someone else. What little talk passed among us before lights went out had to do with allusions to girls and sex, especially homosexuality. Often we heard the stale admonition not to bend over in the shower to pick up a bar of soap. We always snickered in embarrassment.

I discerned the anomie of our lives in response to the threats of punish-ment offered by Bass and Koth. Often they warned us of a coming judgment day for the entire barracks should one man foul up on a detail. But they were whistling Dixie. We lived psychologically, if not physically, isolated from one another and didn't give a damn whether one's behavior had adverse con-sequences for all. We didn't fear reprisals from other men because we un-derstood that there wasn't the slightest semblance of unity among us. No one ever spoke of his identity with or allegiance to Battery C. We shared no sense of a common destiny; we were ships passing in the night.

Undergoing intensive training during the weekdays and pulling guard duty and KP on the weekends, I had relatively little time for recreation. What I had I did not use very wisely. Two or three times I went to the camp theater to see movies, but the antics of the soldiers in the audience allowed little enjoyment for anyone. Twice I took a bus to Houston. I knew my way around downtown Dayton, but Houston was about twice its size, and I felt overwhelmed. I walked around in a daze, taking my pleasure in the consumption of milkshakes and hamburgers. I was not ready by nerve or experience to seek out women of easy virtue. I was at my bravest and most imaginative in Houston when I attended a theater to see a live performance by the Ink Spots.

It was in Galveston one Sunday that I passed through the spirituous rites of manhood. Early that day several of us boarded a bus for the city. Once there, we wandered around aimlessly for a while, our steps at last taking us to the Peacock Restaurant where I ate a steak and pronounced it excellent.

Then we drifted down to Murdock's, a huge beer hall resting on piers on a beach along the Gulf. Here, it seemed, all the trainees had gathered, and among them I met two Miamisburg boys. They and their friends were drinking beer and laughing raucously. I had tasted beer but once or twice in my life and did not like it, but the price of admission to the circle was hoisting beer and sharing in the laughter. So I sat down and soon was caught up in the conviviality.

I drank one beer, another, another, and another until I had only a few dollars left in my money belt. I did not feel any intoxicating effect and managed to rejoin my traveling friends and catch a bus for downtown Galveston.

Again we ate at the Peacock — and now I learned that the wages of sin is death. Increasingly, I became befuddled and nearly choked on my food, which did not taste nearly as good as what I had eaten at noon. Leaving the restaurant, I sent a spray of food and the beer from Murdock's into the gutter. The vomit splattered over my shoes and onto my trousers. Pedestrians looked on in disgust. I beat a wobbly path to a bus and rode alone back to Wallace sick and humiliated, my head aching, my stomach rolling. At that point, I did not believe that malt did more than Milton can to justify God's ways to man.

Arriving at Camp Wallace, I lurched and staggered to my barracks and collapsed into my bunk. For hours I thought I was near death. No one was there to offer me succor. There was no balm in Gilead. Now I knew that God's punishment was sure, if not swift. The next morning I dragged myself out of the bunk and somehow got through the day. As my pain gradually subsided, I vowed total abstinence from strong drink. The lips that touched liquor would never be mine.

After about thirteen weeks, our training was coming to an end early in May. To give it a crowning fillip, we had to go through a final parade, a grand review, something that hearkened back, I supposed, to ancient military traditions. It seemed odd and ironic. As our reward for hard training, we had to labor more.

In any event, we put on our khaki uniforms, even ties, and slung our rifles with bayonets fixed over our shoulders. Never before had we drilled with them unscabbarded, but I felt no alarm at the new order. I should have. Once on the parade ground, we joined a mass of soldiers in one great formation. We passed routinely by a reviewing stand where dignitaries of some sort acknowledged our eyes turned to them. Then, to my horror, the command came to bring our rifles to port arms and run in step. So there we were, a mass of thousands, I thought, running with rifles fixed with bayonets. What would happen if someone fell? Would he impale the man in front of him, or would he be trampled to death? Fortunately, no one fell, but I died a bit with each step.

Though our training ended in a grand and fearful flourish, we had little idea of what awaited us. Considering the rumors emanating from the latrine, we should have resorted to divination of a chicken's intestines. One story in persistent circulation had us receiving more training and forming a new battalion that would stay in the United States, go to England, or go to Australia. Another was that we would join existing battalions in Europe and the Pacific. Still another had it that we would go overseas without a furlough. That, we all agreed, could not happen. The Army had to give a furlough; no one went overseas without a fourteen-day leave. Rumor piled on rumor, and we waited, knowing that wherever we went, we would see home first.

We thus felt a sense of disquiet when the cadremen, offering no information about our destination, marched us out of Camp Wallace and into railroad cars at the siding where we had disembarked three months earlier. Entering relatively new cars, Pullmans at that, we momentarily put our tenseness aside. Then the train pulled away, following the sun to the west. We sat relaxed in our seats, viewing the land of the Southwest as we played cards, wrote letters, and ate. Despite the uncertainties of our journey, I slept peacefully in the very comfortable Pullman berths.

More and more we fastened our attention on the topography as we approached and entered California at Needles. Continuing northward through desert and farmland, we arrived at Pittsburg, on the San Joaquin River about forty miles above San Francisco. Descending from our cars carrying our cumbersome duffel bags in all manner of positions, we then walked, or shuffled, through the streets of Pittsburg to the Pittsburg Replacement Depot. The name was scary, ominous—replacing whom, why, where?— and the camp was dreary, a collection of small dark shacklike barracks that bespoke impermanence and made the barracks at Camp Wallace seem palatial.

We did little or nothing at the depot, as though we needed respite before some hard going. We grubbed around for things to do and even welcomed a few minutes of drilling. The one weekend we were there, three of us hitchhiked into San Francisco. But we saw little of interest except the Oakland Bay Bridge and did little outside of eating at Lefty O'Doul's restaurant. We were too fresh, too naïve to pursue a rake's way. Yet we missed the bus that would have returned us to the depot before our passes expired. When we did reach camp, we slipped past an unattended gate and congratulated ourselves on our derring-do.

No one was giving us the slightest hint of our ultimate destination, and we were still repeating the claim that we could not go overseas without a furlough or delay en route that would permit us to return home for a few days. Our faith in what was required of the Army was touching, but it was gradually diminishing. We became more apprehensive when a sergeant came to the barracks and ordered us to pack our duffel bags and prepare to leave. Where were the orders for furloughs? Again we stumbled down streets with duffel bags in tow. Our journey, fortunately, was quite abbreviated, taking us only to Camp Stoneman, a stone's throw from the depot. It was quite mystifying. Why had we not gone directly to Stoneman? Why the layover at the depot?

No matter the deviousness of the Army, we should have read a warning from the barracks at Stoneman. They appeared clean and little used, and many were empty. Obviously soldiers did not linger there — and neither did we. The tip-off came for all who would accept reality when we had to test our gas masks in a small building permeated with tear gas and file by medics administering a series of shots. On the second day at Stoneman, the word came. We would leave the next morning. Again the Army would not provide us with an itinerary. But now we feared that indeed we were leaving the country; the brave assertions about furloughs rang hollow. That night, we learned later, twenty or thirty men tried to scale the fence around the camp to say farewell to wives and sweethearts. A few went over the hill, AWOL.

The morning saw us silent and tense as we put on our khaki uniforms and stuffed our duffel bags. Then we marched out of the camp, no band playing, down several long streets to a steamboat. Appropriately, forebodingly, we had to walk a gangplank to board it. It presented no aspect of the life of gaiety and romance historically associated with its kind — no beauteous belles walked decks overhung with Gothic gingerbread; no young handsome men stood tall and strong on a Texas deck; no roving gambler hastened to the gaming table; no sweating muscular black sang "Old Man River." Far from it. The ship was a dirty, pedestrian tub. We seemed to occupy every inch of space on it, our packs and duffel bags constantly clashing for possession of territory. After an hour or so, as we grew increasingly weary, the boat steamed off toward San Francisco. No one talked now about the furloughs we had to have. The little boys had a voyage to make, miles or leagues to sail, and oaths of patriotism to keep.

"No More Maggie's Drawers" 2

The Voyage, The Men of the Battery, Pain and Pleasure, Trial for Combat

On reaching San Francisco, we disembarked and walked to a corrallike area by a large wharf, tied to which was a huge oceangoing vessel. Originally called the *Kaiser Wilhelm*, or something like that, and now named the *Republic*, it had supposedly been seized from Germany by the United States during or shortly after World War I. Certainly it was old enough, and some of us thought that the Germans had the better of the deal, even though presumably they had received nothing in exchange for it. It was a grim ship, bearing the marks of wear everywhere—paint peeling off bulkheads and smokestacks, rusting decks, seams ripping loose on yellowing hammocks.

Nothing but a war could have justified the use of the *Republic* as a troopship. Owned and managed by the Army but manned by sailors, it could accommodate about five thousand men (fifty thousand seemed to be aboard) only because the commanding officers, evidently trained at concentration camps, squeezed us into every nook and cranny belowdecks. Our bodies spilled everywhere. Along with about a hundred men, I plunged into the innermost depths of the ship, into the bilge, taking a hammock in the outer brig. The hammock was the highest one in a pile of six or seven. Climbing a mountain would have been easier than pulling myself up to it, and I always feared falling out of it; consequently, I spent little time in it. Worse yet was the stench of flesh jammed against flesh.

Our voyage, beginning on May 23, took eight days, going on eight months. Nothing redeemed the pain and suffering of that passage. The food was an affront to every short-order cook in the nation, and our experience in shortstopping proving of no avail, we had to sweat out long lines to get at it. Often I went without meals. Moreover, I was usually seasick and constantly had the urge to vomit but could not do so, probably because I was not eating much. The water for washing ran off our bodies as though it were slime, and the water for drinking tasted as though it had salt laced in it. Surely the Navy did not use water from the ocean for the troops; surely the

Army did not acquiesce in its doing so. But we knew that we were sheep to be shorn and that neither the Navy nor the Army had any great concern about our comfort. We exercised but infrequently and then in a desultory fashion. We began taking Atabrine to protect ourselves against malaria; it left a foul-tasting residue on the tongue. We feared, or hoped for, a Japanese submarine attack. Even a week out, we had no idea about where we were going, but anywhere would be a relief.

Our only recreation on ship was taunting the sailors with our deliberate misuse of nautical language. The "bow," in our terminology, became the "front," the "stern" the "back," the "portside" the "left," the "head" the "latrine" or "toilet." The sailors were sensitive about our defiance of their standards. But our words became, after a few days, flat, weary, stale, and unprofitable. Soldiers seldom realized that too much of a good thing can become too much, but excess can become a way of life in the Army.

On the eighth day of our voyage, in late morning, we reached our port, the harbor of Honolulu. We were in the Hawaiian Islands, the land of the lei and the luau. For the moment we rejoiced, believing that no enemy awaited us, that battle for us was not imminent. Of course, the American Army could make the islands less than a peaceful sanctuary for us.

Disembarking near the famous Aloha Tower but not receiving the greeting of leis and kisses customarily accorded tourists by native girls, we walked to railroad cars that came right out of the cartoon strip *Toonerville Trolley*. The cars, boxcars cut in half, and the steam locomotive were for a narrow gauge track and ordinarily had been used, we were told later, for the hauling of pineapples and sugar cane from the interior of Oahu. Accordingly, it followed that we had to be packed in the cars like so many pineapples, with only occasional pockets of space among us. Again we huddled together, insecure in our ignorance of where we were heading.

After about an hour of traversing flat fields and winding around low-lying hills, our comic train stopped at what was obviously an Army base. It was Schofield Barracks, later to become the central scene in James Jones's novel *From Here to Eternity*. As we alighted from the cars, we could see the pinkish barracks at Schofield and assumed that we were to walk to them. Instead, we began a hike up a continuously rising asphalt road, the very road that Jones had Private Robert E. Lee Prewitt trudging up to Kolekole Pass in "full field pack . . . extra shoes, helmet and all" as punishment for his alleged insubordination. Dragging our duffel bags, lumbering along for nearly a mile, we finally reached a gathering of large ragged pyramidal tents. They were the first of many thousands that I would see in the next thirty months, one of man's great inventions bridging the gap between savagery and civilization.

On the hike and as we entered the makeshift camp—for that was what it was—we noticed red dust collecting on our shoes and trousers, an

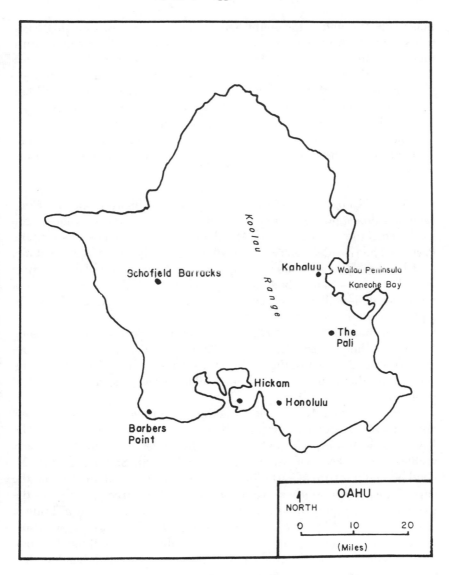

Oahu, Hawaiian Islands.

enveloping red blob that seemed to have a life of its own. Every step, every movement brought more to our clothing and our bodies. We were under attack, of course, from the ubiquitous, infamous red volcanic dust of Schofield. Despite the dust that sent us into the showers two or three times a day and despite the abominably bad food, life at the tent city was not unpleasant. There was no drilling or guard duty and little KP. I even found time to play a round of golf on the Schofield course. It wasn't much of a golf course, but it gave me an opportunity to return to a yesterday of pleasure under the sun.

In the three or four days after our arrival at the tent city, men were gradually leaving, assigned, I assumed, to various units in the islands. When and where would I go? As usual, I had no hints. Then on about the fifth day, along with two of the Wallace trainees, including the smartass Rennler, I was told to prepare for departure. Early that afternoon, a sunny day in June, a pickup truck wheeled into the motor pool, and we climbed in it for our ultimate trip.

After winding and wending for an hour or so on highways passing along cane and pineapple fields and penetrating clumps of tropical forest, the truck began to deliver its cargo. At a thickly forested area overlooking the Pacific—I had no idea where I was—Rennler and the other soldier left me. Now I anxiously awaited the next stop. It came a few minutes later at a strip of land curling out into a body of water. What I viewed as I climbed out of the truck defied all my perceptions about Army installations. Along an asphalt road meandering to the right and left up a slight incline for about four or five hundred yards were small dark wooden shacks, perhaps twenty. Other than their similarities, they hardly implied that soldiers lived here; they were reminiscent of the cabins at a summer camp near Miamisburg. Called huts, they housed five to six men, affording ample space for them and their gear.

Soon enough I understood something of the geography of my new home. I was on a peninsula jutting about five hundred yards into Kaneohe Bay on the windward side of Oahu. About five miles across the bay, clearly visible to the naked eye, lay the Kaneohe Naval Air Station. A large fish pond behind our strip of earth formed a small inlet. About a mile from the base of the peninsula—there was no isthmus—rising precipitously was the Koolau Range, a spiny mountainous range separating the windward side of the island from its leeward side. The road giving ingress to the peninsula stretched on the right to the north shore of Oahu, to the left, the direction that I usually took, for about five miles to Kaneohe City and then for a few miles to a junction with a road to its right.

What a road it was to the right! Crossing a narrow piedmont, it then ascended a series of hairpin curves nearly two miles to the Nuuanu Pali, a walled precipice commanding at its peak a panoramic view of the windward shore to the north and of the outstretched Pacific. King Kamehameha had pushed his enemies off the Pali more than a century before; I always prayed not to follow them. Down the gradually descending road was Honolulu, about twenty miles from the peninsula. I would trace the route between them many times before I departed the islands.

Scene in camp at Wailau Peninsula, 1943.

The peninsula bore various names, none of which, happily, derived from a military legacy. Hawaiians living in the minute community at an edge of the peninsula—actually an admixture of Filipinos, Chinese, Japanese, Portugese, and Hawaiians—called it Wailau or Lihikai. *Haoles* (mainlanders from the United States) knew it as Libbyville because the Libby company had once operated a small canning facility there, and parishioners of the small Episcopal church at the base of the peninsula, Saint John's-by-the-Sea, used the name of their church to identify it. Whatever name it went by, it was a small jewel, a luxuriant patch of ground crowded with tropical trees, flowers, and bushes.

Here it was that I joined my outfit, the Headquarters Battery of the 866th Anti-Aircraft Artillery Automatic Weapons Battalion—so my discharge recorded it. As our name indicated, we directed, coordinated, and serviced a battalion of antiaircraft batteries—four of them—ever ready to fire their .50-caliber machine guns and .40-millimeter antiaircraft guns against the Japanese. Almost all of the men in my battery had been drafted late in 1940 and early in 1941 after the enactment of the Selective Service Act of 1940. Many were original members of the battery at its organization in the spring of 1941 at Camp Davis in North Carolina as the Headquarters Battery of the 95th Coast Artillery Battalion. Many were with it when it arrived in Honolulu only a few weeks after the Japanese attack on Pearl Harbor. At full strength, the battery numbered about ninety men and seven officers.

The men of the battery were a fairly nondescript lot. No unusually large number came from one state, much less from one city. Though many were natives of midwestern and northeastern states, especially Wisconsin, Michigan, and New York, a large handful were sons of Georgia, Mississippi, Louisiana, and Texas. Probably the majority had lived in large cities — Boston, New York, Philadelphia, Baltimore, Cleveland, and Chicago, among others. But a few were dirt farmers from Kansas and Nebraska. If there was any common bond among them, perhaps it was religion. At least half or more were Roman Catholic — men of Polish, Irish, and Italian descent. Only one was a Jew. Except for a Seventh Day Adventist, a source of no little trouble, the Protestants were of the mainline denominations — Methodists, Presbyterians, and so on. Only a few had attended a college or university; and clearly, excepting what the Army might do for them, most would become blue-collar workers or low-level white-collar employees in the civilian labor force. Not one expressed his intent to pursue a career in the Regular Army at the end of the war. Scarcely any verbalized a belief that the war was a grand crusade, a struggle against tyranny. They were quintessentially civilian soldiers.

Besides my duffel bag, I brought to the battery the baggage of vague and stereotypic notions about the character of non–Anglo-Americans. Nurtured by a community where an ethnic coherence had created a narrow parochialism, I was held hostage to biases that I now regret and reject. I used them as prisms for viewing the men who composed the battery and usually confirmed them by what I thought I saw. The big-city boys, I believed, were arrogant, brash, and impersonal. Nonetheless, I wanted but could not actively seek their approbation, standing as I did in awe of them. As a Protestant from a small town, I saw the many Catholics as somehow alien to American life. When they went to Mass on Sunday en masse, their affiliation almost an affront to the men left behind in isolation, I did not know whether to feel envy or anger. Though no one ethnic group was numerous, of course I had no hesitancy in identifying the several sons of Italy as distinct characterological types: emotional and temperamental, talkative with their hands, short and swarthy.

Even when only a few men represented a geographic section or ethnic element of the nation, I discovered in them confirmation of my secular understanding of universality. One man, a tall rawboned Mississippian, was the apotheosis of the backwater South. He drank too much, was not very articulate or well educated, disliked the urban Yankees around him, was prideful and consequently quick to take offense. In consonance with my adolescent views of the world, I comprehended all Indians in the person of a half-breed from Oklahoma. Like the Mississippian, he was not secure or comfortable among city men and was in a perpetual quarrel with them. He took to strong drink too often and then lost control of himself, his red face becoming redder, his wide nostrils flaring. We all gave him a wide berth. No wonder, I thought, that whites had moved the Indians to reservations. In our sole Israelite, I faced a challenge to old assumptions. Far from being assertive and intelligent, he was servile and almost dim-witted, fit only to serve as the officers' orderly. Yet I found in him the avarice I looked for when he boasted that he was saving nearly every penny from his monthly pittance and refused to lend money to the chronic gamblers among us. I did not know what to make of his amusing certainty that another Depression would follow the war and that against it he would arm himself with a toaster for the breadlines. Was he serious? I had never known any blacks in my all-white Miamisburg but "knew," as did everyone in the community, that they were shiftless and shuffling (we had all seen Stepin Fetchit), dirty, and inferior. I met none in our battery, so I could safely hold on to my racist views. At a distance, moreover, I saw them driving trucks for the Quartermaster Corps, sufficient evidence of their insufficiency for war.

At a different level, I observed the men in the battery as a study in varying qualities and attitudes. Some were persistently indolent or inert, some insouciant, others innovative in meeting or skirting the demands of the Army. Some earned respect or envy for their indolence, others contempt; it depended on the verve with which they maneuvered around the regulations and red tape of the Army. Some elicited emulation for their temerity, but usually the copy was ersatz, lacking the substance of the model. As the months passed, I increasingly understood and appreciated their conduct as a minute mutiny against authority.

I remember the men of the battery by the score, and they still rattle around in my mind. For better or worse, they are yet a part of me. There were the comedians — they were precious assets — like John Black. The battery clerk, Black touched all our lives. He was an irreverent, wisecracking man who always seemed able to put the Army in its place.

Cut from a similar but more colorful cloth was Ray Maller, a private the same age as I. A delightful rogue, he was a picaresque character who could have graced the pages of a novel by Henry Fielding or Tobias Smollett, outrageously yet disarmingly brash in his relations with men over him, sergeants or officers. He relied on personality or stretched the truth into outright lies to avoid what he considered onerous duty. I still have in my mind's eye his image when infrequently we all had to turn out for morning calisthenics. As we did jumping jacks in unison, Ray, positioned at the end of the formation, threw himself into a wild contortive motion joining jitterbugging and the Charleston. Snickering, the jumpers would lose their concentration, and the routine became a farce.

Joe Ranzo mystified everyone by his trademark: as he walked, wherever he was, he would stop periodically, bend forward to his waist, lift one leg in a horizontal position to his rear, and spread his arms outward. No one ever knew, no one every asked, what he was doing.

Frank Collier, from Texas, was a source of a different, perhaps vicarious, amusement. Nearly forty, slightly cross-eyed, and utterly potbellied, he regaled us with stories of his visits to Honolulu that always included his going to a whorehouse for a "trip around the world." If we saw Collier as an amusing old glandular goat, we envied James Leese as a true sexual athlete. Handsome, supple in speech and muscle, and daringly carefree, he had probably won the heart of many girls stateside in the backs of automobiles and elsewhere, and certainly he had continued his romantic career in the peninsular village. There he had met a maid named Tillie, and nearly every morning he crawled exhausted from her bed and returned to the battery to take up his military duties as best he could. A prankster too, altogether he was another picaresque figure, a Roderick Random or Tom Jones in our midst.

In contrast to the comedians, a few men were sullen in the extreme. Deeply gloomy and morose was Rudy Raymond. The war had ended the world for him when his fiancée in Milwaukee sent him a "Dear John" letter. Mario Manzano seemed consumed by a silent rage. What accounted for his anger we did not know, but we all thought that we knew that A. D. Robertson was sour, silent, and reclusive as a result of his years of sheepherding in Montana. He spent many hours alone at the edge of the fish pond playing a fiddle. Perhaps he was our "mute inglorious Milton."

Among the several distinctly eccentric men were "Baby" Snook and "Little Joe" Roher. A farm boy from Pennsylvania, Robert Snook could have had no other nickname. At the time, Fanny Brice's celebrated radio character, Baby Snooks, was a fixture in American popular culture, and anyone with a surname remotely resembling Snooks had to endure allusions tying him to her. But the name was not inappropriate for our Shook. His face devoid of any trace of whiskers, he was a baby in appearance — and behavior. His peculiar problem was his refusal to shower. About once a month, at the petition of his suffering bunkmates, our first sergeant (more about him later) would carry Snook off to the showers and scrub him down. Becoming latrine orderly for the battery, Snook pushed his aversion to cleanliness (or nudity) to another strange point. He gathered up all used wet towels and hid them in his footlocker. Joe Roher, a short, pudgy, owlish-looking man, was another problem child. He disdained the Army and barely tolerated its intrusion into his affairs. His duty, it appeared, was to sit on his bunk and read, day-in, day-out. He would not write home, except when about every six months the first sergeant, acting on orders from Army officials who had received inquiries and complaints from Roher's parents, ordered him to do so. Certainly Snook and Roher did not stand alone in the battery in their bizarre behavior, but they stood conspicuous in it.

Just as the Snooks and Rohers were predictable in their eccentricity, some men were predictable in their conventionality. Often priggish, they lived by the rules and expected others to follow suit, dressing in stuffed khaki shirts. Showy and obsequious in their conventionality, they were the Uriah Heeps and Mr. Bumbles among us. I recall Sergeants Bonner and Johnson as examplars of their kind, quick to demand reverence for regulations and ever ready to subscribe smilingly to instructions from above. Perhaps they and a few others like them gave some necessary stability to the battery. They gave little else.

Our first sergeant, Jerome "Jerry" Sarver, was, thank God, all that one did not expect to find in the realm of sergeancy. A big man, six feet four inches and about 230 pounds, he had been drafted and had little stomach for the order and discipline of the Army. We recognized his insufficiency for the exercise of power and shamefully exploited him at times. One of the boys, he did not command respect by the habit of command. He could become angry on occasion, but pumping blood into his reddening face was, we knew, the heart of a pussycat. Yet in a sloppy way he held the battery together, and at bedrock, notwithstanding all the platitudes about respect for stern men of authority, we did admire him, even loved him. He was, I believe, one of nature's noblemen, one of the kindest, gentlest men I have ever known.

I met another kind of nobleman in a hulk of a soldier who joined the battery for a few months after I came to it. Though I can't remember his name, he gave me a valuable gift. He had attended Stanford, was perhaps a graduate of that university, and wore the mantle of intellect. He lugged around a box of books, mostly American novels, and nearly every evening perched himself in a chair in front of his hut and read one. He was the object of some ridicule, even scorn, but persisted in his reading, which separated him from many of us. Perhaps seeing me as a kindred spirit, he urged me to look through his books and read them at my leisure. I did so and kept alive my childhood interest in the world of books.

As for the officers of the battery, I remember little beyond their names. As personalities, they were eminently forgettable. A fellow named Rowe, a first lieutenant, commanded our battery, a husky, stout man who remained isolated from us as though we had the plague. He and his fellow officers were shadowy figures who had virtually nothing to do directly with our everyday lives. They and other officers in the battalion had their whiskey, women, and steaks and dreamed of higher command and the preference that shoulder straps might give them in civilian life. Theirs was a different Army, a different war, from ours.

Whatever their virtues or vices, the comedic, the dour, the bizarre, even the prosaic sort and many others in the battery had identity, even status. If I aspired to create a place among them, I had limited prospects. I was still a rookie, a snot-nosed kid with only a few months of training behind me. I had no unusual experience, skills, talents, or knowledge, no distinct mien that might set me apart from the ordinary run. Except for scratching my rear, I had no unusual personal traits. I could expect, at least at the outset of my life in the battery, no preferential treatment, no easy details; I would have to be a hewer of wood and a drawer of water.

Thus I could hardly complain when after a few days with the battery, I found myself assigned to an ammunition detail. Along with another private, I rode in the bed of a two-and-a-half-ton truck to an ammunition dump and loaded artillery shells on the truck—my first real duty in the Army, something that would really contribute to the smashing of Hirohito. I could see the shells crashing down on the Japanese. They were heavy, but I loaded them with relish, knowing that I could be, was, a hero at a remove.

After we unloaded the ammunition at our batteries, we returned to our huts late in the afternoon. I showered, whistling in bravura, and trudged wearily but eagerly to the mess hall to join my new comrades and tell them, as we ate, of my patriotic labor.

No opportunity presenting itself, I slowly walked fifty yards or so to a postage-stamp-size shack that served as our PX. I thought that I might mingle with the men there, start becoming one of them. I drank a weak syrupy liquid passed off as Coke and sat on a bench with three or four of the old soldiers. After some idle chatter, I began to rise to get another Coke. But I could not straighten out, my spine seemingly locked at a ninety-degree angle. Though I felt little pain, I remained in a fixed position. Almost immediately, the men gathered around me began to laugh and scoff at my distress. Already they perceived me as a goldbrick. But perhaps—I didn't appreciate the possibility at the time—they were ridiculing me for resorting to what they considered an unimaginative ruse for evading continuation of a toilsome duty.

I hobbled along in a semistooped hunch to my hut and literally rolled into my bunk. The next morning I was able to straighten out and, placed on sick call by Sergeant Sarver, walked more or less normally to the dispensary. Here I began to learn something of the way of the world—or at least of my outfit. First the medic, a flap-eared man known as "Jazzy"—

Jazzy Dee—examined me for a second and gave a form to the battalion doctor, who seemed quite oblivious of my presence. Though implying that I
was a malingerer, he did declare that I should not go on any more heavy
work details for a while. It was truly humiliating, but there was no use to
protest my innocence, that I had indeed been unable to straighten out. I
still did not understand that some men in the battery might fault me for an
insipid performance in goldbricking.

I had expected to be nearly alone on sick call. I had seen no one the
previous evening who was obviously ill, had heard of no aches and pains.
Yet there were ten or twelve men at the dispensary, all appearing to be in
some distress. Jazzy gave them a quick look-over, and they left and returned
to duty. What was happening? That very evening I had the answer to my
puzzlement. Jazzy had given all the men an ounce or so of raw alcohol for
ailments that he seemed particularly able to discover and diagnose. In the
evening, undoubtedly following his prescription, they mixed the alcohol
with Cokes at the PX and subsequently became a little tipsy but presumably
cured of their afflictions. A few men also had access to the barber's after-
shave tonic, which, often at the price of great discomfort, met their peculiar
need for John Barleycorn.

It was the beginning of a series of revelations about the nature of war
in the Hawaiian Islands, at least for the Headquarters Battery of the 866th
Anti-Aircraft Battalion. A few days after straightening myself out, I pulled
guard duty. I had abhorred it at Camp Wallace. I had walked my post there
in a stiff military manner, ever prepared to recite my orders, always fearing
a court-martial for a breach of regulations. The very security of the nation
had rested on my shoulders, on my rifle at the ready.

Guard duty at the battery, in contrast, was an astonishing exercise in
laxity, a lark. I shared duty with a tall lanky man named Taylor who had
recently returned from detached service on Christmas Island. We had to
walk two hours, each taking a post about two hundred yards long, before
two more guards relieved us while we slept for two hours and then returned
to our posts for another two hours. At our meeting as our duty began, Taylor
said, "You sleep first." "Sleep first? What do you mean?" I asked. "You sleep
in the latrine while I walk both posts. Then I'll sleep while you walk them."
I could hardly believe what he was proposing, demanding. But here was an
experienced veteran, and I wanted to become one of the boys. What should
I do? Argue with him, refuse, or acquiesce? I flopped the test of duty. Reluctantly, apprehensively, I went to the latrine and lay on a bench, envisioning
Japanese overrunning the peninsula because I was sleeping. I could not sleep
and felt great relief when the two hours passed without my dereliction discovered. Then I fled to my hut for an honest sleep of two hours.

My ordeal, though, was not at an end. As the hour neared for me to
walk both posts, Taylor, who had been gambling at the rec hall, came to my

hut to awaken me. I should, he said, go to the mess hall and help myself to some bologna ("horsecock") and cheese; if I needed a taste of alcohol, I might try the lemon extract. Never mind, he insisted, about walking my post. No one ever did. Just walk around the battery once in a while. He virtually ordered me to the mess hall. Again, reluctantly I acquiesced in his command. Choking down a sandwich, I hurried off to my post in defiance of Taylor's words and walked it like a good soldier.

Like several other details that I pulled after my debacle as an ammunition man — KP and policing the battery area among them — guard duty was not physically demanding. Meanwhile, Jerry Sarver was looking for duty for me of a steady nature, something that would utilize my abilities without taxing my body. Recognizing my limits, he placed me on permanent KP. At first, I was appalled, seeing such duty as ignominious, but soon realized that it had certain compensating rewards.

First of all, the hours were not burdensome. Like the cooks, I was on duty twenty-four hours, from noon to noon, and then was free for the next twenty-four hours. If I wanted to be off an entire day, I could usually get a morning or afternoon off. Moreover, the work was not particularly onerous. Awaking at 4:30 A.M., I started the fire to heat water for washing mess equipment. Then I prepared the coffee; "prepared" was a euphemism meaning that I threw a sack of coffee into a thirty-gallon container of hot water. After assisting the cooks in serving breakfast to a chow line, I had to clean the gas burners for the cooking stoves. It was dirty but not difficult work. Then I often sat down with one or two men assigned to KP for the day and peeled potatoes. Far from a benumbing task, this time-dishonored labor gave us an opportunity for leisurely swapping stories of various sorts, usually about our pre–Army lives.

Only one chore did I find repugnant. About once every ten days, two boxes of frozen chickens, plucked but not eviscerated, arrived at the mess hall, a delivery from the Quartermaster Corps. It fell to me to clean them, usually about thirty. If the chickens had not thawed enough, I had to pull and tug the entrails out, sometime roughing my knuckles against the cold bones. If the chickens had thawed excessively, I could not grasp all the viscera slipping here and there.

Diminishing in my mind the indignities of *l'affaire du poulet* was my occasional opportunity to join the cooks in the preparation of an exotic dish for the battery — say, Spam rolled around dressing. I won a measure of distinction as a master of eggs. About once a week, we had fresh eggs, and the cooks fried them to order — sunny-side up, over light, or hard — as the men moved through the line. It took some time for the men to pass the grill, and when the cooks discovered that I could break an egg in one hand and deposit the yoke and white on the grill, they pressed me into duty as cook. The line moved more rapidly, and I became a kind of folk hero. I had the privilege too of helping myself to seconds and thirds from the supply of pastry, which, unfortunately, was not usually very good.

I received another dividend from KP in a change in my living quarters. My old hut was adequate but hardly as spacious as the cooks' hut into which I moved. Here I ensconced myself in a large corner affording me considerable space around my bunk. Above the bunk was a large shelf for storage that became the receptacle for all kinds of odds and ends.

Except for Rudy Raymond, the cooks were an affable lot. Don Boeam, the mess sergeant, had little time for the mess hall, spending days and nights with a family in the village that had taken him to their bosom. He was an excellent bugler, and on a doubly rare occasion when Sergeant Jerry could find him in his bunk early in the morning and could roust him from it, he played reveille in place of Jim Pate, who, though the battery bugler, blew incredibly sour notes. On rare occasions, we saw Boeam in the mess hall drinking coffee and ordering supplies. Two buck sergeants were in charge of the shifts — Raymond one, Ed Miller the other. I worked for Miller, a tall gangly man, gregarious and friendly in the extreme. Another Ed, Bowers, was pleasant but taciturn and thus was almost perfectly suited to work for the laconic Raymond, who cared little for idle chatter.

As the weeks and months wore on, I gradually became integrated into the life of the battery. I had a degree of visibility and was participating in numerous off-duty activities. Our recreational life seemed incongruous in the light of the battles taking place in the Pacific. While thousands of Americans were fighting in the Marshalls, the Gilberts, and other island chains, we played.

Nearly every week in that summer and fall of 1943, twenty or thirty of us, obtaining trucks through the easy hand of Jerry, went to Honolulu to see the Seventh (Army) Air Force baseball team play. Composed of established stars like Joe DiMaggio and Joe Gordon, both Yankees, and coming stars like Ferris Fain and Bob Dillinger, the Air Force squad regularly demolished the Navy and Army teams, each of which had but one or two major leaguers on their rosters. Fall also saw many of us bowling in a league in Honolulu. At the battery, we often played softball and organized Ping-Pong tournaments. On my afternoons off, I played marathon Ping-Pong games with Black. Gambling was another source of recreation, but I had neither the money nor the nerve for it.

Despite our varying activities, time could weigh heavy on our hands, and like children at play, we sought to create new and novel means of entertainment. We reached a certain perverseness in our search for play when we attempted to enhance the sexual life of two battery dogs, Herman and Hazel. Herman was a small, low-slung multiple-strain dog, Hazel a much larger animal of dubious origins. Realizing one day that Hazel was in heat, we looked for ways to facilitate the coupling of the two. That seemed quite unlikely, though, because of the very considerable difference in the heights of their sexual mechanisms. But someone had a brilliant thought. Why not put both dogs on the pitched roof of a hut, Herman above Hazel in a position enabling him to mount her? It was a fool's errand but the source of much raucous laughter and vulgar talk. Herman, despite our vigorous encouragement, made no attempt at coupling. Hazel crouched in fear. Both dogs were terrified. Finally we removed them from the roof and sent them on their way to practice their own devices.

The holidays that should have been festive breaks from routine were, behind their celebratory masks, reminders of happier days with our families at home. Better than Christmas, I remember Thanksgiving at the peninsula. Gathering at an old corrugated tin church that the villagers had made available to us, we celebrated the day. Perhaps viewing the villagers as the Pilgrims did the Indians, we invited them to share our turkey and the traditional trimmings. A few men knew them well, had spent countless hours with them and their daughters, but many of us had never met or talked to them and thus looked forward to meeting them. They were appreciative guests, and we were gracious hosts. After we cleared the table of the remaining scraps of food, a quartet of our men sang a few songs, and several nubile *wahines* performed a hula for us. At the surface, we seemed to enjoy ourselves; nonetheless, our hearts were thousands of miles away—in Ohio, New York, Massachusetts.

Whatever the day meant for us, it came to an unpleasant end. Some liquor was floating around—perhaps some officer had shared his largesse with the troops—and one James Kaye, always a tense young soldier, had taken more than his share of it and was expressing his contempt for the Army in a loud voice near the barn. Told by Jerry to shut up and return to the battery area, he rushed to his hut, took his rifle from the rack, and fired it in the air. Startled, everyone at the dinner became restless, and some soldiers, curious about what was happening, began to leave the barn. Jerry and three other men, all armed with rifles, confronted Kaye and ordered him to lay his rifle down. At his refusal, they began advancing on him at a distance of about ten feet. He kept retreating and retreating as they advanced and talked to him. Only when he reached the very end of the ramshackle pier at the end of the peninsula did he finally surrender his rifle and himself. By that time, the dinner was ending in a shambles, soldiers silently returning to their huts, distraught villagers to their homes. Kaye spent the remainder of the day—and many more days—in a hospital and eventually received a medical discharge.

In our search for recreation and entertainment, we could leave the battery on a pass two or three times a month. I did not use mine very wisely. Usually, I went to Honolulu, ignoring other points of interest on the island. Hitching a ride, often in an Army vehicle, I typically arrived in Honolulu

Downtown Honolulu, 1943.

by around nine in the morning with little idea of what I would do for the next six or seven hours. Mechanistically, I walked around the downtown area, going in and out of retail stores, particularly the two bookstores there. I always walked near the curb staring straight ahead, Zombielike, as though I could see nothing to the left or right. Thus I intended to avoid saluting an officer every five or six steps. An officer once nabbed me and ordered me to salute him — the bastard. After that, I delivered snappy but contemptuous salutes of defiance to the ninety-day wonders. Evidently fearing that the thousands of servicemen on the islands would soon breed a famine, I interrupted my steps every two or three hours at a dirty grill at streetside to force a greasy hamburger down to my stomach. One day, breaking with stale routine, I tried the native dish, poi, a pastelike substance made out of taro root into varying consistencies — one-finger, two-finger, or three-finger poi. "Poi, my boy," said the local lore, "will make a man out of you." I agreed. The stench and taste of the stuff drove me gagging down the street.

There were several establishments abutting the sidewalks where one could have his picture taken with a girl in a hula skirt coiled around his body like a snake. Many times I gawked at the sailors and soldiers making fools of themselves before I decided to do likewise. Seeing the embarrassing results and feeling crass, I never sent a print home. I did mail one to my brother, who for many years threatened to blackmail me with it.

Ordinarily I had time to get down to Waikiki Beach. There I walked near the beach and explored the lobbies of the two old-line hotels, the Royal Hawaiian and the Moana, soaking up the ambience I thought was there. On three-day pass, I stayed overnight at the Moana, hoping and waiting to find something or someone to enliven my existence. Nothing happened. Often I took in a movie at the Waikiki Theater and had dinner at Trader Vic's. Once I found my way from the beach to a public library and read for a couple of hours, which I could have done at the peninsula.

All sailors and soldiers in Honolulu had some thought of whoring after Babylon. And Babylon was there. On Hotel Street a row of whorehouses stood ready to minister to the needs of the flesh. A few houses also plied their trade on Nuuanu Avenue. Men in uniform lined up in front of the houses on Hotel Street from noon to evening every weekday awaiting the madam's call of "next," signaling them to move closer to the shrine of love.

I knew of the houses but for many months resisted a desire to visit one. But gradually the hormones took their toll, and, what the hell, I thought, I was a man at war. Would it do for me to die a virgin? Early one morning, well before anyone was stirring inside, I approached the door of a house on Nuuanu (Nuuanu was less conspicuous in the business and hence, I thought, less immoral), found it open, and nervously ascended a flight of steps to a second-story landing. I rang the bell, and a bleary-eyed madam answered my ringing. She told me to wait and ten or fifteen minutes later beckoned me into a dingy parlor. I paid three dollars and took a few hesitant steps to a small bedroom, there taking off all my clothing except, for some strange reason, my cap. In a second my woman joined me. I recall absolutely nothing about her. Surely she and the madam must have laughed at me later as a classic example of a youth on his first foray into the bedroom. I was obviously tense and hasty in my love and did not even remove my cap. Certainly I had no pleasure out of the encounter, (it was no more than that), indeed felt revulsion. Even the slightest pleasure would not have been worth the pain that I met at the pro station. I hastened there to receive the medical treatment intended to protect me from a "distemper," as Ben Franklin once put it. The medic employed a medieval instrument of torture, a long needle that he thrust into the male appendage. The pain was excruciating. It cured all my thoughts of purchased love. Never again did I attend the painted ladies of the night, day or night. My brief and embarrassing life in illicit sex had ended, a casualty of antisepticism.

Because the Hawaiian Islands were an important hub in the movement of sailors and soldiers throughout the Pacific, servicemen often met friends and relatives in uniform there, particularly in Honolulu, by chance or by prior arrangements. Such meetings were the occasion for animated conversation about adventures, friends in common at home or in the service, and the past and present in the home community. Thus the hometown could come to one's fingertips.

One day I had the good fortune of running into Billy Bennett in Honolulu as he came out of the YMCA. He was a year younger than I and had been a classmate of my brother's. Though I had not known him well, we had a pleasant visit as we re-created scenes of the Miamisburg we both knew.

My meeting with "Uncle Sam" became a part of family folklore. A younger brother of my mother, Uncle Sam was about ten years older than I. He had been close to my family during my childhood, and I welcomed the opportunity to meet him when his naval unit came to Oahu. Through the crisscrossing of letters among our families, we were able to arrange getting together in Honolulu. We met at the YMCA, talked at length, and had lunch. It would be appropriate, we agreed, to have a picture taken together to send to our families. Arm in arm, we appeared on the snapshots that we mailed to our homes. Almost at the moment that they received the pictures, the proud families sent copies to the Miamisburg *News* and the Dayton *Daily News*, both of which ran columns on "Boys in the Service." The Dayton newspaper dutifully published the photograph, noting in the caption that "Boyhood Chums Meet in Hawaii." To this day I call Uncle Sam "chum."

No one could count on meetings with friends and relatives for sustaining lifelines to home, and like nearly all soldiers, I read letters for creation of the past and present there. Thus mail call, though a routine event, could become a soldier's solace or sorrow. At Camp Wallace, as I noted earlier, it had been a chaotic affair. The battalion clerk, surrounded by a hundred or more men, read names of men receiving letters or packages, then passed them through a chain of outstretched hands to the recipients. Often it seemed unfair, a few men getting the lion's share of the letters, many receiving one or none at all. In any case, then we stole what minutes we could from our training for a hasty reading. At the peninsula, our mail came to us in a more civilized manner. Each day Black personally delivered letters and packages to each hut, and we always had time to read the letters and open the packages at our leisure.

My parents wrote to me at least once a week, sometimes twice, my sister when the spirit moved her, my brother about once a month. My parents and sister described the routine of their lives—what was happening to my friends, who had gone into service, and what was going on in Miamisburg. Often they gave me news of my brother. John had gone into the Army in the summer of 1943, taking his basic training at Fort Benning, Georgia, ostensibly as a vehicle maintenance man. But he never became a mechanic working on Jeeps or trucks. Instead, he found himself serving as a rifleman and in a mortar crew in the 85th Infantry Division, which fought for months against the Germans in Italy. We were always worried about him, though our letters never overtly raised fears for him. He wrote to me regularly, except for the periods when his outfit was engaged in intensive fighting. He survived the fighting in Italy, recalling later that his closest call to a Purple Heart came when a German artillery shell hit near him and nicked his shoe. Almost incongruously, though truly a rough and tough football player and a case-hardened combat veteran, he went on to become a librarian, ever gentle and kind.

My mother often sent me cookies and candy. Invariably, the cookies were a crumbling mess and extremely stale. Other men received such damaged goods, and we took great delight in comparing the state of our cookies. For months I did not apprise my mother of what was happening to the cookies; I did not have the heart for it. At last I did, and she began to send fruitcakes, which retained their shape and semblance of freshness. At the taste of a fruitcake today, I always recall stale cookies.

Besides the letters from my family, I looked forward to reading the local newspaper, the Miamisburg News, a weekly compendium of the recent history of my hometown. Reading it from stem to stern, I learned about the births, deaths, marriages, parties, meetings, sales, crimes, and more in Miamisburg, the whole spectrum of public life there. I followed the goings and comings of soldiers and sailors from the community, many of whom I knew. Though at times the columns about servicemen implied that only Miamisburg boys were winning the war, they often offered reasonably accurate accounts of local men fighting in Guadacanal or flying over the Ploesti oil fields.

In one celebrated column, one that became a part of local lore, the News became an unwitting party to a soldier's deception. Appearing early in 1944, it told of the exploits of Junior Knee, a boy I had known slightly. Home on furlough, this "distinguished son" of the community addressed a noon meeting of the Rotary Club and recounted a tale of high adventure. He had served, he said, as a radioman and turret gunner in a bomber attacking the enemy in the Mediterranean. His aircraft shot down by the Germans in "heavy action," he was wounded in the leg, miraculously survived the crash landing, subsisted on tropical berries, and with the aid of African natives returned to his base. Then he had gone on to fight the Japanese in the Asian theater. He had found time too to serve as a special guard for Franklin D. Roosevelt and Winston Churchill at a secret meeting in Turkey. Naturally, he was beribboned beyond measure—service ribbons galore from all theaters and the Purple Heart. The Rotarians were proud to host such a hero!

After reading the story, I wrote to my parents, perplexed and perhaps envious. Junior, I noted, was two years younger than I and had had little time for the adventures he recounted. Besides, virtually no soldiers were moving from the European theater to the Asiatic theater in 1943. A few weeks later, my father sent me a clipping reporting that Junior had bent

Ulysses' bow a bit, that he had lied. Though he had been in the Air Corps briefly, he had never left the United States. When he appeared before the Rotarians, he was AWOL. The "distinguished son" was less distinguished in the stockade.

As the months of 1943 passed by, we continued our pursuit of pleasure and our unsoldierly conduct. A small number of men were becoming weary of duty in the island paradise and were quite willing to move on to a new scene that might be more exciting and dangerous. The majority, though, were content and expressed no interest in coming closer to the fighting in the Pacific.

Inspections, in consonance with the tenor of our laxity, were a wonder to behold in their variance from conventional military behavior. The officers conducted them only because of a faint adherence to duty, and the men turned them into comic operas. One inspection in particular exemplified the state of discipline in our world of nonchalance. On hearing word of an impending inspection, the men in our hut made a perfunctory tightening of bed covers and sweeping of floors. No one feared the coming of the officers. Indeed, when Lieutenant Rowe entered our hut accompanied by an entourage of lesser officers and Jerry, we stood at limp attention, indifferent to if not contemptuous of them.

They made a quick sashay past our bunks, but for some reason Rowe stopped at Raymond's bunk and reached above to the storage platform. Rummaging around, he knocked over a half-empty can of beer; down it came, striking him on the head and spilling its contents on him. Now, I thought as I held back my laughter, here would come real punishment, even in our slack outfit. But the commander gave Raymond the gentlest rebuke: "Be a little more careful about your beer, Sergeant Raymond." Perhaps he knew that the sergeant did not readily suffer censure of any sort.

Almost fittingly, the one really serious inspection imposed on us — at least we foresaw it that way — triggered an emotional eruption. Captains, colonels, and even generals from the Inspector General's office, Jerry told us one day, would be descending on the battery for a rigorous inspection of the men and their equipment. It seemed liked earnest business (even the title of the inspector was threatening), and we quaked a bit. So we began policing the battery area and cleaning rifles a few days before the scheduled visit. On the day before, we were all giving unwonted attention to our huts, washing layers of dirt off windows and finding lost socks and other personal items under beds.

As we worked, somehow we learned that A. D. Robertson, the ever-silent sheepherder who rarely left the peninsula — usually he scratched his fiddle alone on a hillside on his days off — had asked for a pass for the following day. Lieutenant Rowe, who never concerned himself with such a mundane matter, had told him that he could have it if the entire battery passed muster at a preinspection tour to be conducted later in the day. Apparently for some minor deficiency, Rowe found the battery wanting and denied A. D.'s request for a pass.

That evening, as I lolled in a wooden chair in front of my hut, A. D. walked by. Striding purposefully might be the better way to put it; certainly he seemed more determined than ever before. Curious, I asked him where he was going. "I'm gonna hit the battery commander in the nose." I was much amused, never having heard him express anger or satisfaction about anything. I thought little of his words and remained amused when on retracing his steps, he declared in response to my question about whether he had seen the commander that he had seen him and struck him. Still I was amused.

A few minutes later, three soliders, their rifles at the ready, hurried along the path in front of my hut. "Have you seen Robertson?" they asked. I told them of his passing and learned a moment later from other soldiers that he had encountered the battery commander, another officer, and Jerry as they came out of the rec hall. He had hit all of them—bloodied Rowe's nose, blackened the other officer's eye, and cut Jerry's lip quite badly, so badly that he had to go to a hospital for emergency treatment.

The soldiers corraled A. D. with no trouble (he had no quarrel with them) and hustled him off to the military police in Honolulu. Eventually, he was discharged with a Section Eight as mentally unfit. What a deal, we noted: He had creamed two officers and ended up with a discharge that took him home to Montana and his sheep. Sooner or later, unfortunately often later, the Army lay bare the weaknesses of men it so easily embraced as draftees.

The inspection that followed the next day was anticlimactic. For all the intensity of our preparation for it, it was an abbreviated affair. The inspection officers rushed through the battery as though they were headed for some wanton *wahine* at Waikiki beach. Of course, we read some reassurance in the officers' haste. A few men had interpreted the inspection as a foretoken of a radical change for us, perhaps a departure from the islands. Now we dismissed it as meaningless sport.

If the inspection had presaged some new setting for us, our "firing for record" soon thereafter could have reinforced our fears but for the fact that Jerry treated it as an unwarranted intrusion into his pacific routine and the battery's way of life. Early one week Black had posted a notice on the bulletin board stating that on the following Sunday the entire battery would go to a firing range thirty miles or so down the road and fire our rifles for record—become marksmen again.

Jerry was not pleased. He observed the Sabbath as a day of rest, though not of reverence, and did not easily suffer the Army's interference with his personal time and affairs. Moreover, he had to arrange transportation for us, get food to us, keep records, and make reports — simply too much to expect of him and Black. Having no choice but to complain bitterly, early on Sunday he shoved us into trucks and led them in a Jeep to the firing range. The firing went routinely. Everyone fired, and the privates and corporals manned the butts. About ten men, I among them, did not qualify. Maggie's drawers rose repeatedly after I fired, as though an automatic and necessary cause of the effect, the missed target.

Jerry was quite displeased with the results. Though only about ten of us had failed, he again had to make arrangements for us that would interrupt his Sabbath. But he had to arrange, and we had to go. We fired again, and three or four men, I among them, again failed to qualify. Jerry said little, obviously irritated by our incompetence, which would require another, though smaller, break with his sabbatical routine.

Early the next day he collared me. "You will qualify next Sunday, Becker!" "I don't know how, Sarge," I whined; "I flinch when I fire." "Never mind, you will qualify. No more Maggie's drawers for you." Naïve as I was, I was mystified and fearful. How in the name of heaven could I hit a target that I could barely see as I flinched? Unlike Sisyphus, I could not even roll the stone halfway up the hill. Soon enough on Sunday, I understood, I knew. Jerry himself went to the butts and supervised marking the targets. Again and again, all of us hit the bull's-eye or close to it. The result tabulated, I became a sharpshooter. What a transformation! It was not very comforting to me, though, as I speculated what would happen if I had to fire on the enemy.

Perhaps Jerry envisioned the same scene. A few days after my success on the range — too coincident with it, I believed — he designated me as one of the two battery grenadiers. A grenadier had to carry a rifle equipped with a grenade launcher and pouch containing three rifle grenades. He might fire the grenades at gun emplacements or tanks, large targets that presumably did not require him to be an unerring marksman. For nearly all my remaining service, I carried the grenades in the pouch that became almost a part of my body, an ugly growth at my side that I feared might explode at any second. I hated it. Withal, the duty had its reward. The table of organization for the battery called for the rank of corporal for a grenadier. By incompetency, then, I rose to that high level. I had expected and was satisfied to remain a private in the U.S. Army. Then for a moment the taste of rank was in my mouth. But the fancy passing quickly by, soon enough, like Housman's poetic swain, I was "quite myself again," content to remain as I was.

Soon, along with the other men in the battery, I was put to the test of using grenades. No doubt the exercise was another link in the chain of our preparation for combat. We boarded our trucks one day and followed a twisting asphalt road to a forested patch of land in the center of the island. There, everyone had to stand in a protective pit and lob a grenade at the imaginary enemy in front of us. Everyone feared dropping his grenade in the pit after pulling the pin; that would put an end to one's passion for glory. Fortunately, we all pitched our grenades out of the pit without incident. But the men standing to our rear, some 20 yards or so, did not have proper shelter, and at least 10 suffered minor cuts as the fragments of grenades flew in every direction. The Army had been recklessly careless in exposing us to such a hazard, so I thought, but perhaps, I reasoned later, the training officers were attempting to give us a taste of things to come. I also had to fire a rifle grenade. The firing gave my shoulder a terrible jolt, so much so that in the recoil I was unable to see where my grenade had struck. I prayed that never again would I launch a grenade, in Oahu or elsewhere.

Grenade lobbing and launching at an end, a few weeks later everyone had to demonstrate his ability to swim under conditions of combat. When I first heard of the test or training or whatever it was, I was alarmed. We were expected to swim a hundred yards with packs on our backs, rifles on our shoulders, as though we were pursuing the Japs up a jungle stream. As a child and boy, I had detested swimming. My eyes and nose could not tolerate submersion in water, and I always feared drowning. I knew, though, that what we had to do might be far less demanding than what we had been told that we had to do. And as a matter of fact, the swim was an exercise in frivolity and futility. We carried our packs and rifles, all right, but the stream approximating one in combat was only about a foot deep, a mush of mud blanketing its bed. I flung myself into the water and dog-paddled the course. It was laborious, but as we saw ourselves slopping around in the roily water, all we could do was shriek in laughter. We came out a muddy mess, facing a horrendous cleanup of ourselves and our equipment. War could be hell.

Not many days later, we took what our officers called a forced march. Once again we were attacking the enemy, the perfidious Japs. It was the only hike the battery took while I was with it. From the outset it was a fraud. We put our packs on — nothing in them — and slung our rifles and gas masks on our shoulders. Led by Jerry, we struck off from the peninsula at about nine in the morning, walking along the asphalt road stretching out to the north shore of Oahu. Our pace was easy, punctuated by frequent breaks and idle chatter. Then Lieutenant Rowe, playing soldier, suddenly shouted "gas" and ordered everyone to put on his gas mask. As we ripped our masks out of their packs, apples, oranges, and candy bars fell out and littered the ground. Rowe was beside himself. At noon, after we had covered seven or eight miles (hardly a "forced" march), we had a lunch of C-rations in picnic fashion among a stand of palm trees. By two in the afternoon, we had retraced our steps to the peninsula, barely fatigued but permitted to rest the remainder of the day. Rehearsal for war could be frightening. What the hell was the Army thinking of going through such a charade?

Ironically but perhaps appropriately, even as I was failing miserably as a rifleman and grenadier, I was seeking to become an officer. Well, it wasn't quite like that. At the time, though life in the Army was bearable for me, I longed to return home for at least a visit. Often, as I went to bed, I pondered the means by which I might get back to Ohio. But I could not discover any, even far-fetched ones. A man in the motor pool, Baysacker, had gone home at the death of a member of his family, but I was not prepared to wish or ask anyone in the family to facilitate my return that way.

Then, as though God had given me a personal hearing, a window of opportunity opened for me. Calling me into his office one day, Jerry made a surprising announcement to me: Alone among the men in the battery, I met the requirements for possible appointment to West Point. Each year, he informed me, the Army could appoint several score enlisted men to the academy. That year eight men would come from our command, the Pacific Ocean Area. By virtue of my score on an intelligence test that I had taken months before, my marital status, and other factors (I did not know what they were), I was one of 30 men in the command who could seek a berth at West Point.

I stammered out my willingness to be a candidate. Of course, I was all puffed up at the distinction and basked in its glory, especially as I came to the realization that everyone in the battery, learning of my candidacy, accorded me status as an intellect. It was heady stuff. Little did they know that I had failed plane geometry in high school and that algebraic equations frightened me to death. No doubt, though, they understood that I equated an appointment to West Point with a ticket home, and certainly I viewed it that way.

My quest for the appointment went swimmingly at first. I spent a day at Fort Shafter near Honolulu taking a thorough physical examination. I passed it with flying colors and figuratively thumbed my nose at the Navy when the ophthalmologist declared my eyesight perfectly normal — I was not color-blind. Then I took some kind of written test and evidently did reasonably well; at least I became one of the final eighteen candidates for the eight appointments. The odds, I figured, looked good for a return trip to the States.

Finally, I braced myself for the concluding and conclusive trial for the Holy Grail — an interview with a board of Army officers, all graduates of the Point. I did not know exactly what to expect but could have expended some effort at preparation. I could have read, for example, could have gone to the Honolulu public library and read something of West Point. Indeed I should have. Though my remembrance of the officers is terribly blurred, I vividly recall their opening, their decisive questions, and my fatally defective

responses: "Where is West Point?" "I dunno." "Why is it called West Point?"
"I dunno." "When was it founded?" "I dunno."

Egg covered my face, dripped everywhere. The officers, protectors of
the alma mater from ignorant intruders, were dismissing me, I could see,
as a serious aspirant for lodging at their West Point. Within a few days, their
word came to me: I would remain with the Headquarters Battery of the
866th Anti-Aircraft Artillery Battalion.

So ended my path to glory. But I lost little status at the battery for my
failure, for I still retained the singular distinction of standing alone among
the men as a candidate for a high place. Probably it was for the best. All ap-
pointees had to spend six months at Amherst preparing for entry to West
Point. Surely I would have failed a branch of mathematics at one of the in-
stitutions, as I had in high school, would have been assigned to an infantry
unit, and would have been killed in France or Germany. Thus I read the
outcome as a providential decision. Yet I continued through the years to
have visions of myself as General Becker, U.S.M.A., 1948, Chief of Staff,
Defender of the Nation.

The great inspection, the firing for record, the grenade lobbing, the
swimming, despite our nonchalant view of them at their termination, did
have significance for us. For evidently they were movements in a train of
changes leading us to scenes far from our idyllic peninsula. In March 1944,
after the battery had spent two years at Lihikai, after I had been there for
about ten months, we received orders to move to an Army camp at Barbers
Point on the leeward side of Oahu. Many of us feared and a few hoped that
we were now linked to a large venture, one that would see us leaving the
islands for a theater where the war might be like a war.

Barbers Point was no paradise. Here on a scrubby plain near the ocean
we exchanged the quasi privacy of our huts for a large barracks with double
bunks, forcing us tightly together. There was little leisure time for recreational activity. The battery was kept busy servicing all the gun batteries,
which were spending more and more time firing their guns in practice runs.
We took our only pleasure from following Woody Woodpecker as he cavorted
in the cartoons we saw at a wretched little theater. Life was entirely dull,
and we were reduced to speculation about where we were headed.

Speculation centered on fighting fronts when we excerpted a week
from our routine for "jungle training" led by a crazy Marine at a remote site
in central Oahu. Presumably it was intended to toughen us up for combat,
to get us ready for the enemy. But at the end of the week I was no readier
for combat than I had been the first day of the week, for I had managed to
avoid the training sessions. All I learned from the training derived from accounts of other men, who told me of forced marches, defending themselves
against infiltrators at night, climbing cliffs by rope, mock fighting with

knives, practicing the art of jujitsu, subsisting on vegetation of the jungle. At the first notice of the training, I had resolved to evade it—it sounded too rigorous and violent for me. Within certain limits, one could control his destiny in the Army, and I did not foresee mine as training for fighting, so I mobilized all kinds of excuses and explanations for Jerry why I should not participate in it—equivocated, maneuvered, and manipulated. Though classified as a grenadier, I was still pulling duty as a permanent KP. The cooks, I insisted, required my help all day, and every day in a new camp the stoves were quite dirty and needed a special cleaning, I had to peel the potatoes by myself. What a line! Jerry knew what I was doing, but he didn't push me, preferring to let a sleeping KP lie. And so I lived the week in the mess hall.

After we had completed our week in ersatz combat and returned to Barbers Point, we expected to ship out for the real thing. But we remained in place for a month or so, and then late in the spring, for reasons the ordinary soldier could not comprehend, we moved to Hickam Field. It was quite a different setting from Barbers Point, a permanent Air Corps base with all kind of facilities for easing the soldier's life. We had pleasant accommodations in small frame buildings. In the mess hall, we used various labor-saving devices—meat slicers, potato-peeling machines—and received daily rations of pastry from the Hickam bakery. The theater showed first-run movies, and two or three times a week the Seventh Air Force baseball team played at the base. Bob Hope and his troupe entertained all base personnel one evening. I was in the packed audience but was so many miles away from the stage that all I could see was the stage and all I could hear was the laughter of the soldiers near it. We had no illusions about staying long at Hickam despite the signs of stability around us. Our battery was obviously marking time for another move.

Sure enough, in midsummer of 1944, as we followed the news of the American campaign in the Marianas, we moved to a tent city at Aiea Heights a few miles from Hickam. A staging area perched on a ragged hillside, it presented to the eye a miserable collection of discolored pyramidal tents, jerry-built mess halls, and makeshift latrines. A good wind could have and should have blown all away. By the thousands, 40,000 or more, we milled in and around a dirty PX where some rowdies slopped in their beer, quiescent men slaked their spirit in syrupy Cokes, and (predictably) fights were commonplace. Tension mounted as we awaited departure, again to what place on the map we knew not. Rumors floated around, taking us to every atoll in the Pacific, to the Philippines, to Formosa.

Surely something big was coming. We had heard that Roosevelt, Admiral Chester Nimitz, and General Douglas MacArthur were meeting in Hawaii, apparently to discuss military strategy in the Central and South Pacific. We were right. As I would read years later, Nimitz, commanding the Pacific Ocean Area, and MacArthur, commander of the Southwest Pacific Area, met with Roosevelt at a palatial home overlooking Waikiki Beach. There for two days the great officers contended for the president's support for their respective plans. Nimitz argued for an invasion of Formosa. MacArthur, invoking logic and self-righteousness, demanded an assault on the Philippines. He had promised the Filipinos that he would return, and evidently Roosevelt gave at least his tacit support to the general.

Even before their meeting, we met the architects of our fate, sort of. On a sunny morning late in July, we arose, dressed in our best khaki (even neckties), shouldered our rifles, marched en masse to a highway, and stood in line on both sides awaiting the advent of the wise men from the East and the West. After an hour or more of boiling in the sun, we heard the order to come to attention, our rifles at present arms.

Down the highway moved a mammoth limousine bearing our leaders. As they passed, everyone furtively shifted his eyes around his rifle in a desperate attempt to see them. I had a glimpse of a blur—a long cigarette holder, a civilian hat, and service caps—and thought that somehow I was seeing history made or making history. Surely my comrades and I were about to take part in a mighty military campaign. Returning to our dusty and dirty tent city, we viewed it as an inappropriate, even obscene, point of departure for a grand expedition. Did the Romans, I asked myself, begin their campaign against the Carthaginians or Gauls in such circumstances?

We lingered, however, for more than a month in our canvas slum, suffering in the sun, before we received an order early in September to strike our tents, literally and figuratively, and prepare for departure. Soon we were stripping bunks, packing duffel bags, and posting letters home. Some of us, envisaging the blood and guts of great battles, went to the ten or twelve men remaining behind (a rear echelon that would join us later) with crated equipment and asked them to hold our small valuables, notably rings. If we survived the impending battle, they would return them to us on their arrival at our destination; otherwise they would send the rings and things to our parents. I entrusted my cameo ring to a friend named, fittingly as it turned out, Henry Feuerstahler.

About September 12, we went from Aiea Heights to a dock at Pearl Harbor, there to board an attack transport named the *J. Franklin Bell*. Our movement was a tribute to the logistical skills of the U.S. Army in meshing men, materials, and machines in a chaotic jumble. Pushed into trucks with our rifles, packs, and duffel bags, we rode to a large open area near our dock. There, under an increasingly red-hot sun, we huddled, sat on our bags, walked, and waited—from late morning to late afternoon, with little water and no food.

Not until the sun began its descent did we begin to board ship. The boarding took hours, but the relief of rest quieted our complaining and tempered our umbrage at our realization that we were on a floating hotel close in accommodations to what we would have found in a Bowery flophouse. Our narrow, dirty hammocks were uncomfortably close to one another, the heads dingy and smelling of urine and excrement (we called them piss and shit), and the deck afforded little space for movement.

As we settled down and waited for the *Bell* to weigh anchor, we heard a chilling, ominous report. One soldier, on boarding and reaching the deck, immediately flung himself down to the dock below, killing himself instantly. Probably his fear of what might be in store for him exceeded his hatred of the Japanese. Perhaps, jested an insensitive soldier, he knew that he could not endure another voyage on a troopship. In any event, his act hardly constituted an auspicious beginning for an army of heroes.

"Eyebrow Easy, Eyebrow Easy" 3

Another Voyage, The Invasion, On the Beach,
At the Observation Post, Return to the Battery

Only hours after the suicide—men and machines paid it little mind—on September 15, sailors cast off lines, the capstan raised the anchor, and the *Bell* slipped slowly through the waters of Pearl Harbor, gradually erasing our view of the island paradise—paradise lost. We all felt a sense of excitement and fear, heightened as our ship joined other ships in a large convoy. Sensitive to the demands for patriotism and manhood, we had perforce to act the role of brave men at war. We thirsted for the combat that certainly was near at hand. Certainly we would teach the Japs a lesson. They would now remember Pearl Harbor. I held myself a real soldier. We now lived in an atmosphere of war. Nearly every day we went through a drill for abandoning ship in event of a submarine attack. We anxiously scanned the sea for periscopes and listened carefully to officers and sergeants warning us not to throw paper and garbage into the ocean—the wily Japanese would follow it as a trail for finding and destroying us.

Our apparent courage notwithstanding, we were apprehensive, fearful men and boys. Had we voiced our real feelings, we would have diminished ourselves in one another's eyes. We did not remember cowardly acts of the Japanese. We remembered and longed for our families, girls in our arms. We wished for an immediate ending to the war that would send our ship in a peaceful direction to the United States. But nothing could stop the onrush of our history.

As usual, the Army commanders did not share their plans for us with us. The rumor mill ground exceeding fine and reground old rumors. The great grain of truth, so we thought, had us becoming part of a task force invading Truk, an island group in the Caroline Islands in the western Pacific. It was a sobering rumor because Truk reputedly was a great fortress. One report had us headed for the Philippines, but usually we discounted it, our armchair generals declaring that the islands were beyond our reach. Still another floating story, not one of common currency, portrayed us landing on Formosa.

Speculation on our unknown venture was unending and bootless, but there was little else to talk about. Life on the ship was monotonously routine — drills for abandoning ship, exercising, more drills. Unless one had the initiative and daring for shortstopping, he spent a good part of the day in a chow line that took him literally to mess, an oversized compartment where everyone ate standing up from metal trays that slipped and slopped on high metal tables as the ship pitched and rolled. Suffice it to say the food was nothing to write home about, though I did so. Playing cards was the staple of recreation. Probably craps would have been more popular, but the officers vigorously enforced a ban on it, evidently fearing that throwing the dice would lead to cheating, disputes, and fighting. Similarly, they forbade poker. So we played rum, hearts, bridge, and particularly pinochle. All over topside, soldiers queued up to play various kinds of pinochle; three-handed cutthroat was especially popular. We liked the speed with which we could play any variety of the game, and it lent itself to gambling that could be hidden from eagle-eyed officers.

We also read a great deal. Some men had brought paperback books with them and were willing to share them with friends. A small library belowdecks dispensed a wide variety of Western, detective, and other adventure novels in paperback. The novel in greatest demand, though, had nothing to do with cowboys, sleuths, or adventurers of any sort. It passed from one soldier to another until all copies were dog-eared and fragmented. It was James Farrell's *Studs Lonigan*. Perhaps not many other titles had much literary merit. In any event, men evidently identified with Studs and the life of frustration he led in Chicago. Evidently too, they discovered just enough sexual innuendoes in *Studs* to excite their hormones.

After about ten days of sailing the Pacific, we reached a harbor in the Marshall Islands ringed by atolls. Around our ship were scores of naval craft and troopships. Something was up, no question about it, but what? Amidst our speculation and much to our surprise, Jerry announced that we could go ashore for a beer party. Whether we wanted beer was beside the point. We had to get off the ship and test dry ground. We had to escape the clutches of the nautical creature. So down the netting into landing craft we went by the thousands one morning. It never occurred to us as we approached the beach that we were rehearsing for a landing on a hostile shore.

Of course, the atoll on which we landed could never have justified the expenditure of one drop of blood, of any sweat, toil, or tears. Called Roman or Romanzov Atoll (after the war, Wotje), it was a spit of sand a few hundred yards wide and 700 or 800 yards long. Aside from a few palm trees extending out of the sand in clumps, it was barren. But no soldiers there were worried about its esthetic qualities. We were there to be on land and to drink six beers — or in my case, the ration of six Cokes and the Cokes that I could exchange for my beers. About 15,000 men were on the atoll at one moment nursing and inhaling their beers. I expected to see a few brawls but noted only a few loud arguments in the three or four hours on the sand. I began to lose faith in the American soldier as a fighting man.

The brief sojourn on Roman Atoll yielded an unexpected dividend for me. Just as I was about to step into the landing craft for my return to the ship, I heard someone calling my name. He was Charles "Monk" Shank from Miamisburg. A Seabee stationed in the Marshalls, he was seven or eight years older than I but had often played golf with me. I always beat him. The next day I returned to the atoll, and Monk and I engaged in a long nostalgic conversation about the Miamisburg we had known and our golfing abilities. I also enjoyed a good mess with him; the Seabees were a kind of aristocracy who usually ate nothing but the best.

After two or three days lying in the harbor, the *Bell* weighed anchor again on September 28, now joining a larger convoy. A latrine rumor began to circulate almost at the moment of our sailing, one so controversial and hence so widespread that it overwhelmed all other stories. The Pacific commanders, as we heard it, had initially intended for us to attack Truk, but MacArthur had called for and won a change in strategy. He would return to the Philippines, as he had sworn to do, and we would return with him. He was a truly generous man.

Our speculation was close to the truth. According to the historical record, early in September, a little more than a month after the meeting of Roosevelt, Nimitz, and MacArthur in Oahu, the Joint Chiefs of Staff directed MacArthur to prepare for an invasion of the Philippines on December 20, at Leyte, southeast of Luzon. MacArthur's staff had already readied plans for a December landing at Mindanao in the islands.

The Joint Chiefs had also ordered Vice Admiral Theodore Wilkinson to lead the 24th Army Corps, the Yap Attack Force, out of Oahu for an assault on Yap, an island cluster in the Caroline Islands, about 500 miles southwest of Guam. The assault there, they believed, would open the door wider for the invasion of the Philippines. Our battalion was one of the many units in the Yap Attack Force.

Then, even as we were boarding the *Bell*, a dramatic change in plans occurred. Admiral William "Bull" Halsey, concluding that carrier attacks of his Third Fleet on the Philippines had revealed a deterioration of Japanese strength, urged Nimitz to ask the Joint Chiefs to cancel the operations against Mindanao and Yap. They agreed, and directed MacArthur to attack Leyte in October. And our task force would go with him, not to Yap.

We heard only the rumors of great command decisions and sailed day after day to wherever we were going. At least and at last, I was developing real sea legs and was feeling half comfortable on deck. At night I often slept, at least half slept, on a hatch cover as I watched the stars overhead pulling us on and on and thought of them as taking me to a monumental meeting with destiny. One could become dramatic and blubbery, even on a miserable tub, as he thought of himself caught up in some great historical enterprise.

The second leg of the voyage was devoid of any real excitement, even though we were coming closer to the home waters of Japan. We did enjoy a momentary respite from boredom and anxiety as we crossed the equator. The sailors and some soliders participated in the rites of King Neptune and his court of pollywogs. Our laughter subsided soon enough, though, as the convoy slashed and tubbed through the Pacific toward the Japanese lying in wait for us at some insular stronghold.

Before we could meet the enemy, we had to make another landfall. Early in October, the *Bell* cast anchor at Seeadler Harbor at Manus Island in the Admiralty Islands. Here the convoy took on more supplies and rendezvoused with more troopships. Here too we had another beer party. It dwarfed the affair at Roman Atoll. Thousands of infantrymen, veterans of the fighting in the Gilbert and Marshall islands, and tough, arrogant Marines congregated on a slice of one island, swilling in their six beers, swearing out their obscene language. Unlike the party at Roman, for some reason this one saw fights breaking out everywhere, provoked by the slightest insult or the slightest perception of one. Soldiers assaulted soldiers and Marines, and Marines roughed up Marines and soldiers. They re-created all the barroom brawls, minus the barrooms, ever filmed in Hollywood. Had the Japanese seen the fighting, surely they would have surrendered forthwith. Thousands of beer cans must have littered the island for years, remainders and reminders of the day the Americans stopped to play and fight.

The party ended, we returned to our ship, again speculating on our destination and destiny, awaiting another sailing. On October 14 we received official word on our purpose, a general order, I suppose: We were an expedition that would invade the Philippines, specifically Leyte. Now we started to get serious. We began to write more letters home; we exerted more effort in cleaning our rifles; we spent more time in retrospection and introspection. We were kinsmen, as it were, of the English archers at Agincourt five centuries before who did "sit patiently, and inly ruminate."

As the convoy sailed farther north, seemingly every day more battlecraft and troopships joined it. At its arrival in the Leyte Gulf on October 19, it constituted a great armada, the most powerful naval force of the war, even stronger than the one in the invasion of Normandy. Two attack groups, the Southern and Northern attack forces, constituted the landing force; our battalion was in the Southern Force. The hour was coming for us to win medals.

On the morning of October 20, called A-Day, perhaps because MacArthur did not want to take a back letter to D-Day in Europe, we filed silently into the Navy mess quarters, heretofore off limits to us. The fare, inappro-

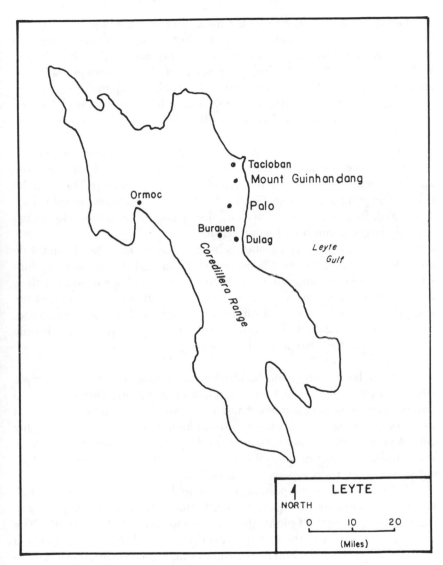

Leyte, Philippine Islands.

priately, might have been prepared for a condemned man—steak, eggs, and beans—nutritious but to what purpose? The steak was thick and tough, but I chewed lovingly and at length. I chewed more intensely as I heard the booming of some guns. Laughingly but nervously, we compared the sound with what we expected from our eating the beans. Perhaps something elemental in vulgarity softened the tension.

Going topside at about eight, I soon made out Leyte at a distance, a faint shape becoming enveloped by the haze of smoke. I observed American aircraft diving toward the island and heard the dull thud of their bombs striking earth and flesh. Battleships, cruisers, and destroyers joined in the bombardment with their salvos. Surely, I thought, the Japanese could not withstand the ferocious attack. Surely our soldiers would wade ashore unscathed, would rout the Japanese still willing to fight, would wear the laurels of the victory.

Around ten, H-Hour, the guns fell silent, and the infantrymen on our ship, men of the Seventh Division, already veterans of brutal fighting in the Pacific, began crawling down the netting into the assault craft. They had the honor of forming the first wave hitting the beach near a town named Dulag. Along with men of the 96th Division, they landed on a three-mile stretch of sandy beaches north and south of Dulag.

I wish that I could remember being envious of them, but I can't. I do recall believing that the great bombardment had made their task easy, their safety fairly certain. Something went wrong. Only an hour or so after their departure, soldiers lying wounded in landing craft were returning to the ship. The Japanese troops had survived the shelling, had not surrendered, had shot back, had inflicted wounds on Americans. I saw real blood. People were getting hurt. What was I doing here?

Late in the afternoon, our battery began the descent into landing craft. I did not want to go, but the Army was not offering options. Our boat pushed through choppy waters to a beach already secured by the infantrymen, but we acted as though the Japanese were immediately in front of us, flinging ourselves into low sandy depressions and abandoned crumbling foxholes. We could hear firing in front of us; it was sporadic, though, and probably not nearly as menacing as we imagined.

At nightfall, an accompanying rain came down. Against it and the dark we had no protection except the earth in which we burrowed. We lay in a dampening ground all night, the rain falling gently but insistently. The rifle and artillery fire in the distance was eerie if not threatening, and when the light of morning reached my earthen vault, I gingerly lifted my body to the surface.

No food, no coffee available, like a rubbernecking tourist in the big city, I began to look around the beach covered with thousands of men and tons of supplies. My undisciplined walk at last brought me within a few feet of a mortar crew lobbing shell after shell at the enemy. I gawked at them, almost as though they were freaks at a sideshow. Standing beside a palm tree directly behind them, I had an excellent vantage point for learning about war. It was great fun.

Then something struck the tree just above my head. A sniper had fired at the mortar crew, and I had nearly paid a price for their traditional vulnerability in battle. The mortar men scattered in all directions. I froze for a moment and then ran like hell.

Returning to the section of the beach where we had come ashore, I met some comrades, not enough, though, to create any semblance of an organization. Later in the morning, Jerry came down the beach looking for everyone and ordered us to remain where we were. Seeking shelter, three of us appropriated a bunker, one evidently once used by the Japanese. For reasons I could not fathom, American troops had ignored it. By its prominence, perhaps it could invite enemy fire. About ten feet high, the bunker commanded an excellent view up and down the beach; inside, it afforded protection from the elements and the enemy and space for sleep. Here we stayed for several days, subsisting on K-rations as we waited for the battery to come together. We heard nothing about the battle inland but assumed that it was going well, hearing ever-diminishing sounds of firing.

Then the war took on a more personal, more dangerous note. On the evening of October 25, we could see flashes of fire in the sky over Leyte Gulf and though we had no certain knowledge of what was happening on the sea below, concluded, correctly as it turned out, that naval forces were engaged in a battle there. In fact, the American Seventh Fleet was in the final hours of a brutal three-day fight with Japanese naval units that, had they won dominion over the Gulf, would have threatened our beachhead on Leyte.

It was still quiet on the beach, but ominously so, as though a preternatural, a malevolent thing from the embattled water had crawled ashore. We all felt dread in our bones. Suddenly a terrible explosion shook the ground, seemingly an inexorable extension of our fear. It raised me, I calculated later, at least a foot off the ground. A frightening series of small explosions followed, something like the detonation of fireworks on July 4th. All night they continued, lighting the sky and sending minute shock waves through the earth. Some men were running wildly from the area, and others were digging themselves into the ground. They expected another attack momentarily, but no one seemed to know the genesis of the great explosion — what it was or where it had come from. Had an enemy battleship or an aircraft struck the beach?

We learned the following morning that a Japanese bomber of some sort had hit an ammunition dump with a large bomb. According to one report, perhaps exaggerated by the terror of the night, 500 men had been killed. I did not, could not, go to the site to verify the figure. We had learned that war could be hell. A man from our motor pool won acclaim (though no medals) for commandeering a bulldozer and using it to bury ammunition even as it was exploding all around him.

All was terribly tense around the beach in the following days. Soldiers were edgy and nervous, ready to shoot at anything that moved. Sailors on ships in the harbor were equally unsteady. Then, on a sunny morning, soldiers and sailors alike exorcised their fear for the moment. I still have the scene in my mind. About a mile to the south beyond our bunker, an American torpedo bomber, a TBF, was flying low and slowly over the naval craft in the harbor. A ship's gunnery crew, apparently mistaking it for a Japanese aircraft, began firing at it, and within a few seconds, every gun on the naval vessels had joined in the attack. The TBF pilot frantically dipped his wings, desperately seeking recognition, and flew toward the beach. There he met a mad reception. Soldiers at machine guns, soldiers with rifles, soldiers with carbines and pistols, began firing at him. They gave him no quarter, no heed to the American insignia clearly visible on the TBF. Like a lighted dynamite fuse, the firing followed the aircraft up the beach until finally it crashed. It was not enough to kill Americans in the air. Firing at low trajectories, the ground troops killed two or three men on the beach. As a final embarrassing note, a Japanese prisoner held on the beach was able to escape during the panic. So much for bravery and coolness under fire! What disillusionment! American soldiers, I had understood, were always calm and brave.

On about the same day, Jerry and the officers, who had been conspicuous by their absence, finally brought the battery together near Dulag. There we raised our ubiquitous pyramidal tents and prepared to support the gun batteries scattered up and down the beach and around the San Pablo airstrip, a hastily constructed strip that lay inland about eight miles near the village of Burauen.

Our stay near Dulag was but momentary. The high command or Jerry decided that all the gun batteries would move near the airstrip at Burauen and that headquarters should follow them. We did not like the decision. On the beach thousands of soldiers remained around us, and we felt strength and security in numbers. Now we were relatively isolated, almost alone, it seemed. Our camp was in a junglelike setting around an abandoned Japanese hangar, and we could easily believe that Japanese troops still lurked among the palm and coconut trees ready to attack us in a banzai charge. Our anxiety heightened at the discovery of a dead American in the underbrush, his body left there by the onrush of the battle. We even took guard duty seriously, warily peering into the darkness from the old bunkers that we crept into at night. Every chirp of a bird we construed as signaling among the Japanese soldiers there.

They were not there, and gradually we became less tense, less fearful of impending disaster. But then we learned again that war could be dangerous. Early in November, as we were preparing for mess call at noon, a squadron of Japanese bombers swept across the San Pablo airstrip and directly over us, dropping bombs and strafing ground troops. They were flying so low that I thought that I could reach out and touch them. Everyone was scrambling for cover. I dove, *ventre à terre*, into a hole that our medical officer, Captain something or other, had dug. A really frightened bird (I was also), he did not want to admit me, but rank had no privilege at that moment, and I forced my body into his protective space.

Fortunately, our casualties were not numerous or very serious. Bill Spurgeon, a communications sergeant, lost a thumb, almost surgically severed from his hand by shrapnel or a machine-gun bullet. The concussion of a bomb knocked Bob Cottle off the hangar, the fall breaking his arm. He was supposed to have been looking for enemy aircraft but gave us no warning. He gave us no relief from his incessant chatter about his fall, as though he had something to do with it. Literally and symbolically, he wore his wound on his sleeve.

After this experience, I understood more about the men on the beach who had been so quick on the trigger. Like nearly everyone else in the battery, I was ready to seek out the nearest hole or depression at any unusual sound; low-flying P38s sent me scurrying for cover. If I had to remain in any open expanse of ground for more than a few minutes, I contemplated digging a hole.

The attack had another consequence for me. Caught by surprise by the Japanese, the battalion officers resolved to improve our capacity for detecting approaching aircraft. Heretofore, only the gun batteries had operated observation posts and only in a uncoordinated way. Now headquarters would maintain a post for all batteries and attempt to provide coordinated warnings to them. Near Burauen was a small promontory offering an observer an unobstructed view east toward the beach, to the north in the direction of an airstrip near Tacloban 20 miles away, and to the south and west along the Coredillera mountain range. It could be an ideal point for an observation post.

Much to my consternation, I was assigned to the post, along with three other men in the battery. We had to take a heavy radio and support equipment to the promontory and there operate "Eyebrow Easy." I didn't want to go. I much preferred to remain within the relatively secure confines of the battery. Despite my considerable skill in manipulation and maneuver, I couldn't wiggle out of the duty. My comrades were equally displeased and equally unable to squirm loose.

There was no disputing the decision. Someone, probably Lieutenant Rowe, had classified all of us by fiat as Intelligence Observers, an impressive denomination signifying that we were qualified for service at an observation post. We were not. We were all novices in the use of the radio and could barely operate it. We had no more training in identification of Japanese airplanes — Bettys and Zekes — than anyone else in the battery. But we were dispensable soldiers, performing trivial tasks for the battery. And the man who called us Intelligence Observers, whoever he was, was a kind of Humpty Dumpty: His words meant just what he chose them to mean, "neither more nor less."

We were boys, buffoons I fear, sent to do men's work. Three of us corporals, one a private, no one had formal or inherent authority over the post. Corporal Bob Lakeman was a big blustery ungovernable Irish American from Chicago whom I liked and feared. Another corporal, Sam Maccone, was a prig obsessed with cleanliness. He vigorously brushed his teeth twice a day. He lacked the ability and particularly the personality to lead us. A model of muscular development, Private John Lavalle was brashly irresponsible, a perpetual candidate for a court-martial who had once taken lodgings in an Army stockade. What I brought to the post was not clear. Perhaps Rowe or someone else, remembering my run for West Point, saw me as an intellect who could outsmart the Japanese and my comrades. The youngest of the quartet and with no record of military accomplishment, I was not likely to become an effectual leader. Competence was not the sign of our four — *miserabile vulgus*.

From the outset, our operation of Eyebrow Easy was an exercise in futility, a disaster. Hitting the wrong switches on a radio that we did not understand, we often lost contact with the gun batteries. We quarreled incessantly about who would perform the arduous labor of turning the hand generator that supplied power for transmissions. Our only shelter was a small pup tent admitting the first and last drops of rain and all between. We had only C- and K-rations for sustenance; novel at first, they soon became unbearable. Already forgetting the recent Japanese attack on our camp and assuming that their decimated air force could not mount another mission over Leyte, we spent unbelievably and unforgivably little time looking for enemy aircraft ("bandits") in the skies around us. Routinely and automatically, we sent out the message "This is Eyebrow Easy, this is Eyebrow Easy; all clear, all is clear."

Rather than scanning the skies for bandits, we sought and found means of diversion. One Ed Jared, a young lieutenant, gave us some moments to while away. Sent to the promontory by the Air Corps to monitor air traffic, he occupied a tumbledown wooden shack about 40 yards from our radio. Early in the campaign, he had won acclaim for his imaginative role in directing carrier-based naval airplanes to safe landings on an unfinished airstrip near Tacloban after their home carriers had suffered battle damage to their flight decks. Slightly arrogant, he enjoyed holding court for us, and though we were envious and even resentful of him, we spent many hours at his feet hearing of his exploits and views of the war. Often he entertained us by singing the lyrics of a currently popular song on the homefront, "I'll Walk Alone," which celebrated the fidelity of a woman to her man at war. We liked the implications of the song.

We were much less passive in our raid of a nearby Air Corps supply depot. Told by other soldiers that security was loose there, Lakeman and I walked into it and hauled away two mattresses and, better yet, several cases of Eagle brand milk. A thick and sweetened condensed milk, it could be eaten with a finger or spoon or spread on crackers. We spared no can in our gluttony. We noticed, coincidentally, a profound and moving change in our bowel habits.

Our propensity for play reached a peculiar level at our discovery of rats, dozens of them, around Lieutenant Jared's shack. Lakeman, often endangering us, shot them at will for a while. Ceremoniously, we buried them with mock military honors and placed crosses of matches on their graves. Maccone refused to participate in the ritual, declaring it filthy and blasphemous. We derisively dismissed his words. Even Saint Paul could not have counseled us to put away childish things.

At the expiration of our ready supply of rats, we gave our attention for a few days to a small contingent of Army nurses who took temporary quarters in a large tent about 300 yards beyond and below our post. We trained our binoculars on the tent hour after hour, certain that sooner or later we would glimpse an ankle or thigh or more. We trotted out all the conventional dirty innuendoes as we smirked and waited for one glorious moment. Our patience and thirst availed us little. All the tease and tantalizer that we saw was a fully clothed body on occasion and panties drying on a clothesline. We did not miss the nurses when they departed after a brief sojourn.

We were more reverent of the persons of two Air Corps fighter pilots who wandered through the area one day. As Lakeman and I threw a baseball back and forth, two men in rumpled but jaunty uniforms walked past us. The ball going astray, one of the men, a short cherubic figure, picked it up and threw it awkwardly to me, noting pointedly that he wasn't much of a baseball player but was good at other things. I recognized him immediately from photographs of him that had appeared in newspapers circulating among us. He was Richard Ira Bong, the leading ace of the Army Air Corps; he had shot down more than 30 Japanese airplanes. Accompanying him was a slender, good-looking man whom I also recognized. I was looking at Thomas McGuire, who had downed nearly as many enemy planes as Bong had. We talked to them for a few minutes, and they walked on. For all our slackness, we felt some awe and admiration for these two men. We had rubbed shoulders with the great and near-great and had enjoyed it.

A few days later, much to our surprise, a Japanese pilot flew his Zero near the airstrip and strafed American positions there. Of course, we didn't see him in time to get to our radio. Almost immediately, a P-38 was on his tail and shot him down in our full view. Later we heard that Bong was the pilot of the P-38. I had a vicarious thrill from his feat. Later we learned that

McGuire had gone down over Luzon. For the moment, the war seemed quite personal to me.

At about the same time, I met some anonymous civilians, a Filipino family from Burauen. I don't remember their names—father, mother, and six children ranging from 6 to 17—but I do recall them as personalities, perhaps as people representative of Filipinos generally. The oldest son, the 17-year-old, came on the promontory one day offering to cut my hair for a peso or so. I needed a haircut and knowing that the Filipinos were an impoverished people, agreed to submit myself to his scissors, though I knew nothing of his abilities with them. He gave me a reasonably good cut until he shaved my neck. Using a mess-kit knife, a dull one at that, and applying some spit to my neck, he proceeded to shave it. He seemed to be pulling out each hair one by one. The pain nearly overwhelmed me; I was ready to go to my knees. But I endured it without complaint, for I did not wish to offend the boy, who seemed anxious to please me. Besides, was I not fighting for equality, the dignity of man, *etc., etc.*?

The young barber invited me to meet his family and join them for dinner. I did so, entering their rickety *nipa* hut late one afternoon. They had brought out all their best dining paraphernalia—worn metal utensils, a handmade linen tablecloth, some chipped plates; it spoke volumes of their poverty and genuine desire to be hospitable. Like the son, the parents were painfully anxious to please, though also quick to bruise. The fare was simple, the main dish *camotes*, a potato with attributes of both white and sweet potatoes. After dinner, the father offered me a drink of *tuba*, which, he told me, was a fruit drink fermented in coconut shells in the tops of coconut trees. Setting aside my pledge not to touch liquor in the face of my host's effort at hospitality, I sipped an ounce or so and declared that it was good. Then he offered to get a bottle for me for a few pesos, and I agreed. Evidently wishing to demonstrate that there was no commercial nexus in his family's friendship, he insisted that I accept a *bolo* knife as a gift from the family.

The next day the son delivered a bottle of *tuba* to me. Something had happened between the dinner and the delivery. The *tuba* was an ungodly witch's brew. One taste of the liquid brought visions of the devil to me, scorched my stomach, and turned it into a hell. Even Lakeman, who was well acquainted with cheap whiskey, could not take it. Once again, I vowed never again to taste the "viper in the glass."

As we dallied the days away on the promontory, the battle for Leyte was continuing. By early December, American arms were clearly prevailing throughout the island. Infantrymen had driven Japanese forces from most of the plain east of the Coredillera range. On the western side, an American invasion at Ormoc, though meeting stubborn resistance, was gradually scattering the enemy. And neither Japanese naval power nor air power seemingly had the strength to challenge our widening control of Leyte. Already grossly inattentive to our duties, we now became even more casual. Ours was a rough existence—poor food and poor shelter—but it didn't seem especially dangerous. We awaited a lesson, a rude awakening from our reverie.

It came on the evening of December 6. We were lying at strange angles in our pup tent, seeking to discover comfortable positions, pulling blankets round us, and arguing about this and that. Hours before, we had left our radio unattended. Then we heard a low buzzing, evidently coming from the south over the Coredilleras. As it became gradually louder, we finally looked in that direction and could make out the shape of airplanes, a dozen or so, apparently two-engine craft of some sort.

Still believing that the Japanese had no strength for Leyte, we saw the aircraft momentarily as American. We heard antiaircraft fire, then saw the flash of the fire in the sky, and at last decided that something was amiss, that the American airplanes were in fact bandits. Frantically, we manned our radio: "Eyebrow Easy, Eyebrow Easy, bandits at one o'clock, at one o'clock!" No response came from our gun batteries, no words, no firing at all. Nor did we hear bombs exploding. Perhaps, we prayed, the enemy had flown on toward the airstrip at Tacloban. The remainder of the night, as we tried to sleep, we heard intermittent small-arms fire. It was not unusual, though, for nervous ground troops to fire their rifles randomly at shadows during the night, and even though the firing was greater than usual, we attached no significance to it.

As dawn broke, we came to an understanding of what had happened. There, five or six hundred yards to our east, draped on trees near the San Pablo airstrip were parachutes. Japanese paratroopers had jumped from the bandits, and we had lain in our pup tents. Had they moved in our direction, we would have been easy prey. Fortunately for us, they had headed toward the airstrip, attempting to disrupt operations there. Joining them, so we heard by rumor, were several hundred Japanese infantrymen isolated in the Coredilleras, who cut through American lines held by support troops between the range and the airstrip. According to one frightening story, the Japanese infantry caught Air Corps men napping and killed them in their beds.

Numbering about 300, the paratroopers, as I read years later, were from the Second Parachute Brigade stationed in southern Luzon. They had jumped from twin-engine transports bearing a resemblance to our DC-3 cargo planes and were supposed to link up with infantry attacking from the west through the Coredilleras. Known as Operation *Wa*, their joint attack had as its goal the capture of three American airstrips on Leyte, Bayug, Buri, and San Pablo. Thus the Japanese hoped to take the initiative in the battle for Leyte and ultimately prevail. Desperation inspired the plan, and poor coordination doomed it. We knew nothing of the Japanese strategy, only that our lives seemed threatened.

Air Corps units and antiaircraft batteries fought off the paratroopers as best they could. One of our batteries won some distinction in a bloody skirmish fought at close quarters. American infantrymen, notably the 11th Airborne Division, came to the rescue and in two days killed all the Japanese troops in our area. Had we been able to read the account of the fight in the *New York Times*, we might have felt slightly abashed. The fight, recounted the report, was the "most colorful" of recent days and was indeed "bitter." Accurately but almost patronizingly, it went on to note that the fighting caused "excitement among rear area units, many of which had never been so close to action."

During the attack, the Japanese cut the road between headquarters and Eyebrow Easy, and at the same time our radio had gone haywire. We had lost all contact with our battery. There Jerry and everyone else imagined and portrayed us as engaged in bloody fighting with the Japanese, defending the airfield to the last man. When the road was open again, Jerry was at our side immediately, seeking personally to ascertain the extent of our fighting and suffering. Though we assured him that we had been in little danger, had not even fired our weapons, he would have it no other way: We had repulsed the enemy. We were heroes.

Soon he had arranged our return to the battery, which, as the campaign was winding down, had returned to a site near the beach. The men there accorded us accolades as heroes of the battery. Jerry manifested a particular concern for me, probably because I was the youngest of the fighting four. He insisted that I take a cot in his tent, stay with him and several other sergeants. For the remainder of my service, except for one hiatus and after Jerry returned home, I was in his tent.

I met one distressing circumstance on my return to the battery. After delays of various kinds, the men in the rear echelon had arrived in Leyte and were with us again. As others had, I sought out Henry Feuerstahler to retrieve my cameo ring, only to learn that he did not have it. Someone, he asserted, had stolen it and other jewelry from him on board ship. I was dumbfounded. I had trusted Henry to be a careful guardian of my ring. He seemed so frank, so open, his face a map of candor, that I wanted to believe him and could not believe talk suggesting that he had converted all the jewelry into cash. I could not fully believe him; I could not fully disbelieve him. His name, meaning "fire stealer," was perhaps instructive.

The loss of the ring was but a trivial and fleeting disappointment in a life at the battery that was reasonably pleasant. There were some routine details for me, KP and policing the area, but nothing especially laborious. Each morning I arose and briefly exercised. As he had in Oahu, Ray Maller reduced our calisthenics to burlesque as he put himself through a cycle of weird contortions. I read a little in the morning or wrote home. Almost every

The battery in Leyte: Ed Pels writing home, 1944.

afternoon I walked on to the beach and threw myself into the breakers striking the shore. The water was dirty, flecked with the flotsam and jetsam of hundreds of ships in the harbor. But what was a little trash after living on the ground near rats and insects? Pleasantly wearied by the breakers, I usually made my way through a grove of coconut trees to a Red Cross tent and there drank a glass of sweet and uncarbonated but cold Coke. Finally I would return to camp, play around with some Spam in the mess hall, and meander through the battery area the rest of the day.

I broke the sequence of my routine for a few days in a vain attempt at

The battery in Leyte: Ray Maller and playmate, 1944.

concocting root beer. My friends in the mess hall had a formula for making root beer, and I decided to try my hand at a batch of it. Somehow, somewhere, I obtained some bottles, made my brew, and bottled it. I had no capper, though, for applying the bottle caps properly. The results were predictable. My product lay exposed to the sun near the mess hall. Soon enough, the bottles were popping their caps. The beer was not fit for man or beast, but my labor gave the men in the battery something to talk and laugh about.

Christmas also offered an interruption to routines. But it was a dreary affair. We put up a few decorative items in the mess hall, among them the remnants of a coconut tree that served as a Christmas tree. I purchased a *bolo* knife and some odoriferous linen napkins, packaged them, and sent them home as presents. No self-respecting Santa would have put them in his sack. It was, of course, a season for reflection. I was now about to enter my third year in the Army and had not seen my family for nearly two years, and the many islands between Leyte and Japan seemed to ensure many more months, even years, of separation. The cliché was true: I hurt too much to laugh but was too old to cry.

My ease, play, and reflection came to an end after a few weeks when soon after Christmas I had to return to duty at a new observation post. Surely the people who selected me for the assignment had in mind the perception of my performance at Eyebrow Easy, not the reality of it. The fastidious Maccone also had to go. Mario Manzano, the morose man, joined us, as did Louis Harcotte, an assertive little figure whose speech rehearsed the patois of his French-Canadian ancestors. We were not a particularly congenial set, but the Army made few allowances on that score.

We had to establish our post on Mount Guinhandang, designated Hill 522 by the Army, just north of Palo about 15 miles north of Dulag and 5 miles south of Tacloban where the Air Corps was operating an airstrip important to air strikes on the Japanese on Luzon. Standing prominently by itself like a sentinel about 2,000 feet above the coastal plain, the mountain, at least in retrospect, appeared to be a stronghold capable of offering formidable resistance to an American advance. On its steep slopes crisscrossed by camouflaged caves, trenches, and emplacements, Japanese soldiers armed with automatic weapons awaited an attack. Nonetheless, infantrymen of the 24th Division, supported by a naval bombardment, had driven them from the mountain in about a day. Here we would look heavenward for Japanese aircraft that might attack the airstrip.

From the beginning, nothing was good, nothing was right about the assignment. We moved our equipment by truck about halfway up the mountain, then packed it on our backs and carried it up a winding trail to the peak. There we put it in a dank wooden shack that the Japanese had apparently once used and somehow had escaped the bombardment of A-Day. It was an exhausting effort that left us cursing our fate.

As soon as the sun set the first day, we all felt uneasy. We knew that Japanese troops had been killed here. We feared that some were yet alive here. The quietness, the pervading darkness — we could see no lights in any direction — created an eeriness, a gloom. Each night two of us stayed in the shack while the other two remained at our base camp halfway down the mountain. Peering into the darkness, we searched for the bandits that did not come — and that could hardly come, for now the Japanese truly had little strength for any offensive action in the Philippines and were being pushed off Luzon. But we had learned a bitter lesson at Burauen and remained alert; and of course we supposed that Japanese soldiers, at least a few, were crawling around the mountain.

Despite our apprehension, we did take an infrequent excursion up and down the mountain. Walking warily along a middle slope one day, Harcotte and I discovered trenches but no evidence of their use by the Japanese. Then we came across a line of skeletons — Japanese apparently caught by artillery fire. We froze in the presence of death. A few odds and ends lay around the remains, including a billfold. Harcotte was ready to pick it up when I noticed a wire attached to it, or what I thought was a wire — a booby trap. I was so tense that I was prepared to see anything. We ran immediately from the scene of death. What cowards we were! I have long regretted our failure to ascertain what was there. Did someone pay a price for our pusillanimous conduct?

Our sojourn on Mount Guinhandang was not long, perhaps a month, but long enough to deprive me of a visit from a cousin. One of my many cousins, Herbie Schenck was an adventuresome character who had been in the Army since 1940. He knew that I was in Leyte with the 866th, and when his outfit stopped in a convoy in Dulag harbor on the way to Luzon, he decided to seek me out for a visit. Locating my battery and learning of my whereabouts, he tried to hitch a ride to the mountain. But the going was slow, and at last he turned back, only to reach the harbor as his convoy and ship were sailing away. Eventually, by scratching around, he caught up with his outfit in Luzon. A buck sergeant, he had been "busted" before, and now the Army again removed his stripes. Later, he allowed that the laughter at family reunions arising out of the tale of his pickle made the pain of his demotion quite worthwhile.

Sometime in February, much to our relief, we departed the mountain and returned to the battery. All was quiet there. The campaign in Leyte virtually over, we were simply waiting for whatever was next. With little to do, the men cast about for diversionary activities. Some sought out women of easy virtue, asking young and old Filipino women whether they would "push-push," but the Filipino women were truly virtuous and spurned the offers of cigarettes, chocolate, and clothing. Others looked for alcohol, found it, and suffered monumental hangovers. Happily, no one got hold of alcohol free gasoline drums, which could cause blindness or death. Many gambled, borrowing hundreds and even thousands of dollars in the mortgaging of their monthly pay. Ray Maller and I expended no little energy in obtaining, one way or another, bread and Spam from the mess hall. In the evening we fried the Spam over a small burner and ate sandwiches until our stomachs could distend no more. We were giants in the earth.

No one seemed able to author any innovative diversions. But in the saga of Virginius Baylor we recognized a real departure from the norm. A thin, short, sallow man from Georgia, Baylor was at least 35 when he joined our battery just before we left Oahu. His late arrival heightened his anonymity among us. For he was a cipher; he meant nothing to us. He had no shred of personality, no verve, no distinguishing marks, nothing. Even his appearance reinforced his nothingness; he was mouselike, his nose sloping down to a zeroid chin. His first name seemed quite right, implying that he had never known strong drink or loose women. No one even disliked him. What was there to dislike? No one knew that he was living; no one cared whether he lived or died. Every outfit in the Army had a man like Baylor. It had nothing to do with rank; even a sergeant, an officer, might be such a man, one who projected no image, had no real identity, was a void.

Yet Baylor was a man, and his time had come as we waited for new ventures. By March 1945, American forces had invaded Luzon and secured Manila. Soldiers in Leyte could obtain three-day passes and, by some arrangement that I never understood, transportation by Air Corps cargo planes to Manila. In any case, Baylor asked for a pass, received it, and went off with several other men from the battery to that city. Of course, he merely happened to be going on the same airplane with them; he was not one of them. Why would he go? we asked one another. He would not carouse, he would not drink, he would not seek out plump partridges. What a waste of time!

While Baylor and the others were in Manila, word came that we had to prepare to move. We had to crate equipment, move it to the beach and onto a ship, take various shots for malaria and other dread diseases. As we completed our labor, the men returned from Manila—except for Baylor. Where was Baylor? Jerry nonchalantly inquired of them. They had seen him every day in Manila, they reported. Every day they had seen him in a jinrikisha, obviously drunk and swearing at the driver. But he had not shown himself, drunk or sober, at the airport for departure. Almost immediately, Baylor won some status among us. We were thunderstruck, astonished. Could it be true? Had he been the wicked rake in the wicked city? If so, what a man!

When we left Leyte, Baylor had not returned. No one in the battery, including Jerry, knew his whereabouts, his fate. Three months later, he joined us in Okinawa. Receiving an official report on Baylor, Jerry regaled us with details. Picked up besotted by the military police in Manila as he argued incoherently with a shopkeeper, Baylor had been hospitalized for many days, recovering from a gigantic case of the delirium tremens. He had looked into the pewter pot and seen the world "as the world's not" or as it is. He had been stripped of his one stripe—no longer was he even a private first class—and his pay for the period. In no other way did his stripes of anonymity change on his return. He was the same old Baylor in bearing, in personality. He gave no hint of having kicked over the traces. But no longer was he a cipher. He had earned an honored place in our hearts and minds. For thumbing his nose at convention and at us, we enshrined him in the hall of Valhalla as a warrior, at least for demon rum. He had revealed himself as more a demigod than a man. Never again would anyone pass him without giving him a quick glance of envy and admiration. With the grace of God, we might go with him, we thought. What a man, and more, this Baylor!

Awaiting the order for boarding a troopship, the men of the battery endured or enjoyed a bizarre epicurean adventure. Since we had left Oahu, we had had no "fresh" meat and did not expect to receive any soon. Then on a Thursday before Good Friday, the mess hall received a shipment of frozen pork chops. The news circulated wildly through the battery. Men literally licked their chops in anticipation of devouring the procine flesh.

But there was a problem — a serious problem. The cooks had to prepare the chops on Friday. There was no choice. We had no refrigeration, and the pork would spoil if we did not eat it Friday. Half or more of the battery were Catholic, and though many had eaten pork or beef on Friday in Oahu, out of indifference to the teaching of the church or by claiming a priestly dispensation, nearly all now asserted that they would not touch the chops on Good Friday. A few declared that the pope could go to hell along with them: They would have the chops. Friday came, and the cooks prepared the pork, its greasy and pungent aroma wafting throughout the camp. We Protestants were gleeful; a feast awaited us. We knew no bounds, no shame. I was one of the joyful. I bolted down one chop, another, another, and another, and then toyed with a few until I finally ceased my gluttony at nine chops. Agape and angry, my Catholic friends saw it all. I praised their church for its loyal communicants, Luther for his break with Rome.

"Banzai, Cat's Eye!" 4

*Still Another Voyage, The Battery in
Limbo and Leisure, The Battery in
Dispersion, The Long Journey Home*

Only a few days after the few feasted on pork, all of us again had to
board a troopship, an unprepossessing vessel called the *Berrien*. As usual,
the Army was sharing little information with us about our destination. One
persistent rumor depicted a voyage to Okinawa, the main island in the
Ryukyus, an island chain extending from southern Japan to Formosa. On
April 1, ironically a day celebrating the Resurrection of Christ and the exploits of fools, American infantrymen and Marines had invaded Okinawa.
Though these ground troops did not initially meet great resistance,
Japanese kamikaze pilots had mounted bloody attacks on the fleet around
the island. Perhaps, we told ourselves, the Navy had a desperate need for
our guns, and thus the rumor of Okinawa carried considerable weight with
us. Once in a great while, some talk surfaced about attacking Formosa, but
now that we were veterans of one campaign and had become military
strategists, we quickly dismissed it, noting that the island, unlike Okinawa,
did not offer a direct route for an assault on Japan.

Almost no sooner were we out of the harbor than we heard the news
of President Roosevelt's death. April was the cruelest month for him.
Momentarily, we were stunned. Certainly we regretted our leader's fall and
reverently joined in a shipwide prayer for him. But certainly too we were
not preoccupied with thoughts of him. Arthur Godfrey could weep as Roosevelt's cortege passed on Pennsylvania Avenue, and the nation could mourn
at length for the fallen leader, but we were more concerned about our skins
and our comfort aboard the troopship and quickly enough returned to old
routines.

The *Berrien* was no worse but no better than the *Bell*, which had
transported us from Oahu to the Philippines. But many of us were better
able to make our way on it. Maller and I devised new methods, usually just
for the sake of devising them, for cutting the lengthy chow lines, for short-

stopping them. I became particularly skilled in pleading with the men at the front of the line that I had special work to do for Jerry. A pottage of canned vegetables and meat—even worse than the infamous SOS ("Shit on a Shingle")—the food hardly merited our efforts. We baited sailors with un-nautical language and infuriated them by suggesting that they were mere seagoing bellhops who knew nothing about the real war. Wearied by repetitious drills for abandoning ship and seeing ourselves as happy-go-lucky veterans of a great battle, we ignored the alarms calling for us to take stations along lifeboats and went about our own business. I languidly responded to calls to attend training sessions for the identification of enemy aircraft. We defied fixed routines whenever we could.

Our ship, of course, was in a convoy. The convoy moved with relative speed before it stopped at Mog-Mog in the Ulithi Islands. Again we attended a giant beer party. Mog-Mog was a miniature island, and the great body of soldiers coming ashore threatened to sink it by their weight. Perhaps satiated by the fighting in Leyte, they behaved for the most part as gentlemen, only occasionally engaging in an exchange of harsh words with one another. Neither Maller nor I liked beer but were more willing than in the past to drive a hard bargain with our ration of it. We smuggled our cans aboard ship and there traded with mess personnel for ice cream. As we ate the ice cream, we laughed hilariously at the sight of half-drunken naval officers returning to the ship. All the while attempting to affect the decorum of their rank, they struggled in a clawing, slipping climb up the boarding net to the deck. In a complementary fashion, the ship's captain looked on without a trace of emotion.

Sailing from Mog-Mog, we were certain that our next port of call would be Okinawa, uncertain about what we would meet there. We relieved tension in playing pinochle, reading, idle chatter for several days, and then in mid–April the convoy cast anchor at a wide-stretching harbor at the foot of gently rising hills of a large island. Sure enough, it was Okinawa.

Ours was a peaceful arrival and disembarkation, but the foot soldiers who had encountered only nominal opposition from the Japanese at the outset of the invasion were now engaged in a bloody battle, especially in the lower end of the island, and the kamikaze pilots were continuing their suicidal attacks on naval craft and were striking at targets on land. Only days before we reached Okinawa, the Japanese had also begun use of the Baka bombers. Essentially a glider guided by a suicide pilot, a Baka approached its target attached to a Betty, a twin-engine bomber, and on release took its power from rockets. With a warhead weighing over a ton, it was potentially a devastating weapon. But the doomed pilot could not easily control its descent, and often he died in the wreckage far from the ship or ammunition dump he had marked for destruction.

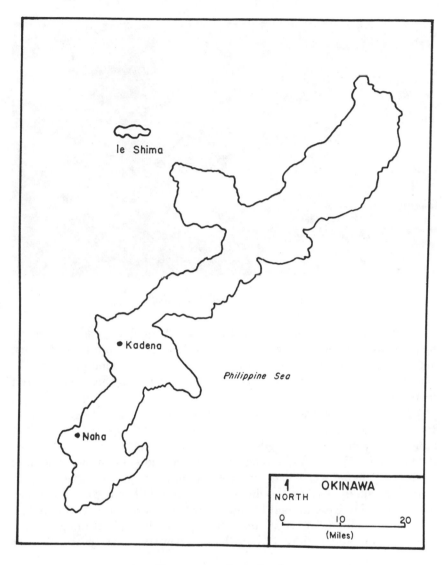

Okinawa, Ryukyu Islands.

So we were entering a maelstrom of fire, iron, and blood. Not quite. As men fought, bled, and died, our battery—all our batteries—lay like the *lazzorone* of Naples doing virtually nothing except moving from one place to another. Organizationally, on paper we remained in the 24th Corps. The Army, we thought, had so many men at its command that it had lost track of us and might not find us before the war ended.

In our first days of the campaign, the battery stayed in pup tents near

Baka bomber, Okinawa, 1945.

the Kadena airfield in the center of the island. Though not engaging in any fighting, we did not live in agreeable circumstances. Rain often pelted us, and rivulets, escaping the small ditches that we dug around our tents, invaded our confines. Our fare was principally C-rations, which we endured more than we enjoyed.

We were at least ten miles from the lines of battle, but every night a Japanese artillery piece concealed behind our lines opened fire on the airfield. We could hear the shells whirring and whining overhead and exploding beyond us. It was frightening. It would be bad enough, we lamented, to die in battle but worse to die inert. Every night too we could view sheets of tracer bullets marking the flight of the firing at kamikazes and Bakas. During the day we searched for the locations where the Baka pilots had crashed. Finding them, we stared curiously and clinically at the wreckage and dismembered bodies. I could hardly stand the terrible scenes but sought them out anyway.

We were quite ready to move when trucks took us to a nearby hollow formed by low hills punctuated with caves used by the Okinawans for the burial of their dead. Whoever had chosen the site for our camp surely had flunked geology. When it rained, as if often did, water slipped down the hillsides and to the flat bed of ground on which we had raised our pyramidal tents, turning the area into a quagmire. We would slog through the mud for a few days until finally, as the sun drenched the earth, it turned into choking dust. Probably the depression did afford us a degree of protection against air attacks.

Remains of Baka pilot, Okinawa, 1945.

An eerie aspect of our setting was the burial caves around us. Constructed of limestone and coral and shaped like a lyre, they afforded an
uneasy ingress through a small opening at the front. Inside the Okinawans
put the bones of their dead in large vases and like the pharaonic Egyptians,
placed personal items, especially chinaware, around them. Acquisitive
Americans did not hesitate to enter these caves and appropriate everything,
even the vases. No one seemed to feel any sense of shame about the ghoulish
larceny. We were simply enjoying the spoils of war — remembering Pearl
Harbor.

We did little there that had any relationship to the war or the battle for Okinawa. We simply sustained ourselves. To that end, every morning I went on the water detail. Climbing into a two-and-a-half-ton truck two of us rode to a supply depot, filled ten-gallon water cans with water, returned to the battery, and unloaded them. On one occasion, I dropped a can on my foot. The big toe on my left foot was sore for days, and to this day the nail is wood- or funguslike, an emblem of my duty in Okinawa.

Almost out of desperation, we hunted for recreation and entertainment. For a while we played volleyball nearly every evening. It was a ferocious game we played. At the net, all was fair. We kicked each other, slugged each other—anything went under our so-called Texas rules. After dark we often walked to a nearby Marine encampment to see movies at the mess hall. A movie might last four or five hours because air raid warnings required the shutting down of the projector. *Laura* did not end until three one morning, warnings sending us scurrying from the mess hall on three occasions.

Still looking around for diversions, we went beyond intramural competition when we arranged a softball game against one of our gun batteries, which like us, was lying inert. The preparation and playing the game bore all the aspects of young adolescent boys at play. We scratched out a diamond and outfield on a scrubby but level field near the camp. Then we "trained" for several days, taking batting practice, fielding ground balls, and shagging fly balls. Everyone, I believe, saw the practice and the impending game as an opportunity to demonstrate that he had been a star at home. I had played a fair game for the Miamisburg Green Hornets as a teenager—ours were marvelous green and yellow uniforms—and won a starting spot for the battery as the second baseman.

From the beginning, the game was wildly flawed and predictable. We had only a few softballs, and they were misshapen and dead from excessive use in practice. The bats were ancient, ready to splinter at striking even a soft softball. Our gloves were poor, but precious because they were few. Each battery chose one man as an umpire. At first the players and spectators were good sports, but soon both sides were acrimoniously contesting the umpires' calls. Players began to rail at one another. The game deteriorated further as the athletes sprained ankles, pulled muscles, and played less ably than they thought they should. I waited in vain for the moment when I would make a dazzling catch at second; no balls came my way. My discomfiture increased as I watched the prim Maccone field his position at third base flawlessly as though his obsession with cleanliness brought him athletic purity. At last, mercifully, the game ended. I do not recall the outcome.

We found distraction and antic behavior in our barbershop—in our case, wherever we had room for a chair. In consonance with military regimen,

The first sergeant and Charles Nuttall in Japanese gun emplacement, Okinawa, 1945.

we regularly had our hair cut in a uniform and prosaic manner—short and even. Probably the Army identified the stolid haircut as a source and symbol of cleanliness and discipline. Still there was something subversive or potentially subversive about the barber's setting in the Army. Men going there, even young ones, could recall that the barbershop was a neighborhood social institution where males commemorated and celebrated peaceful and irregular pursuits and did not chafe under military rules.

Our barber, Burt Harrell, had been giving us conventional cuts for months until Chuck Wolfe struck a blow for independence. A native of Maine and proud of it, Wolfe may have been unconsciously re-creating the democratic tenor of his local barbership when he demanded that Harrell cut an M though his hair. Harrell, perhaps weary of the same old cut, gave him what he wanted. Wolfe became the talk of the battery for the moment, and other men, seeking to emulate or surpass him in his daring, asked for and received bizarre cuts, paths moving through their hair in all kinds of odd patterns, scalps cut nearly clean, and so on. They became a source of considerable amusement. Then Jerry, undoubtedly acting on instructions from the battery commander, ordered an end to the comedic clipping.

Top: **Camp in muddy vale, near Kadena, Okinawa, 1945.** *Bottom*: **Men in battery area, camp near Kadena, Okinawa, 1945 (author kneeling at far right).**

Another momentary diversion, one illustrating the incongruity of our war, came when a Red Cross unit near us conducted a raffle of Japanese small arms and personal items taken from the battlefield. To my delight, I won a rifle. I enjoyed the alliteration: I won a rifle in a raffle. I sent it home and later told friends and relatives that I had taken it from a Japanese soldier I had killed in a hand-to-hand fight. They did not believe me.

John Moore scrubbing a pan at mess hall, camp near Kadena, Okinawa, 1945.

I could not help but see the irony and even the unfairness of the sedentary life of our battery. Here we lolled as ground troops fought bitter battles with the Japanese around Naha and naval craft fended off kamikaze attacks. But I had no passion for glory and did not lament our inertia, especially after seeing the bitter fruits of warfare.

Near our camp was a graves registration unit (or something like that) of the Sixth Marine Division. Here medical trucks bearing dead Marines from the front came each day, turning over their bloody burden to personnel

Ray Maller in front of burial cave, Okinawa, 1945.

who identified the men and sent them on to burial in an adjacent cemetery. One afternoon several of us solemnly watched the arrival of a truck and the removal of three corpses. We were quiet for the remainder of the day and did not play volleyball.

A few days later, I accompanied a soldier in the battery to the Sixth Marine cemetery. His brother had been killed in the first days of the invasion and was buried in the cemetery. A stoic man of Polish descent—I cannot remember his name but retain the memory of his agony—he lingered long at the graveside, saying nothing and taking a photograph of the white cross before we finally walked away. I also was looking for a grave. Jimmy Bussard was buried there. Jim was from Miamisburg, a real Adonis, good-looking, a great athlete, a vibrant personality. We all had envied him but genuinely liked him. Even today I cannot drive in downtown Miamisburg where he lived without recalling Jim. And inwardly I always recite the consolatory words, "Now you will not swell the rout / Of lads that wore their honours out."

I had yet another cemetery to visit, an Army cemetery. There lay my cousin Lawrence. A farmer's son, a good-natured ordinary boy, he worked on his father's farm near Miamisburg through the first three years of the war. He received at least two deferments from the draft because of his occupation, but he did not want to stay on the farm while his friends fought. He longed to be a soldier or sailor, to join in the great cause. At last he persuaded his father to accept his decision to waive his deferment and enlist in the Army. His was a brief candle. Within a few months after going into the Army, he was in Okinawa. There a sniper killed him. I found his grave in the Army cemetery, shed a tear for him, and wondered why he was there. Today he lies in the old cemetery in Miamisburg, as patriotic a lad as ever bore arms for the nation. When I recall Lawrence, I think of Carl Sandburg's prose exploring the death of an unknown soldier at Gettysburg: "Why he had gone away and why he would never come back had roots in some mystery of flags and drums, of national fate in which individuals sink as in a deep sea, of men swallowed and vanished in a man-made storm of smoke and steel."

Lawrence was in good company at the Okinawan cemetery. Only a few feet from his grave was that of General Simon Bolivar Buckner, who had been killed by Japanese artillery fire. Buckner, in a sense, linked the American Civil War to this great world war. His father, also General Simon Bolivar Buckner, had commanded the Confederate forces at Fort Donelson that surrendered to Ulysses Grant in 1862. Several decades later, he remarried and fathered the son who lay near my cousin.

Evidently looking for something that would bear the semblance of meaningful duty for us, someone ordered the battery to create an inspection team to examine records of other batteries in the antiaircraft artillery. Perhaps believing that my intellect was just right for paperwork, Jerry designated me Classification Specialist on the team. In the guise of serious duty, four of us began to travel around Okinawa, especially the northern half, looking at personnel records. We assumed an air of authority as though we really knew what we were doing. We didn't, of course. It was make-work, a boondoggle that would have shamed any WPA worker. I examined one form in particular for the accuracy of checkmarks on occupational classifications. What a secret weapon I was wielding! It was drudgery and contributed to the fighting on Okinawa no more than volleyball.

U.S. Army cemetery, Okinawa, 1945 (author's cousin buried here).

There was an element of danger in our duty, though. Often we were driving over rough lonely roads — one of which, incidentally, brought us into view of Ie Shima, the small island where Ernie Pyle was killed — where the Japanese had ambushed American soldiers moving in small numbers. We feared that prospect and traveled with our rifles ever at the ready, knowing, though, that they would give us little protection against snipers. We survived the drudgery and danger, and someone up there in the Army, someone with a grain of sense, finally ordered a halt to our labor.

Probably the nadir of our service on Okinawa came in June and July as the battle for the island wound down. We had moved our tents near a beach on the eastern coast. There we were doing nothing, as usual, beyond meeting the demands of a ritualized routine — working as KPs, hauling water, and so on. Ordinarily we would be at our complete leisure by mid-morning. Many of us then filed down a sandy path to the beach in a search for seashells. Especially we coveted the so-called cat's eyes, a small shell bearing the likeness of feline eyes. On returning to the battery after a successful hunt, we would shout "Banzai, cat's eye!" and then set the shells in the sun to hasten the decay of the organic matter in them. They stank to high heaven. Once we had thoroughly cleaned them, we made necklaces and bracelets out of them, really believing that our wives and sweethearts would find them attractive. Again it was all quite incongruous: Down the road 20 miles men were still fighting and dying as we idled and played.

Closer down the road was a stark reminder of that fighting, a prisoner-of-war camp. Hostages to a code demanding that they fight to the death, Japanese soldiers had surrendered in small numbers in the Pacific fighting, hardly enough to count, but on Okinawa several hundred had decided that dishonor was better than death. On several occasions, we passed the camp, a compound bounded by a heavy-gauge steel fence and guarded by American soldiers armed to the teeth. The Japanese soldiers we saw standing near the fence, or thought we saw, were a mean, sullen lot capable of the vilest of deeds. Had not their countrymen attacked Pearl Harbor? We interpreted their posture as they walked as representing an arrogant defiance of their captors. They were ragged and unkempt too. Surely they were not merely frightened men who wanted to go home, who had seen enough of war.

Unlike Leyte, Okinawa clearly revealed the scars of war. Everywhere, it seemed, were huge piles of shell casings, the sweat and blood of war congealed in them. Naha, at the southern end of the island, particularly testified to the destructive power of sea and land artillery. Once a city of 60,000 built of gleaming white stone, it lay in ruins. Virtually no buildings remained erect, only their rubble serving as evidence that people had once lived and worked here.

In the countryside in the lower half of the island, we could see Okinawans moving away from the lines of battle. They were bedraggled, a pathetic train of people walking for a while and then huddling together in misery. As we understood their history, we had to feel sorrow for them. Their island had been a semi-independent tributary of China until late in the 19th century when the Japanese annexed it. They had suffered under Japanese rules concerned only about fortifying the island in anticipation of a war with the United States or European powers. They were not Japanese nationals, but they did not welcome us as an army liberating them from the Japanese yoke. Indeed, they appeared no happier than the Japanese prisoners. There was something about them, something almost foreboding, that limited fraternization. American soldiers who usually had no compunction about the limits of their sexual interests did not openly seek out the Okinawan women. Of course, the women seemed terribly unkempt in their well-worn apparel, which, moreover, was so loose-fitting as to imply the neutering of the species.

The European war had ended in May, and many men in the battery had sufficient "points" — a quantitative measure of service based on months of combat and noncombat, the months of combat counting more — to anticipate returning home in a few months. Midsummer saw a few leaving for the States, and we expected an acceleration of departures in the ensuing months. Men with fewer points, I among them, began to worry about going into the infantry and joining in an assault on the Japanese homeland. Rumors of that prospect were continuous and seemed realistic. I became increasingly nervous. I had made my way in my outfit, had even manipulated it on occasion, but I knew that life in an infantry regiment might be something else. So we waited, speculating and worrying.

Dump of shell casings, Okinawa, 1945.

Near the end of June, we again pulled down our pyramidal tents, packed them up, and headed for a site 10 or 12 miles from Naha, in the southern end of Okinawa. We were uneasy about our new berth even though we continued in our life of ease. Japanese troops, though surrendering in increasing numbers, were still offering stiff resistance to American forces, and we feared that remnants of the enemy were yet in our vicinity. At least we could hear the firing of rifles at night and ascribed unpleasant meanings to it. We also heard distressing stories of Okinawan civilians who, believing that Americans would subject them to brutal treatment, committed suicide by jumping off cliffs at the lower end of the island.

It was here that we were witnesses, at a remove, to a sad and tragic occurrence. For some strange reason, the Army assigned to the battery a young sergeant pending his discharge and supposedly was merely awaiting the availability of transportation for his journey. He was an infantryman who had fought in campaigns in the Central Pacific and the Philippines. Though young, he wore on his face the lines of suffering, the wear and tear of fighting. He had seen the elephant. But he was not to go home. Sent on a detail in a truck (he should have been loafing in a tent), he was struck by lightning and killed. We could hardly believe the news. After that, we could not believe that God had an eye on the sparrow.

We had scarcely settled down to our old life in the new camp before the awesome word came: Our nation had dropped an atom bomb on Japan. Following our use of a second bomb, the Japanese surrendered. And the war ended. It was that simple.

In our battery some men questioned the morality of using the horrifying weapon, but many men who otherwise would have gone on to fight in an invasion of Japan dismissed such a concern, noting that the moralists would soon be discharged in any case and could afford to rasie ethical issues. Besides, had they forgotten Pearl Harbor? The naysayers had doubts about our capacity to use an ultimate weapon wisely and well. For support of that argument, they might have pointed out that on the night of the Japanese capitulation, sailors and soldiers all over Okinawa had put their weapons to an irrational use. Celebrating the surrender, they had fired handguns, rifles, machine guns, and artillery pieces indiscriminately and recklessly. They covered the sky with tracers, filled the air with deafening explosions — and killed eight or nine of their comrades who also wanted to go home.

Coincident with the ending of the war, we received a double ration of beer and Coke — 12 beers, 12 Cokes — because we had missed the previous month's ration. Men slopped in their beer all day, none making serious trouble, fortunately, but many becoming adept in the practice of regurgitation. I indulged in my own distinctive excess. By careful trading, I amassed 33 Cokes and obtained ice from Monk Shank, who was on the island near us with his Seabees. The ice would not last long in the summer sun and had to be used forthwith. I lay on my cot all day drinking one Coke after another and replacing each one from a bucket with another until at last I had none left. I raised myself from the cot only to answer the call of nature, which came with increasing frequency as the hours passed. My supply of Coke exhausted, I then proceeded to jam 24 packs of gum — Wrigley's Spearmint, I think — into my mouth at one time. Somehow I managed to chew them all; of course, my cheeks bulged grotesquely. It was a marvelous exercise in excess.

Now the battery really began to break up. Men were leaving every week. We did nothing to mark their departure. There were no sad farewells, no talk of seeing one another later, no talk of shared experiences. Our battery had no sense of coherence, of interdependence, in large part because we had not really faced great dangers together, certainly not in any sustained way, as an infantry company might. No external force had bonded us. Seldom if ever did one man look to another for protection. We weren't even sure that we had helped win the war. We had been near the scenes of bloody combat, but we could not point to any role we had played in winning skirmishes, much less battles. We had simply been there. We had done our duty as directed.

Nor had the interplay of internal life pulled us together. We knew little about one another's families. We would have found it unbelievable if we had seen a movie in which a soldier became well acquainted with the family of another solider through letters. Rarely did we talk about our girlfriends or wives. When, as happened on occasion, someone received a "Dear John" letter, we expressed little concern about it, even if we did learn of it. We did not act as surrogate sob sisters for one another. If we did not form close friendships, we were not, of course, enemies; we were friends — but only for the moment, not for eternity. Certainly I felt no real loss at parting with anyone. I had known people and expected never to see them again. The remaining men had to attend to the ordinary duties of soldiering and had to preside over the deactivation of the battery. We had to put rifles in cosmoline, crate equipment, and dispose of certain records.

Evidently because I had recently worked for a few days in the supply office, not because I had any training or experience for it, the Headquarters officers had me promoted to the rank of staff sergeant in supply, directing me to dispose of excess materials and to requisition day-to-day supplies. For a moment, I took pleasure at the turn of events. I would receive more money and greater prestige when I reached home. Yet then (and now) I was uncomfortable about it. The stripes, which I did not wear, did not give me any status in the battery and created an appearance of authority that I did not really want. In mind and spirit, I remained a corporal, really a private, in my essential being. I enjoyed a freedom from responsibility giving me, as it were, autonomy in the nether regions, indeed a kind of dominion over routine military circumstances. "Better to reign in hell," I might have said, "than serve in Heaven."

In any event, I paid a price for my new rank and responsibility. About 40 of us still constituted the battery in October when a great typhoon struck the Philippine Sea and veered inland. Capsizing ships at sea and tearing quonset huts out of concrete, it left a trail of death and destruction. Only the tail end hit us, but that was enough. For a few minutes, we kept our tents up, and then we saw them blown away, along with duffel bags, clothing, and nearly all our personal articles. Taking refuge in trucks and the burial caves, everyone managed to survive.

I faced more than a loss of clothing and personal effects. Now I had to resupply all my fellow soldiers with clothing, tents, mess equipment, and many other kinds of materials, and I knew little or nothing about the proper procedures and requisition forms for doing so. I was at a loss, flailing around and cursing the luck of rank. Only after soliciting the assistance of a supply sergeant in another battery did I procure the necessary supplies. It was a humiliating experience that devalued the few benefits of the sergeancy.

By December the battery had become a skeletal crew. And early that month my remaining comrades and I boarded the *Alshain* (Alshain is a star in the constellation Aquila) for our voyage to the United States. Again we were on a wretched ship, but it mattered little if we could but endure the long passage. Some of us, remembering the young sergeant struck by lightning, worried that we might strike a stray Japanese mine or might be capsized by a typhoon. We were worrywarts. Taking the northern circle route, the *Alshain* arrived at Seattle on December 24. The next day, Christmas, we disembarked as a military band played a few patriotic numbers for us, albeit in a perfunctory way. There were no cheering crowds, no parades, no Santa Claus, no pretty girls for the heroes from the Pacific. But no one cared. We were nearly at our hearthside—*dulce domum*.

From dockside we rode by truck to Fort Lewis. There we received an issue of olive-drab uniforms, including a heavy overcoat like the one I had received at Fort Thomas. I had come full circle. We had a Christmas dinner with all the trimmings at a huge Army cafeteria manned by German prisoners of war. We rather enjoyed seeing them at menial tasks. That night I crawled into my bunk and lay awake for hours listening to a plaintive rendition of the Gershwin song "Someone to Watch Over Me" repeatedly coming over a loudspeaker near the barracks. I thought it appropriate.

The next day a few of us had time to go to downtown Seattle. Unsatiated by the Christmas dinner, we drank gallons of milk at a small restaurant. At an Army store, I bought all the ribbons and shoulder patches that I was entitled to—and more besides. Suddenly I became a member of two divisions, two Army corps, a Pacific command, and had served meritoriously in several campaigns. I was a splendid-looking soldier.

Two days after arriving at Fort Lewis, I began the next leg of my journey home. It was painful. Along with 2,000 to 3,000 other soldiers, I boarded a train in Seattle that only a war could have put into service. The cars were ancient and creaked without surcease. The seats in the coaches were worn to the threads. There was virtually no heat in the cars, and the sanitary facilities beggared description, so much so that soldiers held everything back as long as they could. The food was a small step removed from the fare of a soup kitchen. We could have endured all without complaint if only the train had rapidly clicked off the miles. But it inched along and multiplied the deficiencies of our accommodations.

Some men slept on piles of duffel bags, some in their seats. I could not sleep anywhere and became progressively weary as we moved snaillike across Washington, Idaho, Montana, and on east on the old Northern Pacific track. We stopped at numerous small towns, and soldiers got off to look around and buy alcohol and food, the former first. Cold as it was in the cars, it was even colder outside. Dreading the cold and fearful of missing the train, I did not venture from my car.

Probably at least one soldier should have followed my example. At one town, he got off, found some liquor, and brought it back to the car for his own party. Becoming intoxicated, he ended up in a quarrel or fight with one of the officers commanding the train, who went to a telephone at the next stop and called the military police. They were awaiting the train at the next town and took the inebriated soldier away. I have thought about him on

occasion. Did he spend some time in the stockade? Or did he get by with
a chewing-out?

As we neared Chicago, the cars moved at an even slower speed. Our
train was shunted to sidetracks for every cattle car, every milk car, every
freight car on the road. From Chicago to Camp Atterbury in Indiana, a
distance of no more than 200 miles, the train ran for a full day—or did not
run. Exhausted, at last we tumbled out of the cars at Atterbury. The stay
there was mercifully brief. Officers rehearsed in a mechanical way the
rewards of remaining in the Army and urged us to enlist. I saw no one doing
so. We took the name Separation Center used at Atterbury in a serious way.
And then we received a part of our mustering-out pay and the great
document— the honorable discharge. Mine read: "This is to certify that
Carl M. Becker Jr. 35 624 032 Staff Sergeant Headquarters Battery 866th
Anti-Aircraft Artillery Automatic Weapons Battalion Army of the United
States is hereby Honorably Discharged from the military service of the
United States of America. This certificate is awarded as a testimonial of
Honest and Faithful Service to this country."

I wished to hasten my way home but did not want to subject my parents
to the long drive through Indiana. Ironically, Arthur Rennler, the author of
my embarrassment at the hands of Sergeant Bass at Camp Wallace, offered
me a ride to Cincinnati with his family. At Cincinnati I took a bus to Dayton
and then at about 9:00 P.M., after calling my parents, caught another one to
Miamisburg. On the bus were two young women who had been girls in my
high school class. I implied that I had been a great hero in the war. At about
10:00 P.M. I reached the station in Miamisburg. My mother and father were
awaiting me there, tearful but happy.

I rode in their old blue Studebaker about a mile to the house that I had
left in January 1943. And late in the evening of January 5, 1946, I again
opened the door to my home. Home at last was the man—at least I saw
myself as one—who had left as a boy nearly three years before on a bleak
January morning. We talked for a while in the old but comfortable living
room, and then I drove over to see my girl, who had waited so faithfully for
me. We embraced. It was good to be home. I slept soundly that night.

Epilogue

"Directory Assistance"

Nearly half a century has passed since I returned home from the Pacific. I still live in Miamisburg, less than a mile from that house of homecoming. Through these years, I have lived a life of some variety and accomplishment, though of no great excitement. I have followed various pursuits. For periods ranging from several months to a few years, I operated a punch press (a mean business), carried mail, administered a detention home for boys and girls, sold insurance. I sandwiched around these stints of labor attendance at several colleges and universities and earned three undergraduate and graduate degrees. I have taught American history for over 30 years at colleges and universities, 25 at a large state university, and have written about 40 articles and books, mostly scholarly works of no great distinction. Especially in recent years, I have traveled through a large part of Western Europe and have returned to the scenes of my duty in Oahu. I count as my special blessings my wife, children, and grandchildren.

Over these same decades, I had made but few attempts to renew connections with the men of my battery. Just after the war, in the summer of 1946, my parents, my brother, my wife, and I drove to Detroit to see the Tigers play the Boston Red Sox, then seemingly the best team in baseball. While there, I called Don Boeam, the sometime mess sergeant. I enjoyed seeing him again, but we did not have enough in common then to sustain a relationship over time and space. Later, in the 1950s, acting on an impulse, I searched out Jerry Sarver, the first sergeant. Knowing that he had lived in Vincennes, Indiana, I called there and finally reached him. He was well, and we had a pleasant coversation. I had the distinct impression, though, that he could barely remember me. We talked about staying in touch with each other, but we did not do so.

As I brought a first draft of these reminiscences to a close, I increasingly sensed a need to recapture in more than my recollective words the memory of my life in the Army and the men I shared it with. I hearkened to a Confederate soldier writing his reminiscences decades after the Civil War. He had envisioned a reunion after life with his fellow soldiers, gray and blue, when they would return to the days of camp and battle, fight, talk and laugh, and say, "Did it not seem real? Was it not as in the old days?" In no way could I invest my experience with such romantic coloration, but perhaps I could revive in talk and laughter some of the days in Oahu, Leyte, and Okinawa.

So I went to the telephone. Again I called Jerry, understanding that he might no longer live in Vincennes, or that he might no longer live. I was elated at getting a number from directory assistance for a Jerome Sarver in Vincennes. I was even more elated when I called the number and heard a voice reminiscent of Jerry's. Yes, said the man, he was Jerome Sarver, but no, he had not served in the Army during World War II. I was looking, he was certain, for a distant cousin, also named Jerome Sarver. He had been in the Pacific during the war and met my description of a big red-faced man. Unfortunately, I could not talk to him. He had died sometime in the 1960s.

Despite this bad news, I continued my search. Ray Maller had in various ways identified himself as a native of Sioux Falls, South Dakota. Again going to directory assistance, I heard the automated voice give me a number for a Ray Maller in that city. I reached the number and a Ray Maller who was the Ray I knew. Ours was an animated conversation. He remembered me well, and we shared stories of our military and personal histories. I was not surprised to learn that he was in real estate and auctioneering, callings that depended on the kind of persuasive and manipulative skills that he had employed in the Army. But I was astonished to learn that Ray, a man who had known his way around the Army, had made himself vulnerable to its demands. After coming home from Okinawa, he had accepted the Army's invitation to join the Reserves. It was a mistake. Soon after the Korean War began, he was again on a troopship in the Pacific, this one sailing to Korea. There, as a line sergeant, he led an infantry company in combat for nearly a year. He survived the fighting and returned to Sioux Falls, a sadder but wiser man.

Ray had recently been in touch with Joe Ranzo, the soldier of Italian blood who had amused us with his strange habit of spreading himself into a horizontal plane as he walked through the battery area. He was living in Elmira, New York. So I called him. Ranzo remembered me, but he seemed phlegmatic and distant, and the conversation led nowhere.

It was a different story with Don Boeam. I could not locate him in Detroit. Recalling that he had dated a woman from Holland, Michigan, I called directory assistance and learned that two Don Boeams, Junior and Senior, lived in the community. The senior was my man. We talked at length and then exchanged calls in the next several weeks. Finally he and his wife visited my wife and me. A retired meatcutter, Don was vibrant, witty, and well, though a little worse for wear from a deteriorating hip. A member of the battery at its organization in 1941, Don knew its history quite well and recounted numerous stories of its men. Later we visited him and his wife in Holland during the Tulip Festival. Coming to join us from Racine, Wisconsin, were Rudy Raymond, the laconic cook, and his wife, who had been exchanging visits with the Boeams for many years. Ray, who had been a pipefitter in Racine, was as dour as ever, but we all enjoyed our small reunion. Ray and Don both knew something of what had happened since the war to the many men from Wisconsin and Michigan who had been in the battery. Several had died; one had endured the suicide of a drug-ridden son; another had become an alcoholic; still another had spent years in a state penitentiary. They had constituted, in short, a microcosm of the sorrows of their generation.

I came away from that visit content to go no further. Especially Don had given my experience additional flesh and substance and had endowed it with greater meaning as he re-created the days when I had been with a company of men bearing the burdens of duty in the U.S. Army. I remembered more vividly the men of my battery by name, by face, and by deeds as "familiar" in my mouth "as household words."

Appendixes

Appendixes

Appendix A: Registration Certificate and Notice of Classification

Duplicate issued 1-8-46

REGISTRATION CERTIFICATE

This is to certify that in accordance with the
Selective Service Proclamation of the President of the United States

Carl .... Monroe .... Becker, Jr.
(First name)   (Middle name)   (Last name)

821 Sennett St., Miamisburg, Ohio.
(Place of residence)

(This will be identical with line 2 of the Registration Card)

has been duly registered this 30th day of ...... June ...., 19 42

/s/   John Knight
(Signature of registrar)

Registrar for Local Board ...... 14 .... Miamisburg, Ohio.
(Number)   (City or county)   (State)

THE LAW REQUIRES YOU TO HAVE THIS CARD IN YOUR
PERSONAL POSSESSION AT ALL TIMES

D. S. S. Form 2
(Revised 6/9/41)   16—21631

NOTICE OF CLASSIFICATION

Registrant ...... Carl Monroe Becker, Jr., ... Order No. 12408

has been classified in Class ...... 1-A (Until further notice, 19 ....)
by ☒ Local Board   (Insert Date for Class II-A and II-B only)
☐ Board of Appeal (by vote of ...... to ......)
☐ President

December 9th, ...,19 42   /s/ John Knight
(Date of mailing)   Member of Local Board.

NOTICE OF RIGHT TO APPEAL

Appeal from classification by local board or board of appeal must be made by signing appeal form on back of questionnaire at office of local board, or by filing a written notice of appeal, within ten days after the mailing of this notice.

Before appeal a registrant may file a written request for appearance within the same ten-day period; and, if he does so, the local board will fix a day and notify him to appear personally before the local board; if this is done, the time to appeal is extended to ten days beyond the day set by the local board for such appearance.

There is a right in certain dependency cases, of appeal from appeal board decision to the President; see Selective Service Regulations.

The law requires you—To keep in touch with your local board; To notify it of any change of address. To notify it of any fact which might change classification.

D. S. S. Form 57 (Rev. 4-13-42)   16—19071-1   U. S. GOVERNMENT PRINTING OFFICE

Appendix B: Honorable Discharge and Enlisted Record

Honorable Discharge

This is to certify that

CARL M BECKER JR 35 624 032 Staff Sergeant

Headquarters Battery 866th Anti-Aircraft Artillery Automatic Weapons Battalion

Army of the United States

is hereby Honorably Discharged from the military service of the United States of America.

This certificate is awarded as a testimonial of Honest and Faithful Service to this country.

Given at Separation Center
    Camp Atterbury Indiana

Date 5 January 1946

E. W. HENRY
MAJOR AC

ENLISTED RECORD AND REPORT OF SEPARATION
(ONORABLE DISCHARGE (

E 14 8 rem/24

1. LAST NAME - FIRST NAME - MIDDLE INITIAL	2. ARMY SERIAL NO.	3. GRADE	4. ARM OR SERVICE	5. COMPONENT
Becker Carl M Jr	35 624 032	S/Sgt	CAC	AUS

6. ORGANIZATION	7. DATE OF SEPARATION	8. PLACE OF SEPARATION
Hq Btry 866th AAA AW Bn	5 Jan 46	Sep Cen Camp Atterbury Ind

9. PERMANENT ADDRESS FOR MAILING PURPOSES	10. DATE OF BIRTH	11. PLACE OF BIRTH
821 Sennett St Miamisburg Montgomery Ohio	5 May 24	Miamisburg Ohio

12. ADDRESS FROM WHICH EMPLOYMENT WILL BE SOUGHT	13. COLOR EYES	14. COLOR HAIR	15. HEIGHT	16. WEIGHT	17. NO. DEPEND.
See #9	Brown	Brown	5'7"	165 LBS.	0

18. RACE			19. MARITAL STATUS			20. U.S. CITIZEN		21. CIVILIAN OCCUPATION AND NO.
WHITE	NEGRO	OTHER (specify)	SINGLE	MARRIED	OTHER (specify)	YES	NO	Stock Control Clerk 1-38.04
X			X			X		

MILITARY HISTORY

22. DATE OF INDUCTION	23. DATE OF ENLISTMENT	24. DATE OF ENTRY INTO ACTIVE SERVICE	25. PLACE OF ENTRY INTO SERVICE
18 Jan 43		25 Jan 43	Fort Thomas Ky

SELECTIVE SERVICE DATA ▶	26. REGISTERED	27. LOCAL S.S. BOARD NO.	28. COUNTY AND STATE	29. HOME ADDRESS AT TIME OF ENTRY INTO SERVICE
	X	14	Montgomery Co Ohio	See #9

30. MILITARY OCCUPATIONAL SPECIALTY AND NO.	31. MILITARY QUALIFICATION AND DATE (i. e., infantry, aviation and marksmanship badges, etc.)
Classification Specialist 275	Not Available

32. BATTLES AND CAMPAIGNS
Southern Philippines; Ryukyus

33. DECORATIONS AND CITATIONS
Asiatic-Pacific Theater Ribbon w/2 Bronze Stars; Philippine Liberation Ribbon w/2 Bronze Stars; Good Conduct Ribbon; World War II Victory Medal

34. WOUNDS RECEIVED IN ACTION
None

35.	LATEST IMMUNIZATION DATES				36.	SERVICE OUTSIDE CONTINENTAL U. S. AND RETURN		
SMALLPOX	TYPHOID	TETANUS	OTHER (specify)		DATE OF DEPARTURE	DESTINATION	DATE OF ARRIVAL	
Jun 44	Jan 45	Feb 45	Flu Oct 45		23 May 43	Asiatic-Pacific	31 May 43	
					8 Dec 45	USA	25 Dec 45	

37.	TOTAL LENGTH OF SERVICE					38. HIGHEST GRADE HELD
CONTINENTAL SERVICE			FOREIGN SERVICE			
YEARS	MONTHS	DAYS	YEARS	MONTHS	DAYS	S/Sgt
0	4	8	2	7	3	

39. PRIOR SERVICE
None

NO FURTHER GUARANTY BETWEEN UNDER TITLE III OF THE SERVICEMEN'S READJUSTMENT ACT OF 1944, AS AMENDED, IF AVAILABLE TO THE PERSON TO WHOM THIS DISCHARGE WAS ISSUED.   ADMINISTRATOR OF VETERANS AFFAIRS

40. REASON AND AUTHORITY FOR SEPARATION
AR 615-365 (Convn of Govt) RR1-1 Demobilization 15 Dec 44

41. SERVICE SCHOOLS ATTENDED	42. EDUCATION (Years)		
	GRAMMAR	HIGH SCHOOL	COLLEGE
None	8	4	0

PAY DATA   Vou 22809

43. LONGEVITY FOR PAY PURPOSES			44. MUSTERING OUT PAY		45. SOLDIER DEPOSITS	46. TRAVEL PAY	47. TOTAL AMOUNT, NAME OF DISBURSING OFFICER
YEARS	MONTHS	DAYS	TOTAL	THIS PAYMENT			
2	11	18	$300	$100	None	$8.30	1366.06 B B CALLAWAY LT COL FD

INSURANCE NOTICE

IMPORTANT If PREMIUM is NOT PAID WHEN DUE OR WITHIN THIRTY-ONE DAYS THEREAFTER, INSURANCE WILL LAPSE. MAKE CHECKS OR MONEY ORDERS PAYABLE TO THE TREASURER OF THE U. S. AND FORWARD TO COLLECTIONS SUBDIVISION, VETERANS ADMINISTRATION, WASHINGTON 25, D. C.

48. KIND OF INSURANCE			49. HOW PAID		50. Effective Date of Allotment Discontinuance	51. Date of Next Premium Due (One month after 50)	52. PREMIUM DUE EACH MONTH	53. INTENTION OF VETERAN TO		
Nat. Serv.	U.S. Govt.	None	Allotment	Direct to V. A.				Continue	Continue Only	Discontinue
X				X	31 Jan 46	28 Feb 46	$6.50	X		

54.
55. REMARKS (This space for completion of above items or entry of other items specified in W. D. Directives) Inactive Service in ERC from 18 Jan 43 thru 24 Jan 43; No days lost under AW 107; ASR (2 Sep 45) 70 Lapel button issued

RIGHT THUMB PRINT

56. SIGNATURE OF PERSON BEING SEPARATED	57. PERSONNEL OFFICER (Type name, grade and organization - signature)
Carl M. Becker Jr	A F EARL 1st Lt Inf C. F. Earl

WD AGO FORM 53 - 55   This form supersedes all previous editions of   WLRD WAR II - I CLAIM

Sources

The preceding derives essentially from my memory of the men I knew and the events I witnessed and participated in during World War II. As a professional historian, I am habituated in my research to the use of written sources—letters, newspapers, reports, and so on. I had few of these traditional sources available and had to let my memory re-create my history. Consequently, probably—almost certainly—I have misread men and exaggerated or misstated the actuality of events. But I have not done so deliberately, and in the main I have, I believe, set forth an accurate account of soldiers in training and in the Pacific four decades ago. Unquestionably, I have permitted my knowledge and experience accumulated in the years since I left the Army to color my understanding of my military past. But I see little room for any other way of going about it; my life did not end in 1945.

At several points I did not depend entirely on my memory. As my Epilogue indicates, I talked to several men of my battery as I was concluding a draft of my manuscript. They provided useful identifying details on persons, places, and things and reinforced my re-creation of certain events. I found important elucidative detail on the Leyte campaign in several secondary sources: William Breuer, *Retaking the Philippines* (1986); John Costello, *The Pacific War* (1981); Samuel Eliot Morison, *History of United States Naval Operations in World War II: Leyte*, vol. 12 (1958); and Ronald H. Spector, *Eagle Against the Sun* (1985). Also, I used a few primary sources illuminating several gray areas in my memory: The Miamisburg *News* for a description of the draftees with whom I left Miamisburg; records from the National Personnel Records Center listing the men in my battery; documents at the Naval Historical Center tracing the movement of the task force out of Pearl Harbor that attacked Leyte; and an account in the *New York Times* of the landing of Japanese paratroopers in Leyte. Remembrance, nonetheless, remained the vital provenance of my story.

Part II

Robert G. Thobaben: A Private

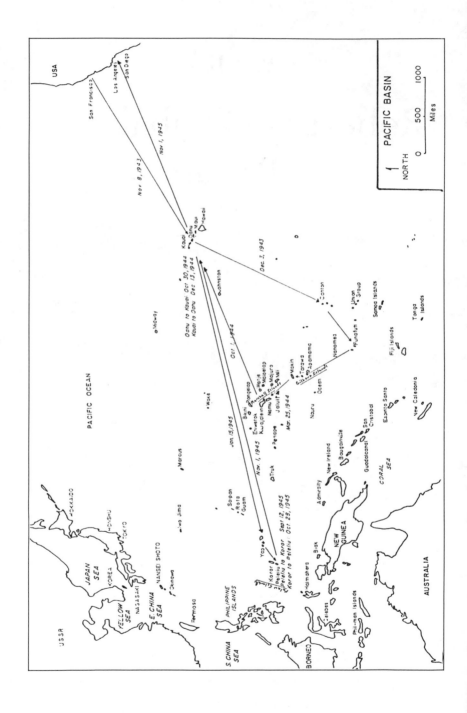

Military Timeline

June 30, 1942	Registered for draft
December 12, 1942	Enlisted in U.S. Army, Army Enlisted Reserve Corps
June 1, 1943	Entered active service
June 1, 1943–June 7, 1943	In transit
June 8, 1943–October 15, 1943	Basic Infantry Training, Company A, 11th Battalion (Camp Wheeler, Georgia)
October 16, 1943–November 4, 1943	In transit
November 5, 1943–September 27, 1945	111th Infantry Regiment (Camp Stoneman, California)
November 8, 1943	Medical Detachment, Third Battalion
December 3, 1943–March 22, 1944	Makin (Butaritari) Island, Gilbert Islands
March 23, 1944–October 1, 1944	Ennylabegan and Kwajalein Islands, Marshall Islands
October 2, 1944–January 14, 1945	Oahu and Kauai, Hawaiian Islands
January 15, 1945–October 31, 1945	Peleliu, Garakayo, and Koror Islands, Palau Islands
November 1, 1945–November 27, 1945	In transit
November 28, 1945	Honorable discharge

Length of Service: Continental service — five months, fourteen days; foreign service — two years, fourteen days; total service — two years, five months, twenty-eight days.

Opposite: **Journeys in the Pacific, 1943–1945.**

Robert G. Thobaben, the author, Macon, Georgia, July,1943, a member of the 11th Battalion, Company A, First Platoon at Camp Wheeler, Georgia.

"Georgia, Georgia"

5

Hometown, In the Beginning, Marching Through Georgia, Trains

The Japanese bombed Pearl Harbor on December 7, 1941. I graduated from Shaker Heights High School about six weeks later, in January 1942. In between we all learned some geography—namely, where Pearl Harbor, the Philippines, Wake Island, and Guam were located. All the boys in our senior class knew we would soon be involved in the war, and we only hoped that the local politicians' predictions of victory over the Japanese in six weeks were overly optimistic. How could they possibly win without us?

Shaker Heights is a suburb on the east side of Cleveland. My parents moved there in 1924 from Cleveland and bought a "two-family house"; we lived downstairs, and my grandparents and great-grandmother lived upstairs. It was a very agreeable arrangement for my sister and me. I never remember having an identity crisis. I always knew who I was because I was constantly immersed in an extended family that continually told me who I was.

At that time Shaker Heights was the wealthiest suburb in Cleveland, and the school system was supposed to be the best. In any event, that's what we were told. It was certainly not a blue-collar, working-class neighborhood. It was generally an upper-middle-class community. One other demographic note warrants mention. The largest single group living in Shaker Heights was white Anglo-Saxon Protestants. There were no blacks in the school system. There was a significant Jewish community and a smaller yet identifiable Italian group. My daily playmates and friends as I grew up came from all the groups mentioned. We all played hard and were expected to perform well in school, and many of us studied music, which implied practice—*every* day. That was life in Shaker Heights.

Growing up in an extended family meant that there were always parents, grandparents, aunts, uncles, and cousins around. We even had family reunions in those days, at a farm that one of my relatives owned or in a hall rented for the occasion. At these big family gatherings there was always plenty of food, beer, and schnapps, and we invariably ended up singing "Look for the Silver Lining," with my father on the piano. Maybe it was the Depression and hope for better times that prompted the song. I never knew. But we always sang it.

My father was a businessman. That's how he earned his living; however, his real love and talent was music. He was outstanding on the piano and organ, and he could play the flute, trombone, and clarinet. He played in theaters and churches in the Cleveland area. He was also a fine craftsman in woodworkng and always kept our home beautifully maintained. I'm afraid he would be disappointed in my lack of skill and interest in this latter activity. My father never graduated from high school. He quit after the 11th grade in a dispute over grades.

My mother was "supermom." She personified all the best human qualities, and she could really cook. (I suspect all sons think of their mothers as gourmet cooks.) My mother graduated from high school and attended Flora Stone Mather College at Western Reserve University for one year. She was artistic (pencil drawings) and a fine seamstress. The marriage was a solid one. The only cross words I ever heard between my parents related to driving the family car—well, not the family car, my father's car. My father just didn't want anybody else driving his car. Eventually my mother, sister, and I internalized this reality, and we bought our own car a couple of years before the war, a 1937 Chevrolet coupe.

My sister, Daphne, was two and one-half years older than I. We always got along fairly well. Sibling rivalry was never a factor in our relationship. We played and fought as I suppose all brothers and sisters do. But most of the time I went my way and she went hers. She was a good student, loved music, and was always very self-disciplined and organized, qualities I may possess but to a much lesser degree. Daphne dated and had a couple of boyfriends in high school, but there was only one man in her life—Don Day. They met in 1939 and after he was commissioned in the Navy, were married in 1944. Don and I worked together at the Shaker Theatre, played ice hockey against each other in high school (he went to John Adams), belonged to the same fraternity at Ohio University, and both loved music. We were good friends.

In politics, the family was Republican, except for my grandmother, who was a strong supporter of Franklin D. Roosevelt (I suspect she is still voting for him in Heaven). There were very few jobs, pay was low, and families conserved in any way they could. Even in the late 1930s and early 1940s, times were still tough. The Depression raged during virtually all of my adolescent years. I clearly remember men coming to our back door asking for any kind of work in exchange for food. The war was about to change all that.

We went to church a lot, but I never thought of my family as deeply religious. I don't remember my grandparents ever attending church, even though it was their son playing the organ each week. I suspect we went to church a lot because my father was the church organist—we were expected to go. When I was small, I used to love to sit on the bench with him while he played. But as I grew older, I never really looked forward to Sunday school and church. Well, I shouldn't say never because later, in my teens, I learned to enjoy church a lot more. I would sit in the balcony with Eleanor Walden, a good-looking girl about one year younger than I, and match pennies or pass notes. Religion isn't so bad. It's the relationships that count.

Even though I was just 17 when I graduated from high school in January 1942, it was easy to get a job. Thousands of young men were being drafted or had enlisted in the armed forces at the very time that thousands of people were needed to fill the vacancies in war production. The contradiction demanded resolution, and it meant that jobs were fairly easy to get. I got a job at Jack & Heintz in Cleveland, Ohio, where I worked for eight months as a plant guide. I escorted visitors through the plant to the offices of the people they had come to see. The plant was big and noisy. Huge presses thundered out their productive message hour after hour. This, along with lathes, drill presses, and small carts rumbling by with parts made it almost impossible to hear in the plant. The war was on, and German and Japanese spies were everywhere (or so we thought)—thus my job. It was a total bore, but it paid good money.

During the summer of 1942 I took a second job, playing trumpet in a dance band at Vermillion, Ohio. At five in the afternoon I would leave Jack & Heintz in Cleveland, drive about 40 miles to Vermillion, play the band job, fall into bed at the band cottage, and do it again the next day. Fortunately, I worked only a five-day week at the plant. These two jobs provided the money for college and enabled me to pay off the debt on a 1941 Ford convertible my sister and I had purchased for $1,140. It was a beautiful car—light blue with blue leather seats, whitewall tires, a radio, and eight pounding cylinders. It even smelled good.

During my three years in high school, I had played trumpet in various dance bands (Bob Good, Phil Peterson, and Bill Porter). I loved every minute of it, and the money was great. By 1942, union scale was $10 for a four-hour band job. I think it was the experience of playing in the big dance bands that ultimately shaped my life and determined my present career. Work and play were so intimately related in playing a band job that although I took the money, I would have done it for nothing. Jobs were usually four hours with one or two 15-minute breaks. There were many opportunities to play as the leader of a section or as the instrumentalist who "rides" (improvises). It was marvelous. There were always food, drink, and pretty girls to go along with the excitement of playing. Sometimes people would just stand in front of the bandstand to listen to one of the soloists. I never forgot the delight of this musical experience, this creative activity, and I determined that I would always seek to duplicate the experience in my lifework, whatever that was going to be.

As I said, during the summer of 1942 I was playing with Bill Porter's band at Vermillion-on-the-Lake. We played from 8:00 p.m. to 12:00 midnight six nights a week; all the great tunes — "One O'Clock Jump," "Skylark," "In the Mood," "Body and Soul," "Stompin at the Savoy." The band was typical of the day: four saxophones, four brass, and three rhythm, plus a singer. I remember the owner, a real creep, always telling Bill to "shorten the numbers, shorten the numbers." He did this because it cost ten cents a dance, and the more numbers we played, the more money he made! Obviously, money and music conflict at times.

When I went to Ohio University in September 1942, I joined the campus dance band the first day in town. I can't remember how the contact was made, only that Bob Good, a super tenor sax man, and I were in the band the first day and played with that group until we both went into the service in June 1943. My only other work experiences were probably the same as those of millions of other boys growing up in America at the time. I had a paper route for two years, sold magazines (most of these to my relatives), parked cars at the Terminal Tower, sold Christmas trees, and for about six months was an usher at the Shaker Theater for twenty-five cents an hour — a miserable job and low pay.

My two best friends were Bob Good and Jack Foley. They were nothing alike; on the contrary, they had very different interests and personalities. We often stayed overnight at one another's home to study (this meant talk), and our parents put up with all this nonsense with grace. Jack and I doubledated a lot because he went steady for a while with my girlfriend's sister, Eleanor "Hap" Harper. Most of these dates involved movies, dances, or just a stop at a hamburger joint. Bob Good, with patience and fortitude, got me through high school physics somehow, and we played in bands together. Sometimes we took our girlfriends to a band job — not too often.

Like everyone, I had girlfriends as well as boyfriends. Barbara Rupert was the first girl I really liked — that was in junior high school. She was a good dancer and rather vivacious. I think she liked me. I know I liked her. Later in high school I went steady with Alberta Best for a few weeks. But my real girlfriend was Barbara Harper. Barbara was blonde, five feet four, good-looking, blithesome, and about one year younger than I. She had a friendly, open personality and seemed to enjoy the same things I did — movies, music, and dancing. Sometimes when a "name" band (Tommy Dorsey, Benny Goodman, Stan Kenton) came to the Trianon Ballroom in Cleveland, we would go with another couple, ostensibly to dance. Instead, we would frequently end up standing in front of the band listening to the songs and humming out the memorized solos of our musical heroes. It must have been "thrilling" for Barbara. But she put up with it stoically. She must have possessed the patience of Job. We went together part of my junior and senior year at high school, and we wrote to each other during the war. We dated, went "steady," argued, broke up, went "steady" again, had lots of fun together, and probably conducted ourselves like millions of other young people. We did some "necking," but everything was quite innocent.

I attended the public schools in Shaker Heights. Academics didn't really interest me very much in junior and senior high school. I took a college-prep program, passed with a minimum of effort, enjoyed my literature and history classes, and disliked mathematics and science (with the possible exception of biology). I was an average student, rarely did homework, "skimmed" by in most of my classes, and spent most of my time on the things I liked—music, ice hockey, dating, and reading. But the Shaker system was good for me. There were opportunities to be involved in all kinds of activities. There was one I shall never forget—the play *Hamlet*. In my senior year a call went out to interested students to audition for parts. Jack Foley was Hamlet. I was given the part of Guildenstern (if you know the play, you realize just how small a part this was). But I tell myself that the director, Robert Freeman, must have recognized my latent thespian skills and talents (which are still latent) because he gave me the part instead of giving it to Paul Newman, a famous movie star the last 35 years, who was on the stage crew. (Yes, Paul Newman and I still have the original program to prove it.) Actually, I can't remember if Paul ever auditioned for a part or simply chose stage crew. He was one year behind me. We knew each other, that's all. But it's a great story to tell one's children and grandchildren. Maybe *Hamlet* was what sparked his interest in theater, who knows?

When the war began on December 7, 1941, I was a second semester senior at Shaker. I remember well the president's speech, broadcast over the school's public address system, asking Congress for a declaration of war. All the boys in the class knew we would be going into the service soon, an event viewed by most, I suspect, rather ambiguously. Adventure, uniforms, shiny boots, travel, glory, and a chance to fulfill one's patriotic duty were internally related to thoughts about death and dying on a field in France or an island in the Pacific. It wasn't clear. It wasn't intelligible. It wasn't something you talked about.

My parents didn't seem to be openly concerned about my entry into the service. They didn't encourage or discourage my involvement in any way. But my grandfather, with whom I lived (because he had an extra bedroom), often expressed his concern to my mother ("Will Bob have to go?"). She told me about this later, and I suspect it reflected her position also.

All the local churches in Shaker Heights, including mine, the Shaker

Heights Christian Church, backed American entry into the war. "Praise the Lord and Pass the Ammunition," a popular song of the day, reflected well the patriotic attitudes of the local clergy and their congregations.

On June 30, 1942, I signed up for the draft at Local Board 50, situated in the Shaker Heights City Hall. According to the card, I was 5′11″ and weighed 140. The card said, "The law requires you to have this card in your personal possession at all times." They didn't have to tell me to carry it. Suddenly I felt older, more mature. I was a boy who had become a man, courtesy of a small paper card. My feet were set on the road to military service that day.

Unlike many of my friends, I had no clear career aspirations — none. Each year I moved on in school, worked in the summer and then did it all over again next year. My parents never talked much to me about college. I didn't even decide to go to Ohio University until one or two months before the 1942 fall term began. If I thought of college at all, it was as a four-year delay in having to go to work full-time. My interests did not change in the summer between high school and college. College was simply my answer to the age-old question "Is there life after high school?" The answer was "Yes — college."

When I went to Ohio University in the fall of 1942, the same behavior prevailed. I cut a lot of tiresome classes and again was an average student, except in my history and law classes. I loved the argument, informal debate, and dialogue in the law classes and was fascinated by the stories on the history of China (my instructor was born and raised in China, the son of a missionary).

On December 12, 1942, I joined the Enlisted Reserve Corps for "the duration plus six months." This sudden surge of patriotism was prompted by a government ruling stating that those who enlisted promptly would be permitted to complete the 1942–43 academic year. I selected the Army rather than the Navy for two important reasons: first, I could enlist in the Army in Athens, Ohio, while a Navy enlistment required a trip to Cleveland; second, I had a date with a town girl the weekend my friends went to Cleveland. These seemed powerful reasons at the time, and since I made it through the conflict, who is to say decisions should be based on more rational grounds?

As the academic year drew to a close in May, we all spent a lot more time in our favorite bar, the 333, drinking beer and talking of the great adventure we were all about to start rather than in the library doing the papers required in our courses. I received my notice to report for duty on May 31, 1943. This was it. Orders were orders. I finished my exams, participated in a final round of boisterous beer parties, and headed north for Cleveland. When I arrived, there was another notice from Uncle Sam. This one granted me a 24-hour delay in my induction into the Army; it was

Decoration Day, and even induction into the armed forces during the war had to give way to national holidays. First things first.

About ten o'clock in the morning on Tuesday, June 1, 1943, I walked to the Rapid Transit from my home at 3413 Milverton. The big day had arrived. I met a friend, Bill Mason, at the Moreland Boulevard stop, and we talked about our new life as we took the 20-minute ride downtown to the Terminal Tower. We submitted to the indignities of a rather superficial physical examination, took the oath of allegiance nearby with 111 other Army inductees, and "marched," as only raw recruits can, back to the Terminal Tower to get the train for Fort Hayes. My parents were there to say goodbye, along with my girlfriend, Barbara Harper. Nobody knew exactly what to say—it was all rather awkward. There was the conventional small talk about writing and calling once in a while, little more. There were hundreds of people in the terminal depot, all doing the same thing we were—waiting. It was an extraordinary moment in the lives of almost everyone there, a moment characterized by its conventionality. In any event, after a few brave goodbyes, some hugs and kisses, we boarded the train.

There we were given small packets containing gum, cigarettes, candy, and soap by volunteers known as the Gray Ladies. Then began the lonely, bumpy train ride to Fort Hayes in Columbus, which took about two and one half hours. When we arrived at the camp, we were met by a minor tyrant, an arrogant Pfc. (private first class) whom I remember with contempt to this very day. He acted as if he were a sergeant. He looked like a skinny wimp. But we were like tiny fragmented atoms at this time, no semblance of a unit at all, so he got away with his pretension and bombast. We talked about him later in our barracks, which housed about 45 soldiers, and came to the conclusion that he was in all likelihood a "kiss-ass" who had a good deal going and was trying to keep his cushy job. In hindsight he was one of the very few insufferable individuals I met in the Army in two and one-half years.

Fort Hayes was a six-day transition site for most of us. Here we began the conversion from civilian to military life. This involved distribution of uniforms, khaki only (no ODs, olive drabs) as it was summer and we were headed farther south, selected immunization shots, and assignment to various training bases throughout the United States (Army Air Force, Artillery, Infantry, Engineers, etc.). There was no effort to teach us anything but how to salute officers. We mastered this in a day or two and took off for a United Service Organization (USO) dance at Ohio State University. The next day the USO sponsored another dance at Fort Hayes. There was a big band (it was the era of the big band), and they played all the music I loved. Army life seemed great—no work, pretty good food, dances, girls—and best of all, we looked like soldiers, or thought we did, in our shiny new uniforms. But it all came to an end on June 7 when we boarded the train for Georgia.

The troop train from Fort Hayes, Columbus, to Camp Wheeler in Georgia took about one and one-half days. Soldiers played cards, read, slept, and talked. There were no beds, and we just dozed in our seats. We had coffee and sandwiches and headed south. At one stop a small black child about five years old did a soft-shoe on the station platform. We all applauded his performance and tossed him a few coins. We finally pulled into the station near Camp Wheeler, and a sergeant boarded the train and entered our car. We had on our "pith" helmets, issued in Fort Hayes, with the straps under our chins. He ordered us to "put those straps back where they damn well belong" and led us to the bus that would take us to our camp.

This was my first encounter with Sergeant Simmons, destined to be our platoon sergeant. He was an unforgettable character. Sergeant Simmons was 5'10", about 170 pounds, had a square face, deeply tanned, and penetrating dark eyes. He was a southerner from Alabama, a buck sergeant, probably about 27. We all got to know him very well professionally but not at all personally. He was tough, not arrogant, just plain tough. He did everything that he demanded we do and more. He was a disciplinarian — he commanded — and he got obedience. He was intelligent, fair, never given to boasting or vanity, and a good teacher, but he tolerated absolutely no foolishness. He knew the Army, was clearly respected by our officers and the other noncoms, and he spoke plain English, English with a southern accent. Many times I've heard him say, "Thobaben, come over cheer" — that's *here* in Yankee. I was in Company A, 11th Battalion, First Platoon, with about 45 or 50 other recruits. I never knew anybody who was personally close to him. Nobody conned Sergeant Simmons. We respected him then. I do today. And if the whole truth were known, I think each one of us feared him. I know I did. Getting chewed out by Sergeant Simmons was a harrowing experience — real pain.

Camp Wheeler was located near Macon, Georgia, the land of red soil, peanuts, mockingbirds, pecans, and tall juniper pine trees. These stately trees were 80 to 90 feet tall and about 24 to 30 inches in diameter. The trunk was usually bare of branches up to about 60 feet. At this point the branches and needles began. Underneath each one was a cushion of long pine needles. They were beautiful and provided a lot of shade. It was a temporary Army facility and no longer exists. In the summer of 1943 there were 18,000 to 20,000 men in training, organized into battalions of about 800 men.

Each platoon (48 men) lived in a two-story frame barracks, two squads downstairs and two upstairs. Our sergeant and corporal had private rooms in the same building. The barracks were painted white with red shingle roofs and were built around a grassy square in which we practiced close-order drill, did calisthenics, took instruction on various weapons, and presented ourselves for inspection. Our platoon was a social contradition—about 50 percent college students from Ohio University and about 50 percent Pennsylvania Dutch farm boys from towns like Pottstown and Kutztown. Little in the backgrounds of the two groups suggested that we could ever be a unit. Different languages (many spoke German), religions, educations, and ways of life made our first encounters uncomfortable. We were the college boys. They were the Pennsylvania Dutch boys. I know that we initially prejudged them, and I suspect they did the same. We started our training isolated and estranged from one another. But three and one-half months later we were a genuine unit. We were bound by a hundred common experiences. We had become friends. I know that I would have preferred to go overseas with this group rather than the one I eventually joined. The relationships we established generated a trust and mutual respect that was never duplicated. This platoon was, in my military experience, my psychic home.

Drilling and marching are two separate things for an infantry soldier. Drilling, what we called close-order drill, involves marionette precision and constant tedious repetition. Practice and more practice is the key. In drilling we were silent, alert, and always prepared to obey one of the many orders of our sergeant as he called out "*hut*-two-three-four," "to the rear . . . *march*," or "by the right oblique . . . *march*." His goal was to make all 48 men appear one body—in step, all rifles at the same angle, even the same position of one's head. It sounds paradoxical, but close-order drill, when thousands of soldiers are involved, can be an awesome individual experience and sight. One is reduced to a mere part of a larger organic being, a living, breathing thing, that transcends the individuals that compose it. Close-order drill was never fun. It was sometimes more of a "religious experience"—particularly when done with bands playing, flags snapping in the wind, rifles with fixed bayonets, and thousands of soldiers in a battalion block.

A long or a short march is quite another thing. Here we marched from 5 to 25 miles, in the cold rain or hot Georgia sun, during the day or night, covered by the red dust kicked up by thousands of boots, and were weighed down with a 60-pound full field pack. But once out of camp, and given the order for "route step," we carried on a constant banter, occasionally sang a song, and looked around to see if there was a pretty girl in sight. Although route step did not demand that each of us pay attention to staying in step, we did. We stayed in step because it was easier to march and make smooth progress than to stumble along at a pace different from that of the others in the platoon. If somebody did get out of step, the one in front or back of him might "politely" remind him of the trouble being caused. Usually the language would be "Hey, Charlie, for chrissake, get in step." We would march three and one-half miles in 50 minutes, and then the sergeant would say, "Take ten." That is, we would flop down along the road and smoke a cigarette, talk, and have a drink of water from our canteens.

During the marching, drilling, instruction on weapons, and assignment of duties throughout my military career, both continental and foreign service, there was a gap between theoretical and practical command. It was always the same. It was my sergeant, not my "commanding officer," who ruled. This reality, this virtual absence of a relationship between officer and enlisted man, this dissociation of men in the same unit, was even further exacerbated overseas. I knew who my immediate officers were, cared little for them, and today can only conjure up a very hazy image of our company, battalion, and regimental officers. They meant little or nothing to me then. They mean nothing to me today.

What I remember of my contacts with a number of Army officers and a few Navy officers is at best neutral and in a few instances negative. Perhaps this is how it is supposed to be—I never knew. Our lieutenant might march with us, or he might not. Sometimes he, or the company commander, would pull up in a jeep, speak to the sergeant, wave to the platoon, and drive off. Maybe he was involved in high-level decision making. We knew only that he wasn't involved much in our day-to-day lives. Perhaps it was all part of maintaining military discipline and being a leader of men. But there was definitely a difference in the way most of us viewed our immediate leaders, our platoon sergeants, and our officers. Unwarranted privilege and genuine respect are inversely related.

We were issued gas masks at Camp Wheeler but were required to carry them only on specific occasions. It wasn't a thing we carried every minute, like our rifles and packs. They were clumsy to carry, and we hated an exercise where they were necessary. This usually occurred in a tactical exercise. For example, we were taught the proper tactics to take a village, and sometimes we would be suddenly "bombed" with tear gas. When that happens, it is important to put the gas mask on quickly because tear gas really burns the eyes, can cause vomiting, and is irritating to the throat and sweaty skin.

Once or twice during our training we were exposed to still another dolorous exercise. We would march out to an area that had four or five one-floor barracks constructed in the middle of an open field. There we were ordered to put on our gas masks and prepare to enter each building. Everybody bitched: "Not that again, God—not the gas treatment." Georgia in July is hot and humid, and with a gas mask on, it is almost intolerable. But there was no escape, no refuge, no way to "goldbrick" (escape duty) your way out of this enriching experience. We usually did this by squad (12 men). In any event, after we were all in Building 1, we were told to take our thumb and forefinger, grasp the rubberized part of the mask at the jawbone, and lift it out about one inch. Naturally, this exposed us to some of the gas in the room. Each of us smelled the gas, let the mask close tight against his face, and left the building.

We were exposed to five different gases—lewisite, phosgene, mustard, chloropicren, and tear. I can remember to this day the odor of phosgene. It smelled exactly like new-mown hay. The other odors are lost to me in the mist of time. The only other time I ever touched my gas mask was two years later, in the Palau Islands. I was cleaning up my equipment one day and found the mask had been infiltrated by small cricketlike insects. I cleaned them out, put the mask back in the pack, and never again looked at it until the war ended and I turned it in.

We fired all kinds of weapons: light and heavy .30-caliber machine guns, .60- and .81-millimeter mortars, carbines, .45-caliber pistols, BAR's (Browning Automatic Rifles), rifle grenades, hand grenades, shaped charges, and most important of all, the M-1 (Garand) rifle. We lived with that rifle in our hands. We broke it down, cleaned it, shot it, carried it; and, God forbid, if we dropped it, we were required to march around the barracks that night, stop at each of the four corners, present arms as defined in *The Manual of Arms*, and say the words "I love my rifle." We could break it down blindfolded. For the first few weeks in camp we only carried and cared for the rifle. About the third or fourth week we went to the shooting range. Here we were taught to fire the rifle from the prone, kneeling, sitting, and standing positions at ranges that varied from 100 to 500 hundred yards.

I did fairly well, except for the 500-hundred-yard range, because I had done a little target shooting as a boy. My father and grandfather occasionally shot a .22-caliber rifle in the basement of our home as recreation. Once in a while I was invited to participate. The lessons I learned at home applied in the Army: sight picture, solid grip, hold breath, and squeeze off the shot. But there were many in my platoon who were firing a rifle for the first time in their lives. And to compound the problems associated with shooting any rifle, this one kicked like a mule. The problem with a sharp kick was twofold: first, it tended to make the shooter flinch, which in turn seriously affected the accuracy of the shot; and second, it produced a number of black eyes, swollen lips, and injured thumbs. This was a consequence of failing to have a really full and firm grip on the rifle with the right hand.

It was quite a sight on the firing range—scores of soldiers shooting, sergeants pacing behind their charges like mother hens, targets going up and down, and frequently, all too frequently, "Maggie's drawers" being waved by those recruits working in the pits. Maggie's drawers is a red flag used by the person working the pits to indicate to the shooter that not only did he miss the bull's-eye but missed the entire target. There was a lot of laughter, growling sergeants, and intimidated recruits on the firing line.

Sometimes when we left the range, we would be ordered to an area for bayonet training. We never did much of this, and I for one certainly hoped I'd never be in a position where I had to use what I was taught. We were usually simply ordered to "fix bayonets" and then instructed to stick some straw-filled sack or dummy. There is a simple technique involved. One holds the rifle firmly and then thrusts forward with both arms, impaling the straw dummy on the bayonet. In sum, for the infantry soldier the rifle is an extension of his being.

Twice while I was at Camp Wheeler I went to Macon, Georgia, on a pass. Macon is about 75 miles south of Atlanta. The center of town is the intersection of Cherry and Third streets. On a small grass square at this intersection was a monument to the Civil War. The focal point was a seven- or eight-foot bronze statue of a Confederate soldier standing at attention atop a white granite column. Macon retained much of the ambience of the Old South since many of the mansions in its older residential sections were spared by Sherman in his march to the sea.

Cherry Street was a wide boulevard with a grass-covered divider and a concrete promenade down the center. On each side of the concrete walk were shade trees. The bus station where soldiers arrived from Camp Wheeler was only a couple of blocks away, and we invariably headed up Cherry Street for the Dempsey Hotel, one of our favorite (and more expensive) watering holes.

In 1943, Macon (like the Army) was strictly segregated. I never saw a black person on Cherry Street. It was whites only. There was a second "main street" for blacks, one block away. Military Police (MPs) would stop any soldier headed toward the "wrong" main street. In Cleveland, blacks and whites lived in segregated communities, but one saw many blacks shopping in downtown Cleveland at Higbee's and May's. This was not the case in Macon. Cherry Street was for whites only.

The Dempsey Hotel was a 10-story building that dominated the other three- and four-story squat brick buildings in Macon. As one entered the hotel, there was a huge photograph of some local Army Air Force hero. We looked at it briefly, but we had more important things to do — drink beer. I'm sure there were a number of fascinating historical things to see in Macon (antebellum homes, museums, art exhibits, etc.), but at 19 I was interested in beer, the music of the big bands, girls, and little else.

Everyday life at Camp Wheeler included a number of mundane activities. Some took a few minutes, some hours. Assignment to work in the kitchen (KP) for a day was an ever-present fear of every member of the platoon. It started at 4:00A.M. and ended at 9:00P.M. In the kitchen, the company cook was an absolute autocrat. He was an overweight, balding, sweaty tyrant who delighted in ordering people around. The jobs on KP were completely destructive to the human spirit: peeling hundreds of potatoes, washing pots and pans encrusted with burnt grease, cleaning the mess hall after every meal, and doing whatever else this "czar of the kitchen" could think of. It was a long, long day when one had KP.

Another delightful task was latrine duty. It didn't take long, but the atmosphere left something to be desired. All the commodes, washbowls, and mirrors had to sparkle, and we cleaned the chrome and copper pipes until they glistened. After we mopped the floor, we wouldn't let anyone in until we had passed inspection. He may have been under extreme tension, but when the cleaning and polishing was completed, we had no intention of letting anyone "screw it up."

Still another job was cleaning our barracks. We were required to keep our bed and footlocker in shape for inspection every day, but once a week we all got on our hands and knees and scrubbed the floor with hard brushes. We turned the pine floor white with soap. Finally, guard duty and "policing up" the area were duties we all performed. Guard duty involved nothing more than walking a prescribed line for a two-hour stint. The best one can say for guard duty is that it was a bore. Time seemed to stand still. Walking your post at two or three in the morning was a numbing experience, rather like some of the classes I experienced in high school where you sat for what seemed to be hours only to be wakened from a semicomatose state by the loud tick of the clock. It just went on and on. Fortunately, I pulled this duty only twice during my stay at Camp Wheeler.

"Policing-up" meant to pick up every piece of foreign matter that wasn't growing. Most of this was associated with smoking. We were supposed to "fieldstrip" a spent cigarette — that is, after extinguishing the cigarette, we were supposed to tear the paper (few people smoked filter cigarettes in those days), sprinkle the remaining tobacco in the grass, roll up the paper into a tiny wad, and pitch it. We policed up the area of our barracks and our exercise area each day. We liked it because we knew that as soon as this task was completed, we would be heading back to the barracks.

Every Saturday we had a film — *Why We Fight* or *Venereal Disease*. In hindsight, I'd say we spent much more time on films associated with illicit sex than why we should kill the Germans and Japanese. Our political indoctrination was limited to a few films entitled *The Rape of Nanking, Bataan Death March* or *German Blitzkreig*. I know Sergeant Simmons never gave us a lecture on politics and the war, and I cannot remember our second lieutenant doing it either. The Army at that time presumed that if they taught a soldier how to fire a rifle and use the various weapons previously noted, he would use them that way in combat.

This is a questionable premise in light of the evidence suggested by the *Infantry Journal* and Mao Zedong's book *On Guerrilla Warfare*. In that small text, written in the 1930s for Mao's guerrilla fighters, he says (and I paraphrase) that anyone can learn to point a rifle; the problem is to get him to do this and fire it at the enemy in combat. To achieve this, argues Mao, one must employ a great deal of political indoctrination. Soldiers must be taught *why* they fight if they are to fight with any intensity. For Mao, politics was primary. In my experience politics was almost totally neglected. I suspect this has changed. If it hasn't, we're in trouble.

The VD films were a different thing. They were graphic, particularly on the consequences of syphilis and gonorrhea, and one could easily be persuaded that a life of celibacy was the only way to go. If the Army had put half the effort into political indoctrination that it put into keeping the soldiers celibate, we would have defeated the Japanese a year earlier.

Another fascinating character I met in the Army was Jock Edmonds. And you just know what that evolved into—right, he was affectionately known as "Strap" to the men of the First Platoon. Strap was overweight. He certainly did not have a savage body. He had a cherubic face and a talent for mimicry. He could duplicate the voice and actions of anyone. His sense of humor was finely honed, and his quick wit and droll burlesque brightened many a bivouac and march. He was, incidentally, a good alto saxophone musician. We played in the same dance bands at Ohio University before and after the war.

One day, while marching down a dusty road lined with pines, we were suddenly attacked by the air cadets from Cochran, Robbins, and Herbert Smart air bases. They flew over us at very low altitude and bombarded us with small sacks of flour. And they were surprisingly accurate. Once, as they made a strafing run on us, we ran for the ditches alongside the road, but Strap was too slow and found himself engulfed in a cloud of flour from a near miss. He was covered from head to toe with flour and looked for all the world like a ghost. But as with everything else, he took it in good spirits, laughed, jumped, and ran down the road shaking his fist at the planes while being cheered on by the entire platoon.

Strap just didn't take anything very seriously. His reaction to anything, a physically painful experience or a psychologically enfeebling event, was to laugh it off. He did more for the high morale of our platoon than anyone else. He sometimes got into trouble because he knew few limits, but he was popular with everyone. Perhaps it was because so much of what we did in training called to mind the stone of Sisyphus. We seemed to labor in vain. So much of what we did might be likened to beating the air—useless. Strap was sensitized to the futility of much of Army life, and his conduct satirized that attribute.

Sometime in early August 1943 I made two moves that seem in hindsight somewhat contradictory. I signed up to take the mental exams for Army Specialized Training Program (ASTP) and the physical exam for the paratroops. If I passed the first, I would go to a "star" college after basic training, and if I passed the second, I would go to Fort Benning for paratroop training. About this time in my training I had decided that ASTP and a return to college sounded rather attractive compared with life as an infantry recruit and that life as a paratrooper, with those high shiny boots and flying instead of walking, sounded exciting.

Although I had never flown, I had always dreamed of flying. This all came from reading and rereading the pulp magazines of *The Lone Eagle* in the 1930s. It was the Lone Eagle versus Baron von Richtofen, and I was always in the cockpit with my hero. As it happened, I passed both exams, the mental test for ASTP and the physical test for the paratroops, and so had a choice of where to go when basic training was completed. There were only a few other men from our platoon who made the move for ASTP or the paratroops, and it was a big decision for me. Ulimately, college, that sojourn through the land of make-believe, won out, and I went before a board of officers for an oral exam, passed, and was assigned to the ASTP contingent from the 11th Battalion. I think I was one of half a dozen soldiers. The die was cast.

As mid–September arrived and our training drew to a close, we went on more extensive bivouacs. *Bivouac* is simply extended camping where we could practice tactics we had learned during the summer. It invariably meant bugs, jiggers, rain, sleeping in a pup tent, and eating from a mess kit. Marvelous experience! Oh, and it meant one other thing—delayed mail call.

Mail call was always a high point of the week, and on bivouac our mail was delayed. In my letters home, I reminded my parents again and again how nice it was to get letters from home. There is some loneliness associated with a separation from home at any age, I suspect. At 19, it is somewhat exacerbated.

The days are delightful in Georgia during September, but the nights can be cold, particularly when sleeping on the ground in a tent. The daytime activity while on bivouac involved firing all kinds of weapons, crawling under live machine-gun fire to get used to the sound of bullets flying over your head, navigating the obstacle course (certainly a creation of some military masochist), and, of course, making the daily march. When we started our training, a five-mile march was a real test. Near the end of our training we would do 12 or 15 miles and think nothing of it. We did one 17-mile night hike that was a breeze because it was cool. The longest march we ever made, and for me it was certainly no breeze, was a 25-mile hike. It meant we would be marching for eight straight hours carrying all our gear.

The worst things to carry were the machine guns, tripods, mortars, and baseplates. They were heavy and awkward to carry, so we passed them around. Somebody would take the rifle of the soldier carrying the heavy weapons, and he would shoulder the burden for a while. The first four or five hours were nothing—we were used to that. But the last hour or two, we walked like zombies, moving our feet mechanically, not speaking to anyone, simply falling in our tracks when the "take ten" order was shouted out. I thought that hike was tough. After a bivouac it was always good to get back to Camp Wheeler—luxury and a Post Exchange (PX).

The end of life as a recruit and the beginning of life as a replacement was about to begin. Only one more ceremonial event occurred—a great parade. Here 10 or 12 battalions (10,000 or 12,000 men) marched in a battalion block past a reviewing stand of officers. Bands played, battalion flags fluttered in the breeze, and 10,000 men slapped their rifles, creating a roar, on the command "present arms." We were officially soldiers. Boys were now men; amateurs were now professionals (or so we thought). We felt we were a unit, a living, breathing thing.

But with the mass review over, it was time to ship out, and this happened very fast. Almost everyone was gone by October 12, 1943. We waved goodbye to our friends as they headed west to Fort Ord in California, waved with a tinge of guilt because we knew, we really knew that their destination (a point of embarkation) and ours (a college) stood in polar opposition to each other. But that was it.

The guilt ended two days later. The Army decided it needed no more college students and canceled our orders. We were back in the infantry.

I was given a 14-day "delay en route" to get from Camp Wheeler, Georgia, to Fort Ord, California. What this meant was that I could visit friends and relatives for a few days and then head west. The Army didn't care what I did as long as I arrived at Ford Ord by October 29. I left Camp Wheeler on October 15, 1943, for Cleveland and spent four or five days with my parents. Then I took a train to Boston to say goodbye to Barbara, who was now a student at Bradford. We spent two days in Boston seeing the sights, and then I returned home to Cleveland with just enough time to have my clothes washed and make the train. It never entered my mind to fly.

Prior to the Army I remember only one trip outside Ohio. My father had taken the family on a trip to the East Coast, and we stayed for a time in the New York City area and then at Watkins Glen in upstate New York. That was it. So the travel I had already done in the Army and what I was to do made a monumental impression on me.

I left Cleveland for Chicago with three friends on October 25, 1943. The train from Chicago to San Francisco took us through Illinois, Iowa, Nebraska, Colorado, Wyoming, Nevada, and California. The entire trip was a wonder to me, but I remember the geography most. The picture I shall never forget is Ogden, Utah. There was a short delay in Ogden, and as I came out of the terminal and up the steps, I faced straight down the main street. At the end of the street was a huge mountain. It was a spectacular sight. When we arrived in Oakland, we took the ferry to San Francisco. We visited and did all the traditional tourist things in San Francisco — Top of the Mark, Fisherman's Wharf, and a ride on the cable cars — and then took a train to Fort Ord in Monterey, California, arriving at about 9:00P.M. on October 29, 1943.

The next day we ran into all our friends from Camp Wheeler. They were glad to see us and reveled in our misfortune. We probably deserved the hoots, gibes, and verbal indignities because we had been a little smug about going back to college while they went off to fight the war.

Fort Ord is a permanent Army post, very well maintained. It had carefully tended lawns, flower gardens, and an enlisted man's club located on a cliff overlooking the Pacific Ocean. I'd seen officers' clubs, but until Fort Ord I had only heard of clubs for enlisted men. With the seals playing on the rocks at the foot of the cliff, the gentle westerly winds, and the graceful seagulls riding the thermals, one might be lulled into forgetting the service.

However, Fort Ord was just "more of the same." Practice on the rifle range, marching in close-order drill, cleaning equipment, and listening to lectures. We stayed there only seven days, and this time our old friends waved goodbye to us as our little group of former ASTP candidates headed for Camp Stoneman at Pittsburg, California, where we arrived on November 5.

Camp Stoneman had an ominous look — more like a prison than an Army base. It had high barbwire fences and watchtowers. Armed guards were posted in the watchtowers to prevent anybody from going AWOL. There were no passes issued at Stoneman. At night bright lights illuminated every foot of the yard between the barracks and the fences. It didn't look good.

There we joined the 111th Infantry Regiment. The 111th had been a part of the 28th Division, Pennsylvania National Guard, but when the Army streamlined the organization of its divisions from four to three regiments, the 111th was the regiment that was dropped. The 28th Division went to Europe. The 111th Infantry Regiment went to the Pacific. We were assigned to the medical detachment. They made all assignments on the basis of one's last name. Some of those whose last names began with *s* or *t* were assigned to the medical unit. We told them we knew absolutely nothing about first aid or the treatment of wounds. Their response was simple: "We'll teach you on the way over."

Two days later, November 8, we left Camp Stoneman so early in the morning that it was still pitch black outside and marched to a ferryboat that took us down to San Francisco. We disembarked and were marched straight to an immense ship, the *West Point*, which we boarded for the trip overseas. About 10:00A.M. we left the dock and just moved about the harbor until 2:00P.M. when we were ordered to our quarters for abandon-ship drill. When we returned to the deck a bit later, we were at sea. Continental service had ended. Foreign service began. But I had already learned a bit about Army life and people:

1. The opaqueness of Army orders is something I will never understand. Many seemed incoherent, some just incomprehensible. The secrecy seemed unwarranted, and "the fog of war," as described by Clausewitz, is surpassed only by the fog of many Army orders.

2. Some people who act tough turn out to be brittle. There were a couple of individuals who talked in training about how they would act in combat, but as we approached the POE, one of the biggest braggarts in camp talked of going AWOL. He did eventually succeed in getting himself a "Section Eight"—a medical discharge.

3. Joining the Army demands that one adopt a new language. I really don't know why, but we used a great deal of profanity. Perhaps it's because we never were asked to abstract about anything higher than the quality of coffee. Our language didn't leave much to the imagination. Profanity had no "shock value"; it was normal.

4. Age and a semigeneration gap seemed very real. We referred to soldiers who were 25 as "Pop," they seemed so old. At 19, a five- or six-year differential in age seems like a generation.

5. Tedious and repetitive activity is the way of life in the Army. The former is inherent in many of the things we had to learn. The latter is associated with discipline and the Army's concern that we behave in a particular manner under any set of conditions.

"A Clean Ship Is a Happy Ship" 6

"Luxury" Liner, The Perils of Volunteering, Tramp Steamer, Butaritari: An Adventure in Paradise

The *West Point* was an immense ship, 723 feet long with a beam of over 93 feet, the largest Navy troopship in service during World War II. On one trip, according to Navy records, she carried over 9,300 passengers. It surely must have been the one I was on. It was packed.

She was originally built as a luxury liner for the United States Lines and entered service for that company in August 1940. Thus, she was just over three years old when the 111th Infantry boarded her along with thousands of other military personnel. She was originally named the *America* but was renamed *West Point* when the Navy acquired her in 1941 and designated her AP-23.

The *West Point* was also very fast (over 20 knots), the only ship I ever traveled on during the war that went without a destroyer or destroyer escort, and I think I sailed on at least 10 or 11. She had two smokestacks; was painted gray, black, and white in a patterned camouflage; and had three and perhaps four levels for troops below decks. Scores of lifeboats and rafts lined the sides of the ship. Above the main deck were the officers quarters. This was "off limits," naturally, to the thousands of enlisted men of every branch of the service who went on this trip from San Francisco to Oahu.

Life aboard ship was organized around meals, two each day. This was a surprise to me, but as I was to learn, this was common practice on all troopships. The meals were good compared to those in Army mess halls in both quantity and quality, even the beans for breakfast. We always ate *standing up* on long narrow boards with raised edges to prevent spillage. We usually ate about 9:30A.M. and 4:00P.M. In between one could snack on a Milky Way or Babe Ruth. The ship's store sold everything from candy bars, toilet articles, and paperback books to cartons of cigarettes., Incidentally, the cigarettes sold for 50 cents a carton (yes, a carton of ten packs). The vast majority of servicemen smoked. At the time we didn't know that smoking was physically damaging, but even if we had known, I suspect the ratio of smokers to nonsmokers would have been high. Why not?

Another eye-opener was the sleeping accommodations. I had never seen anything like the stacked bunks five high. Each bunk was a rectangle of metal pipe, probably about two feet wide and six and a half feet long. Inside this fabrication was a single piece of heavy canvas with metal grommets that served as eyelets to strengthen and protect the canvas from ripping. The canvas was then lashed to the metal framework with manila rope. That was it — a bed. These were then stacked five high. It was the same on every ship I subsequently traveled on. We were supposed to sleep fully clothed with a preserver as a pillow, and the gap between soldiers while lying in these bunks was about four to six inches — if you were lucky. If you were unfortunate enough to have a big heavy person above you, the gap could shrink to zero. That was always an enriching experience.

I felt a bit uneasy the first 24 hours on the ship, but after that I loved the trip. The water was inky blue, and dolphins cruised leisurely alongside the ship. Flying fish, amazing creatures that fly for 50 yards or more, slashed to and fro, and we spent hours leaning on the rail watching all the action. The sea was calm for most of the trip, and the weather was delightful, so we spent a great deal of time on deck just looking, reading, talking, and watching the crap games.

That was something. There was a perpetual crap game in operation on the after deck, different from any I had ever seen. There was big money involved — certain "specialists" did nothing but take side bets (always *against* the roller), and one streetwise soldier managed the game — occasionally taking a cut of part of the pot. Thousands of dollars changed hands. The man who ran the game seemed to decide who would roll the dice and who wouldn't. I never figured this out. The odds were even on 6 and 8, 3:2 on 5 and 9, and 2:1 on 4 and 10. This was accepted without question by everyone. They all seemed to know this, but it was all new to me.

The specialists were the most interesting. They had a wad of money containing hundreds of dollars to back themselves up, and they always bet one way — against the dice. I placed a couple of small bets with them, and I think I even won 10 or 15 dollars, but I was definitely not a high roller. No officer ever made any effort to stop the game, although it went on in plain view of everyone. They were not down on the main deck with us but could easily watch what went on from the upper decks. There were also some Marines on board who were responsible for order on the ship, but they never intervened either. The game was always under the strict control of a single soldier. It was up to him to maintain the peace.

Within 24 hours everyone knew we were headed for Oahu in the Hawaiian Islands. Our officers never announced it. The rumor mill produced it, a much more reliable source. This also made relevant the "code," which I had set up with my parents before I left the States. Just before departure I wrote to them that I would be in Hawaii, Attu, the Solomon Islands, or

Kiska, depending upon which of the first four lines of my letter contained the following sentence: "I miss you folks a lot." When I arrived in Oahu, I simply included that phrase in my first letter. It made a lot of sense then. It seems somewhat melodramatic now.

The ship was blacked out at night—no smoking or lights allowed on deck. Submarines! Entrance to the sleeping quarters or the exit to the deck was accomplished by having a small foyerlike area that acted as a transition or staging area coming to or leaving the deck. This was pitch black and enabled the movement of personnel about the ship with relative safety. In four days we arrived at Oahu and docked at the Aloha tower dock. We stayed on board that night and left the ship the following morning, November 13, 1943. We were on "foreign soil."

The entire regiment, about 3,500 men in all, marched from the dock through part of Honolulu to the train that was to take us to Schofield Barracks. And what a train it was. I'll never forget it, nor will anyone else who rode this fugitive from a Lionel toy train set. It was a narrow-gauge railroad with a small steam locomotive and "boxcars" for the passengers.

Each of the boxcars looked as if the top half had been cut off with a giant chain saw. When we boarded the cars, we were all forced to stand up for the trip, and the only thing that kept us from falling out into a pineapple field was the three-foot wall of the boxcar that had been left intact. I'm sure it was a handy technology for loading and moving pineapples. Frankly, it worked equally well for troops. It was small and slow, but it chugged through the fields for an hour or two without complaining on the trip to Schofield. There were many new things to see. The people that we saw were different, people whose ethnic roots were surely to be found in Japan, China, the Philippines and even (rarely) Hawaii. Then there was the environment—the palm trees, the huge pineapple and sugar-cane fields, each sprinkled with its own workers and their specialized equipment.

As the train climbed up the hills toward Schofield Barracks, we were treated to glimpses of shimmering water in Pearl Harbor, and the mountains were a surprise. I'm not sure what I expected in the Hawaiian Islands, but it wasn't mountains with sharp, jagged cliffs. It was fun, and everyone was together. We were starting a great adventure, and the countryside was truly lovely.

Schofield Barracks, made famous by James Jones's *From Here to Eternity*, is a permanent Army post. It is unusual in that the quarters for troops are three-story concrete quadrangles, four of them. The center of each quadrangle, a grass field, is used for various military formations and drilling. The post also had a large theater, post exchange, an arena where boxing tournaments were held, and a golf course.

One of the most notable geographic phenomena associated with Scho-

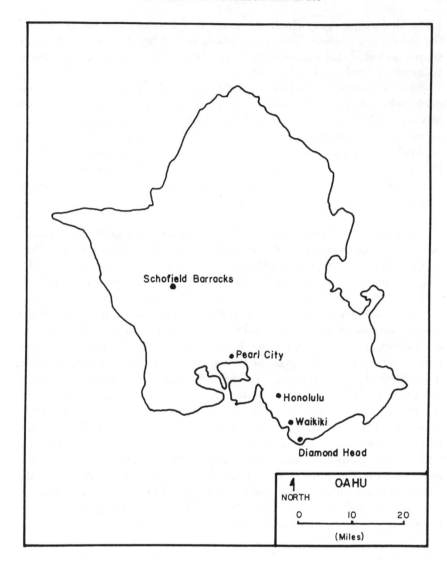

Oahu, Hawaiian Islands.

field Barracks is Kolekole Pass. It was through this pass in the mountains that some of the Japanese planes had come as they headed for Wheeler Field and Pearl Harbor. The road to the pass curves upward from the base and avails the hiker who makes the trip a grand vista.

We were assigned to one of the quadrangles, and the next day all of the replacements, including my friend John Survill and me, were ordered out to the center of the quadrangle and told that we could enter any one of the three battalion medical detachments. There was a bit of scurrying around, and John and I walked into the group that joined the Third Battalion of the 111th Infantry Regiment. It was to be a fateful move. We were assigned to the Headquarters Company of the Medical Detachment because we knew absolutely nothing about caring for wounded or ill soldiers, the principal job of the aidmen assigned to each platoon in a rifle company.

The Headquarters Company (HQ) of the Medical Detachment was a paradox. It contained some of the best-trained medical personnel and technicians and some of the worst, men like John and me with no training whatsoever. Our assignment seemed almost insane to me. We had spent three and a half months learning how to kill people, and now we were supposed to help the injured, all with zero training. There must have been some logic in doing this, there simply had to be, but it was never revealed to me. Such is life in the Army.

We were to learn our new trade while we served on "tech" duty. What this meant was simply that those of us with no experience would watch the trained people handle sick call each day in the Battalion Aid Station, become familiar with proper medical diagnosis and procedure, and then begin to apply our new skills. We were never left alone in the aid station, thank God, there was always someone there supervising us. The men assigned as aidmen with a platoon had experience and demonstrated skills and were in essence the "doctors" assigned to each group. One had to have achieved some level of proficiency to be assigned as a platoon aidman because the platoons were frequently off on their own.

The aidmen had some status in the infantry units. Those of us in the on-the-job training program had none. We really couldn't do anything, but they said we'd learn, and we did. There were about 35 men in the HQ. About one-third of them, say 12 or so, were skilled technicians. The rest of the group served as litter bearers and technicians-in-training. I was in this group. We were embryo aidmen. One final comment: The aidmen lived with their platoon and had little contact with the HQ. Those of us in the HQ lived together as a separate and distinct unit.

The Third Battalion was the "MILK" battalion. I, L, and K companies were rifle companies, and M Company was the heavy-weapons company attached to the respective rifle companies as field conditions warranted. The Headquarters Company, the group John and I were assigned to, established and operated the battalion aid station. We were put there to learn our new trade. Later we were told we would be assigned to one of the rifle companies.

John and I were probably the youngest members of the unit. Most of the others were three or four years older and came from the industrial Midwest; a few from the East Coast, and one or two from the South.

John and I were exactly the same age (born April 3, 1924). John was

Lithuanian. He was about 6', slender, and had a dark complexion and a heavy head of blue-black hair. He was from Bayonne, New Jersey, and I considered him my closest friend during our two years of foreign service. We weren't always together, but most of the time we arranged to do things together. John smoked a lot (we all did), was well liked by everyone as far as I could determine, and wasn't easily ruffled by rumors or unusual situations. In the idiom of the day he would probably be characterized by my grandchildren as "laid back." Things didn't worry him very much. John was always able to look pretty good; that is, in Oahu or on the islands he always seemed clean, the complete opposite to the rest of us. His girlfriend back home was called "Wheaties." He never explained this, and I never asked him to elaborate. We were together from basic training in Georgia until the day we returned to the States. We were friends.

After about a week of drill, calisthenics, movies, and getting new gear and clothing (my B bag was lost someplace on the trip), John and I got a one-day pass and headed for Honolulu. We walked the streets, snacked, drank a beer, marveled at the tropical environment, watched the good-looking girls go by (virtually all of them racially mixed), and finally ran across River Street.

Now this was different. It was unique then, and I've never seen anything like it since, anyplace. River Street was a street in downtown Honolulu lined with two- and three-story buildings, all involved in one profession, the oldest profession. There were soldiers, sailors, and Marines standing in lines outside each one of the bawdy houses, and from time to time one would hear the raucous call "next!" Obviously, the demand for sex was greater than the supply—thus the long lines. There were prophylactic stations located next to or near each building, all clearly marked as such. I have never determined if this was government-approved or government-tolerated, but it existed then, and everyone knew about River Street. It was all "terribly romantic." John and I watched for a few minutes, amazed at what we were seeing, and then left Sin City with its life in the fast lane for Waikiki with its beaches, bars, and buffoonery.

We went by bus out to Waikiki where we got off and went into a bar called the Chicken Coop, across the street and not far from the Royal Hawaiian Hotel. There we treated ourselves to some of the island's best whiskey—Three Feathers. It was terrible, but we drank it anyway. In short order we were drunk, I was terribly sick, and we found ourselves sitting on a bench on the beach alongside the Royal Hawaiian Hotel.

I think there must be some unwritten rule in the Army that a pass to town carries with it the added responsibility of drinking too much. It's possible that there were soldiers who did conduct themselves in a more civil manner, but from what I saw, most did not. "Everything in excess" was our motto. The wind, sun, and water helped, and in a few hours we were able to navigate to a bus that took us back to Schofield Barracks. At the time, our behavior and activities seemed quite reasonable. We had a lot of stories to tell back at the barracks. In retrospect, it all seems pretty dumb—kind of like Tarzan: You always hoped he was brighter than he appeared. Unfortunately, he wasn't, and we weren't either.

Ominous rumors about a move began to fly through the barracks a day or two later. These were reinforced by orders to appear for a series of shots at the aid station. One of them, I suspect cholera, was like being hit in the shoulder with a hammer. It actually made your knees buckle. The rumors at Schofield Barracks were that the 111th was going to move out. It was November 1943, and the first offensive movement in the Central Pacific Area was about to begin.

The rumors were half true. As it turned out, it wasn't the entire regiment, only the Third Battalion that was "going out." The other two battalions were destined to stay in Oahu quite some time. What luck! John and I were particularly overjoyed since either of us could have joined the medical detachments of the other two battalions. But we had lined up with the Third Battalion, so we could stay together.

Well, we stayed together through the Gilbert and Marshall islands campaigns while the other battalions pulled really good duty—guarding Hickam Field and the Oahu coastline.

With rumors confirmed, we began the process of shipping out. We turned in our B bags (all the gear you didn't want to carry on the ship), gave ourselves a farewell beer party, went to the movies on base, bought last-minute supplies at the PX, and generally had a really exciting time. We had spent all of 18 days in the Hawaiian Islands when we boarded the toy train for the trip to Honolulu.

We made the trip in due course and arrived at the dock. There she was, a small cargo ship, a typical tramp steamer, the kind Humphrey Bogart always served on as second mate in the movies. For some strange reason she had two names, *Sea Fox* and *Mormacport*, I never knew why. Later we added still other names that characterized her in a somewhat more colorful manner. But big or small, there she was, and we boarded her quickly. Activity had replaced anxiety.

We had visions of a nice leisurely voyage, not much more to do than read and talk, a chance to log some sacktime and eat some good Navy food. What made it particularly nice for our detachment was that we knew that our sergeant, Arthur A. (Archie) Neumann, would be leaving us at the top of the gangway as he headed for the sick bay. Now, since sergeants run things on a day-to-day basis and ours turned green at the sight of a ship, we knew we were in for a protracted period of rest and recreation. We knew it. He knew it. Everyone knew it.

There were three military groups on the *Mormacport* — the Forty-First Bomb Group, a lot of Seabees (Navy personnel skilled in construction), and the Third Battalion of the 111th Infantry. There were probably about 2,200 to 2,500 men aboard. I was assigned to a bunk in the forward hold of the ship, which was quickly renamed the Black Hole of Calcutta. It was dark, illuminated only by a couple of exposed light bulbs, very hot because it was ventilated only by a small sail meant to catch the wind when the ship was moving, and smelled of perspiration. The Black Hole was a good name. As on the *West Point*, we were to sleep in stacked bunks formed into a square with our B bags piled in the center. It is no exaggeration to say that the pile of B bags was 10 to 15 feet high.

The next day, December 3, 1943, we left the dock and with our escorts, one destroyer and one destroyer escort, headed for the open sea in what turned out to be a 16-day odyssey to the south and west of Oahu. The two escort ships were like greyhounds, slashing back and forth in front of the slow, ten-to-twelve-knot speed of the *Mormacport* and then sometimes sliding up right alongside. We spent many hours just watching the antics of these two ships.

Paradoxically, although we did very little aboard ship, there was a lot going on almost all the time. We no sooner left the harbor at Oahu than the action started, and it kept up throughout the voyage.

Target Practice: Target practice began when a B-26 flew by trailing a windsock on a line about 100 yards long. The destroyers opened up on it (the sleeve, not the plane) and downed it in short order. Another plane flew by, and another windsock bit the dust. We were naturally delighted to see the level of proficiency of the Navy gunners. Later the same day, the ship's public address system blared out the order for all BAR men to report to the bridge. Apparently the commanding officer wanted to employ all the fire-power available in the event of an enemy attack. Objectively, it may have been a great idea. Subjectively, it was somewhat disheartening. Most of the infantrymen knew what a BAR could and couldn't do. It was a fine weapon up to 200 or 300 yards. After that it was quite ineffective. BARs for antiaircraft protection — "You gotta be kiddin'."

Barracks Bag Poker: Gamblers are drawn to each other, and the big games were played day and night in the heat and stench of the hold, on top of the B bags. Soldiers, sailors, and airmen pushed, pummeled, and pounded the B bags into small enclaves that were used as individual poker pits. It was a virtual casino below decks. This was all poker, as crap required a hard level surface. The same people seemed to play most of the time. You could always tell the gamblers. They were chalky white, while the rest of us were tanned from the wind and sun on deck. I watched these games on occasion but never played. I can and did play craps; it requires little or no skill. Poker is quite another thing, a game of art, logic, and science.

Toilet Facilities: Our showers and toilet facilities (the "head" on ships, a term I've never understood) were located on deck. It was a practical place as they both had to be hosed down inside and out frequently. The water in the showers was salt water, and there was salt water soap available for washing up. The problem was it didn't work. When you tried to lather your body and hair with soap, it turned to glue and wouldn't rinse out. It was a real mess. After just one experience we all waited for a rain squall. When one would hit, we stripped off what few clothes we were wearing, lathered up, and rinsed off in the downpour. It was a frantic scene when a squall hit our ship, but it worked well, and few people used the showers after their first encounter. The head was a wooden construction on deck, probably about 10 by 15 feet. As I say, the showers weren't used much, but the toilets were a necessity and were in constant use with over 2,000 men on the ship. There may have been two of these crude, abortive units, no more. The head overflowed onto the deck on a few occasions—really delightful. I can still hear the screams and curses of those sleeping or reading on deck as excrement floated by.

"A Clean Ship Is a Happy Ship": Every day we had abandon-ship drill—not just once, not twice, but sometimes three or four times if we were too slow. Everyone was ordered to his bunk, a claxon sounded, and we put on our life perservers, scrambled for the steep steel ladders leading from the hold to the deck, and tore up the greasy ladder to our assigned places on deck. We had one or two minutes to complete the drill, or we were forced to do it again and again until we accomplished this shin-skinning exercise in the allotted time.

We were hot, sweaty, bruised, and ill tempered when this was over. And it was then that the captain of the ship appeared on the bridge—cool, clean, well dressed, and smiling—commented on our performance, and ordered us to clean the ship. He always ended with a declaration I shall never forget: "A clean ship is a happy ship." This was invariably greeted with groans, curses, and comments on his ancestry by those of us on deck.

I think it was at that moment that the glaring gap between officers and enlisted men, between equality and inequality, was driven home to me in a lesson I shall never forget. It was *we* and *they*. It was an unbridgeable gulf. It was human estrangement, alienation and isolation, in its most exacerbated form. The officers, including the clergy, stood there neat, clean, and elevated on an upper deck, smiling and at ease with the world, while we were packed like sardines on the deck in sweaty gear, bruised and exhausted from the exercise. And then to hear the captain say, "A clean ship is a happy ship" was just too much to bear in silence.

Miscellaneous Activities: Reading magazines and books occupied a large part of my time. I lived on deck, and with my blanket I could sprawl anyplace, open my book, and be lost in it almost immediately. I'd always loved reading. We would also lean on the rail for hours on end—just looking.

Again, it was a strange paradox as I think of it. The ugliness and the beauty of the trip were like two sides of a coin, held together in a kind of dialectical tension. The beauty of nature was everywhere—the water, the flying fish, the dolphins, the spray off the bow of the ship, the clouds, the gray escort ships tearing through the waves. The ugliness was the *Mormacport* with her human cargo. It was strange to see the two so close and yet so far apart.

One of the most unseemly and odious events was the fights that were arranged. Boxing matches were organized on a number of evenings during the trip, on top of the foreward hold. This organized interservice rivalry in the ring was supposed to be a useful "safety valve" on the long tedious voyage, and the volunteers were cheered on as they beat each other's brains out. "Hit 'im, kill 'im!" we screamed in support of our particular fighter.

What a sight. What an absolute absurdity. Two nameless hulks (Army, Navy, Marines, Air Force, Merchant Marine) beating themselves into a bloody pulp as they moved into an area where they could be killed any day in an accident or by enemy action. It must have been for the glory of the unit they belonged to. Or perhaps we are genetically encoded to fight. In any event, I've never seen so much displaced aggression.

We made three stops and crossed the equator two times on our way to Makin Island (in the Gilberts)—Canton Island, the Ellice Islands, and Tarawa. Canton Island is a desolate sliver of sand in the middle of the Pacific. It has no trees, only an airstrip and the most beautiful turquoise-blue and green water I've ever seen. We stayed only overnight, long enough to take on food and water, and then we headed for the Ellice Islands. There we picked up some specialists and headed for Tarawa. We arrived on the afternoon of December 17, and the Forty-First Bomb Group and the Seabees disembarked. It was luxurious. We had room. We had the ship to ourselves—all 1,200 of us.

The battle on Tarawa had just ended, and it must have been terrible. Not a tree was spared. Pillboxes, litter of all kinds, damaged tanks (Japanese and American), and landing craft were scattered like toys on the beaches. It was one and a half miles of tortured earth, torn metal, and ravaged plant life. The next day, December 18, we left Tarawa for the short trip north to Makin Island—the native name was Butaritari. We arrived on the morning of December 19 at 10:00A.M., left the ship in landing craft, and were ashore just after noon.

The Gilbert Islands are situated near the point where the international date line crosses the equator. The islands are atolls composed of coral reefs, generally with a lagoon on the eastern side. The average temperature is 80

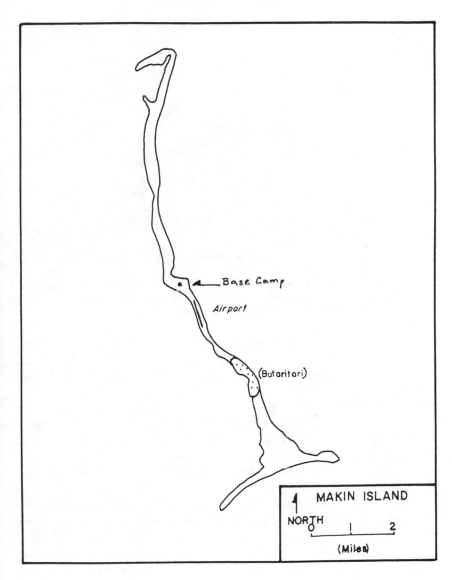

Base Camp

Airport

(Butaritari)

MAKIN ISLAND

NORTH

0 1 2

(Miles)

Makin (Butaritari), Gilbert Islands.

to 85 degrees , and brisk easterly trade winds blow throughout the year. The people of the Gilbert Islands are Micronesian and are thought to have come from Samoa. About half are Protestant, half Catholic. In the latter part of the 19th century the British annexed the islands. But the Japanese seized Tarawa, Ocean, Abemama, and Butaritari during World War II, and they

Makin Island (Butaritari), the Gilbert Islands, December 1943. The Japanese seaplane shown here was located on the lagoon side of the island near the beach where the 111th Infantry landed (source: National Archives).

remained in their hands until American troops seized them in November and December of 1943.

A huge four-engine Japanese seaplane, her tail assembly destroyed and the tip of her right wing buried in the shallow water near shore, was the first thing we all noticed as we waded ashore. As we were marching to our bivouac area, we passed troops of the 165th Infantry, the ones who seized Butaritari, heading in the opposite direction to board the *Mormacport*. They called out the traditional Army salutation, "You'll be sorry," and we responded in kind, each certain the other was headed for the most noxious circumstance.

There were a few damaged tanks, landing craft, and vehicles along the road, and then we saw the first natives. They looked at us, and we stared at them—stared because of their clothes, or rather their lack of clothes. Most of the men wore nothing but a cloth sarong around their waist, tied in a knot in front, that hung down to a point just below the knees. A few women wore the same type of sarong, but most of them wore grass skirts that were tied around their waists, just below the navel, and hung down their legs just shy of their knees. That was it. They were all bare-breasted. We were astonished. There were a few whistles and a lot of inelegant asides such as "Nice build," "Look at that one," "Man, that's really nice." But our officers kept us moving, and we soon arrived at our temporary area.

Neumann ordered us to "dig in" and prepare for air attacks. He did this because we were only about 150 miles from Mili, one of the many atolls in

Makin Island (Butaritari), the Gilbert Islands, January 1944. A young woman of Butaritari in sarong instead of the more common grass skirt.

the Marshall Islands held by the Japanese, and Butaritari was a strategic as well as a convenient place to bomb because of its airfield.

Survill and I decided to work on a foxhole together. The problem was that the soil was composed largely of coral rock fragments, sand, and tree roots, and it made digging very difficult, particularly with our entrenching tool, a small shovel with a hinged blade that theoretically converted into a hoe-type instrument. The setting of coconut palms and pandanus trees that grow prolifically on Butaritari was lovely, but the digging was pure drudgery. We were forced to put all our strength into the effort, and the payoff for straining every nerve was minimal.

We were working next to two married men, Charles Toll of Pittsburgh, Pennsylvania, and Bill Ford of Canton, Ohio. For some reason they were more motivated and made a lot more progress than we did. John and I smoked a lot, drank coconut milk, put up our pup tent, ate our K-rations, talked about the pretty girls we'd seen, and occasionally tried to dig a little. But time passed, darkness fell, and we decided to give up any further excavation even though our dual "shelter" was only about ten inches deep, if that. It was just too much work. The hell with it.

We were asleep when the air-raid siren wailed its warning of approaching enemy planes. Survill and I got up and sat on the edge of our shelter. It was kind of exciting, but not much more. In a little while a number of our searchlights were turned on and quickly picked up one or two of the Japanese bombers—two-engine Betty bombers, I believe. We could see them easily, so I'd estimate their altitude at about 3,000 or 4,000 feet.

No fighter planes were sent up to intercept the bombers, but some of our 90-mm and 20-mm antiaircraft batteries opened up on the planes. The 90-mm shells seemed close, but the 20-mm tracer shells missed the planes by a country mile. We did nothing, just sat and watched, fascinated by the entire spectacle. We heard some bombs land far away and took little notice of this.

We continued sitting on the edge of our shelter with our feet in the hole. At that point our ankles and perhaps our shins were protected—little else. Then suddenly there was a *swoosh*, followed immediately by a *very* loud explosion, then a number of other *swooshes* followed by more explosions. No one had to explain to us what had happened. We understood immediately. The bombs were hitting closer to us.

John and I tried desperately to press our bodies into our long shallow shelter, but to no avail—there was just no place to hide. So we leapt into the shelter the married men had dug, right on top of them. They protested vehemently (in the idiom of the day, "Get the fuck out of here") but we stayed anyway. At this moment we were interested in our physical well-being, not in gaining their respect.

The action was over as quickly as it had begun, and we sheepishly left our guest accommodations. All night you could hear the clink of shovels digging. Ours clinked right along with the rest of them. I don't remember being scared during that first bombing until after the close encounter with the bombs. Frankly, I was too stupid. But my anxiety-fear level was raised very

Makin Island (Butaritari), the Gilbert Islands, December 1943. Photograph of the author (far right) and three members of the medical detachment of the Third Battalion during the construction of a bomb shelter.

rapidly during the next few days as I began to see and understand the tangible consequences of the bombings.

My next lesson in living began the following afternoon. As I said, I'd been eating the meat and drinking the milk of coconuts since we landed, and the price I paid was a bad case of dysentery. It was awful. I was sick. I couldn't make it to the latrine and ended up throwing away a lot of my clothes. Then, in the midst of my trauma, we were ordered to move to a new area just a little past the northeast end of the airstrip, which ran in a northeast-southwest direction.

Fortunately, the plague lasted only about 24 hours, so I was able to help in constructing our new bomb shelter. This was a project everyone was interested in completing, including me. The one I worked on held about six or seven men. We dug a twelve-foot-by-twelve-foot square in the ground about four feet deep and lined the bottom and sides with sandbags to prevent collapse of the sandy walls from concussion. Then we cut and placed coconut logs across the top and covered these with a layer of sandbags and camouflage. The entrance to the shelter was a trench about four feet long. We told

Makin Island (Butaritari), the Gilbert Islands, January 1944. The author holding a spear loaded with fish, a gift from a native fishing party.

ourselves we could take anything but a direct hit, and in hindsight we were right. Experience was the basis of our newly discovered good judgment.

As I mentioned, Sergeant Neumann was no sailor, but he was in his element when it came to building bomb shelters. He organized the work party, and in this activity as in everything else he worked harder than we did. He was a farm boy from Illinois, about 25. He was as strong as a bear, about 6', 200 pounds, had a huge barrel chest and curly brown hair. He ran things in our outfit. In retrospect, I'd say he was very disciplined. In the two-year period we spent together I never saw him drunk or out of line in any way. He was just a dependable person, a guy with a lot of common sense. I have no idea how he was viewed by our officers, but he was well regarded by virtually every enlisted man in our outfit. He wasn't loud or given to barking out orders like my drill instructor in basic training. He never tried to harass or intimidate anyone. He rarely used profanity and was never rude or cruel. Like any outfit, we had a clown, a goof-off, a neurotic, a psychotic, and a con man, but Neumann seemed able to handle them all. He was a good man.

This chapter might have been entitled "Adventures in Paradise" because at the time (and in the 40-odd years since I was there) I thought of Butaritari as a paradise — the people, the climate, the lifestyle. If there were political relationships among the natives, it was not apparent to me. I saw no evidence of local police or any effort at coercion. What was the point? Everything was free. This was a society of abundance. The temperature was absolutely perfect, so there was no need for clothing or any shelter other than that needed to protect one from rain squalls or midday sun.

Fuel was everywhere, the consequence of native pruning. And food was plentiful — coconuts, pigs, chickens, fish, and a sweet-potato type of root that was collectively cultivated. What little agriculture that went on was done by the men in a group.

Fishing was an activity for the entire community. I once saw about 60 or 70 natives — men, women, children, young and old — walk out into the lagoon, each carrying one or two metal spears about three feet long. They formed a semicircle with the shoreline and started thrashing the water with the spears. As they did this, they began to close the semicircle like a purse seine. As the semicircle got smaller and tighter, the water literally began to "boil" with fish. At that moment all began jabbing their spears through the fish until they had 20 or so on a spear. They then cast the fish up toward the shore, and the process continued. They talked, laughed, and worked (if that's what it can be called) until all the spears were loaded. Then they just walked ashore, picked up the short spears loaded with fish, and headed for the village. I asked one of them for a spearful and was given the spear as well as the fish (see photograph). The whole process was over in 30 minutes. It was an amazing "fish story" to me then. It is a wonder to me today.

Makin Island (Butaritari), the Gilbert Islands, December 1943. A father and son who frequently visited our company to collect coconuts.

Their homes were constructed of local material and provided the necessary cover from the elements. I can personally attest to the cleanliness of the village and its many homes. They looked better and held up better than anything we built on the island. They had all the necessities of life right at their fingertips.

Other native behavior patterns warrant some comment. They were skillful at bargaining with the troops for grass skirts and mats — cigarettes were the medium of exchange — yet they were a kind and generous people. I have mentioned the gift of fish, but they also would scamper up a tree for coconuts if we indicated we wanted one, and they would give us whatever they had gathered. They could husk, clean out, and eat the meat of a coconut like an automated machine.

They dearly loved our movies, riding in one of our two-and-a half-ton trucks, singing and dancing. Sometimes we would dance and sing for each other after a movie. It was something to see. They laughed at our animated jitterbug dancing, and we enjoyed their group dancing. I can still hear and see in my most inner ear and mind's eye their dancing and singing. The music particularly was a kind of whole-tone harmony, really haunting.

Life on Butaritari was at once attractive and repulsive. The native culture and climate were certainly agreeable, but the constant threat of danger, violence, and destruction to nature, man, and material was repugnant. But no adventure (the war) would mean no paradise (the island of Butaritari).

On December 23, 1943, I was assigned to KP. It was to be a memorable day — and night. But first I'd better comment on the physical setting of this story. Our mess hall was a long one-story wooden building located right next to the beach. There was a grove of tall, stately coconut trees all around it providing some shade for the building and workers in the area. The company movie screen was mounted on the low roof at one end of the building, and we sat on the ground — the playing field of our volleyball court — facing the screen, the building, and the ocean to watch the movie. All of our recreation and entertainment was focused in this one area — volleyball, movies, and swimming. That was it. About 150 yards from the mess hall, on the other side of the volleyball court, was our aid station. This was simply a pole tent, open at both ends so the air could circulate, and lined on two sides with cots, boxes, and shelving with medicine, alcohol, and bandages. We kept our litters stacked around a palm tree just outside the tent. My air-raid shelter was located a short distance from the aid station, just outside the pyramidal tent in which seven of us slept. This entire setup was, as I said, about 200 yards north of the airstrip with its fighter planes, dive bombers, fuel-storage and maintenance buildings.

But back to KP and the story. We had just about finished our work at the mess hall, and two of us were carrying out a 50-gallon GI can to empty it in a waste pit near the shoreline when the air-raid siren went off. It was about 7:15 P.M. Although we had experienced a few air raids, we had been on the island only five days and didn't yet understand the normal time period between the wail of the siren and the appearance of the Japanese bombers. So we dropped the GI can and ran for the nearest dugout right

Makin Island (Butaritari), the Gilbert Islands, January 1944. Troop mess hall, movie screen mounted on the roof, and volleyball court with a game in progress (facing the lagoon side of the island).

next to the ocean. It must have been constructed by disgruntled kitchen workers who planned never to use it. They had dug a hole about three feet deep and eight feet square and then put five or six sections of coconut logs on top of the hole for protection from shrapnel.

We got inside and scrunched down into two of the corners. The sand walls of the shelter were already beginning to collapse because they hadn't been reinforced with sandbags. We could easily see through the large cracks between the logs to the mess hall, volleyball court, and aid station on one side and the ocean (the tide was out at the time) on the other. It was dusk, not daytime or nighttime. I could just about see where our shelter was located, but I was afraid to make a break for it because I didn't know if I'd have enough time to cross the big open area.

Both of us decided to sweat out the raid in our temporary "reject" shelter. We had to wait about 15 minutes before the first bombers came. (I can only assume that the radar picked them up very early.) "And did they come," I wrote in my diary. "I thought every bomb was on top of our trench. From where I was though, I could see the bomb flashes hit about 75 yards inland in a string from the air-strip up through our (company) area."

I knew there was going to be trouble and casualties from that string of bombs that "walked" right through the area where all our tents, shelters, and equipment were located. There was no way our area could have escaped the stick of bombs that flashed like diamonds exploding as they hit. I could also hear bombs dropping up at the end of the island where Captain Carver's troops from I Company were based. Planes were flying over, Japanese and American, our 90-mm antiaircraft booming out scores of shells, 20-mm tracer shells slashing into the sky—generally a wild scene.

The raid went on and on, long after darkness fell. I couldn't see my watch anymore. Then suddenly there was the familiar *swoosh, swoosh, swoosh,* followed by the flash and explosion of bombs landing *very* close. I could actually feel the shock waves of the bombs, and the entire shelter seemed to be moving. We were literally turned topsy-turvy inside the shelter, and the sand walls with the coconut-log cover began caving in on us. We had sand in our eyes, hair, mouth, clothing—everyplace.

We didn't talk to each other during this incident, but my coworker blurted out, "What's happening—for chrissake, it's caving in!" I was terrified—I really thought it was all over. The crashes of the bombs seemed to be right on top of us. But it began and ended fast, no more than four or five seconds, while we frantically grabbed at the ground, the sides of the shelter, anything in our effort to hold the logs in place.

When it ended, we lay shaking in the sand, too scared to move. Shortly after this episode, maybe 30 minutes or so, the bombing ended, and the all-clear signal sounded at 10:00 P.M. I couldn't see anything, but the next morning I went down to the beach, and there were five bomb craters right in a row about 25 or 30 feet from the shelter we had been in. They had walked right down the beach, like five steps of a giant, past our shelter. I ran back to the aid station, and it was a wreck. What was left of it looked like a sieve, and all our equipment in the aid station was destroyed or scattered all over the area.

They began to bring in casualties, and the technicians started treating them immediately. There was a lot of fast movement and orders being given, but I saw no panic. It was just first things first. There were a number of wounded, but nothing like what I expected. I thought the entire unit had been wiped out. We finished work at about 1:00 A.M. on December 24 and went to bed. Our tent was perforated and just kind of hanging there, but we were exhausted and fell asleep.

At 2:00 A.M. we had a second raid and at 4:00 A.M. a third. But no bombs were dropped in our area on either of these raids, for which we all said a fervent prayer of thanks. As I wrote in my diary, "We were raided two more times, once during breakfast and once during the dinner hour." In my mind the entire 24-hour period blurs together, and I think it did for everyone else. We always talked about it as that wild Christmas Eve, though it began December 23.

McGarvey Combs, a feisty, good-natured briar from Lexington, Kentucky, found a puppy, which we named, in a burst of creativity, Makin. Actually he bought him from one of the natives for one pack of cigarettes. In any event, he was the center of attention at our Christmas dinner the next day, which consisted of turkey, sweet potatoes, carrots, raisin bread, coffee, and punch. Believe me, this was a feast, a meal not to be duplicated, as our usual fare was Spam or something euphemistically called Vienna sausage. In a letter home, after commenting on the dinner, I asked my parents to try to locate a wind-up Victrola so we could listen to records. Music, particularly the music of the "big bands" of the 1930s and 1940s, had always been one of my passions (it still is today, a half century later). I continued this theme in a number of letters to my folks, and somehow, somewhere, my dad located one, packed it up, and shipped it to me. It arrived in good shape in a month or so, along with half a dozen 78-rpm records by Harry James, Benny Goodman, the King Sisters, and so on. Someplace I got hold of some vinyl-type records, probably the forerunner of the present 33-rpm discs, called V-Discs. One by Glenn Miller I remember to this day was "The St. Louis Blues March."

Our tent became a kind of poor man's USO on many an evening. We didn't have a lot of records to listen to, but we played the ones we had again and again. Sometimes there would even be a little spontaneous jitterbug dancing by some of the troops, particularly if we had recently received a beer ration. My letters and diary vary on this, but it seems to have been a ration of four to six beers per week—when we could get them. Music and letters from home were therapeutic. They cured our dis-ease.

In late January and February, virtually half the battalion came down with dengue fever. Dengue fever is caused by mosquito bites, and these were impossible to escape. We were issued mosquito bars, which we hung over a crude T-frame nailed or tied to each end of the bed and then tucked in under the mattress cover. But even this did not provide the necessary protection. Dengue fever is called "bone-break" fever. It lasts about seven days, and anyone that gets it is bedridden for the entire time with a high fever and aching limbs. As I say, about 50 percent of the troops caught the disease, and our only treatment was aspirin and time. There was nothing we could do to prevent it. I don't remember anyone getting it twice. Apparently the first siege immunized the individual. Had the Japanese launched a reinvasion around the middle of January, it would have been a cakewalk because we were decimated with the disease. It hit us, knocked us out, passed on, and was forgotten in the intensity of living we experienced those few months.

In retrospect, virtually everything we did was associated with airplanes and bombing while we were on Butaritari. We played some volleyball, pulled tech duty at the aid station, did some swimming, collected "cat's eye" shells to make jewelry, went on a few details like burning garbage and spraying standing water to cut back on mosquitoes, and of course attended movies in the evening, a high point for everyone. But our daily life was dominated by airplanes, the ones going out and the ones coming in. Consider the following four activities and perhaps it will be clear:

1. We frequently visited our own airstrip. It was just a short distance from our area, and we liked talking to the flyers and just looking at the airplanes. We had 30 or so A-24 dive bombers, our favorites because they hit the Jap bases at Mili and Kwajalein almost daily. One day Combs and I went down to the airstrip to visit the pilots and gunners on the A-24 dive bombers. While we were there in the middle of the day, the air-raid sirens went off. We didn't quite know what to do—run for our area, which was a couple of hundred yards away, or climb in the nearest shelter. We decided on the nearest shelter. Again, it was a sloppy piece of work, but it was handy. We were looking out through some big cracks in the logs that covered the hole when we saw a big black 90-mm gun begin to raise up out of its protected pit. It looked like "Big Bertha" from World War I to us. I didn't like it, and Combs didn't either. We sat looking at each other and the gun for a minute, and then one of us, I forget who, said, "Let's get the hell out of here." We leapt out of the shelter and started running as fast as we could toward our own area. It was wild—the sirens, the guns, the bombs—as we ran, dodged, and ran some more. We made it and dove into our shelter. Never had we been so happy to see our friends. "Where the hell have you guys been?" said somebody. We told them, and they just said, "What jerks." You didn't get much sympathy for a stupid act.

We also had P-39s, Aircobras, that escorted the dive bombers on their missions and also took off to strike enemy bombers attacking Butaritari. Later on in January, as preparations for the Marshall Island invasions got under way, eight or ten B-25s and a few B-24s also operated out of our island. Once we had a flight of Navy Corsairs land for refueling and maintenance. We even had eight or ten old P-40s that were fitted to carry two 500-pound bombs. Again and again I noted in my diary the number and type of plane going out on a raid. We knew the planes so well that I could lie on my cot, count the planes, and tell what kind they were by the sound of their engines. Airplanes were simply important; they were the form our military effort took at this time and at this place in the Central Pacific Area. Besides, they were taking off right over our heads.

2. We had to deal emotionally, not just physically, with the air attacks by the Japanese. I noted all these attacks in my diary because they were very important to me at the time. In fact, nothing was more important. As close as I can count from the data in my diary, we were subjected to 35 to 38 air attacks. Some lasted 30 minutes, some three hours. We spent a lot of time in the shelters. But the intensity factor, in thinking about our behavior, was the changing relationship between the number of bombings

and the general level of anxiety-fear. It is inversely related; that is, the more bombings one experienced, the less the anxiety-fear level. Perhaps the following graph describes the relationship better than words. Near the end of the attacks, in late January and early February of 1944, a couple of us

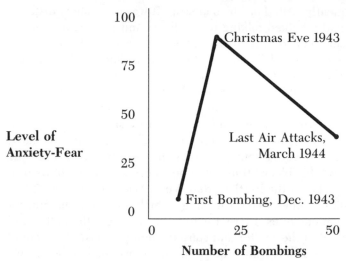

would frequently stand in the trench leading to the shelter, driven by sheer curiosity, to watch what was going on. We saw Japanese planes shot down and were totally indifferent to the fate of the crew. In fact, we would cheer with glee as we saw tracers smash into the enemy bomber. "Look at this, look at this!" we would holler to the guys in the shelter. They were more bored than anything else and were deeply involved in playing checkers.

3. We spent so much time in the shelter that we reinforced it with a second layer of logs and sandbags and then blacked it out so we could take an electric light in with us. Many games of checkers were logged in that shelter. I even wrote some letters in the shelter.

4. One couldn't ignore the very high level of air activity as it escalated in preparation for the invasion of the Marshall Islands. The attacks on Mili, Juliet, Wotje, and Maleolap were incessant. We even had an aircraft carrier lay off our island, which added to the commotion. F6F and Corsair fighter-bombers joined our Army Air Force pilots in attacking the Marshalls. February was a month to dish it out. On February 21, 43 Corsairs landed at Butaritari. We had a few air raids in early March but nothing of consequence, and our fighters prevented the Japs from approaching.

Around the middle of March, the rumors began to fly that we were moving out, going to the Marshall Islands. On March 20 we pulled down our tent and packed all our gear, and on March 23, 1944, we left Butaritari and boarded our ship, the *Sea Pike*, for the trip to Kwajalein.

"Mop-Up" and "Rest-Up"

7

The Way to Travel, No Good-looking Girls,
It's Show Time, Pathetic Prisoners,
Hut City, No More Practice Runs—Please,
"Keep on Truckin'," Together Again

We boarded the *Sea Pike*, anchored off Butaritari, on the afternoon of March 23, 1944. We were the only troops aboard, so there was plenty of room. As usual, many of us tried to sleep on deck, but we were rained out, and I was forced down into the hold to sleep in one of the five-tiered bunks. Though we found relief from the storm and the sheets of water that poured down on the ship, we were forced to experience again the aggravation associated with crowding.

Noise, perspiration, lights, arguments—all combine to make the hold a place to avoid if at all possible. Only the worst storms drove me below-decks. The food was good on the *Sea Pike*, standard fare, which meant beans for breakfast frequently, but the arrangements were the same—two meals per day and "stand-up" dining. We did nothing aboard ship except read, lean on the rail, and play cards. We were free to do as we wanted, and the tedium of shipboard life gradually took the place of the frantic activity associated with the move.

We lay at anchor to finish loading on March 24, headed out at 4:00 P.M. on March 25, and two days later we entered the South Pass (also called Gea Pass) of the Kwajalein Atoll and anchored off Ennylabegan Island, which guards the pass. There are five atolls in the Marshalls close to Butaritari: Mili, Jaluit, Wotje, Kwajalein, and Eniwetok. Army and Marine Corps troops captured the major island bases in Kwajalein and Eniwetok in February 1944 and bypassed the other three atolls and their military bases. We left the ship in Higgens boats and landed on Ennylabegan on the afternoon of March 27. Once ashore, we set up our pup tents and this time really did dig in.

The basic military task of the battalion during our stay in Kwajalein was to "mop-up"; that is, we were assigned the job of capturing many of the small

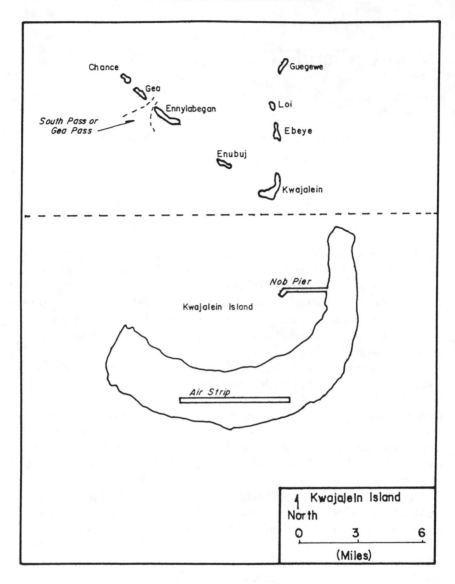

Kwajalein, Marshall Islands.

islands adjacent to the main base at Kwajalein. (To clear up any confusion, Kwajalein Island is just one of the 93 islets and islands that make up the Kwajalein Atoll, which forms the largest lagoon in the world.)

Ennylabegan is about one and a half to two miles long and from one quarter to one-half mile wide. The climate is very similar to that on Butaritari, 80 degrees to 85 degrees with a constant trade wind blowing.

One welcome difference was that there were no mosquitoes, thus no dengue fever. The people in the Marshalls, like the Gilberts, are Polynesians, but we were never in a position to observe or contact them very much. In the contact we did have, they seemed somewhat different physically and significantly so culturally. The Gilbertese were a more handsome people, and their civic culture was definitely more advanced.

Near the end of March we moved to our permanent area located in the center of the island. We chopped, dug, and blasted out what amounted to a company street, which we then lined with our pyramidal tents, each holding five or six men. Because we had cut so many trees of all sizes, and with the lumber left by the Japanese, we erected railings around our tents to let in the cool breezes and catch rainwater. We tied the tent flaps to the railings, creating a gully in the flap; when it rained, and it really poured in those tropical squalls, the water ran down the tent into the gully in the tent flaps and from there into empty 50-gallon drums. It was not unusual to collect 100 gallons of fresh water in a single storm, and on occasion we collected more than that.

We used the water for laundry, washing, shaving, showers — everything. We didn't drink it; we washed in it. We did virtually all our laundry and washing in our steel helmets. They made perfect washbowls. We built a small rack to the rear of each tent and lined up the five or six helmets of the men who slept inside. Initially, we had only candles for light at night, but later we would all "moonlight requisition" a used battery, and in a couple of weeks most of the tents had one or more electric reading lights. We made fresh-water showers out of 20-gallon cooking tins. We simply punctured a four-inch circle in the bottom of the tin, and voilà, a shower.

All this care and attention we gave to our personal welfare as individuals (collecting fresh water, constructing washbowls, reading lights, showers, etc.) was matched by the neglect and disdain we showed toward duties associated with the group. We would spend hours, even days, tinkering and fixing up our individual sleeping and washing facilities, yet if asked to work on a project like building the aid station for a few hours, we complained. Worse yet, if we were assigned to KP or garbage detail, our bitching knew no bounds: What a travesty of justice. What a waste of our talents. What a base and heinous assignment. Incidentally, we built a wooden aid station out of lumber from old Japanese warehouses. It was about 15' × 15', with a screened door, located at the end of the company street, almost on the beach. We were in business in a couple of weeks. It was a project that would have made Frank Lloyd Wright cringe in pain.

Drawing on our experience with air raids in the Gilberts, we built two good-sized shelters for our entire group, each well constructed, solidly sandbagged, and covered with a double layer of coconut logs and camouflage.

Ennylabegan Island, Kwajalein Atoll, Marshall Islands, April–May 1944. The company street scene is typical of the living arrangements for troops based on these Pacific islands.

We had a few air raids while we were on Ennylabegan, but nothing of any consequence. We saw the Japanese planes a couple of times, but not a single bomb hit our island while I was on it. The extremely limited resources of the Japanese on the three Marshall atolls they still controlled simply dictated a very limited bombing schedule. There was really little point in wasting bombs on our island. It wasn't the main American base. In fact, there was absolutely nothing of strategic importance on the island. Its only value lay in its relation to the South Pass to the lagoon.

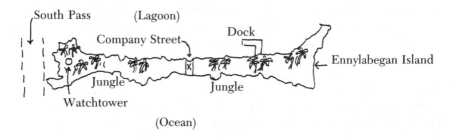

Recreation on Ennylabegan focused on volleyball, movies, swimming, and horseshoes—in that order. Our medical detachment was a small group, but we had a first-rate volleyball team. Most of our wins were due to a fellow named Ray Broomfield from Cleveland, Ohio. Ray was tall, blonde, and usually drove the detachment Jeep for Captain Dobbs, our M.D., but his real skill was as a "spiker." If he got a good setup at the net, he would drive the ball down the throats of our opponents. He was great. I never quite had the timing to spike well, but I played as a regular on the team and loved the game (still do).

Swimming was another popular pastime. We did most of this off the dock located on the lagoon side of the island. The water was perfect except for one thing, the occasional jellyfish. If you ran into a jellyfish, your daily swim was over; the long transparent "filaments" the jellyfish extends out from its body feel like a whip across a swimmer's back or legs. The stinging didn't go away for an hour or so, and we could find no medication to relieve the pain. Swimming while the tide was in could be dangerous. I once saw a large shark caught right on the small L-shaped dock where we swam. But this was no deterrent to most of us. We dove off the dock and went swimming there frequently. Nobody had seen the movie *Jaws*, and it wouldn't have made any difference if we had; swimming helped dull the edge of boredom, and it was a refreshing interlude. Movies and horseshoes rounded out our recreation program.

Sailboats frequently stopped at Ennylabegan. They were simply beached near the dock. One or two passengers could travel with the crew of two, but they were primarily used in trade and transportation. The boats were about 20 to 25 feet long with a three-foot beam, an outrigger that extended about seven feet, and a 20-foot gaff-rigged spar. They were fast, pointed well to windward, and with the wind on the beam they reached like a dolphin because of the small wetted surface. When a strong breeze was blowing, one of the passengers or crew would move out on the outrigger to hold the boat down. I have no idea how far these little craft ventured, but I am confident that they could sail with little trouble between all the Marshall Island atolls and certainly down to Butaritari in the Gilberts. They were sturdy, not overcanvased, and probably moved about eight or ten miles per hour.

As I mentioned, our primary military task was to mop-up the remaining Japanese troops on the nearby small islands. Frankly, I had forgotten the number of patrols we sent out during our stay on Ennylabegan, but here my diary has proved indispensable. I know that I probably didn't note all the groups we sent out, but I show ten dates where troops were sent out to capture various islets or islands. Sometimes they went out for one day, sometimes longer. Once, I note in my diary, a big group went out for six days. This contingent included two platoons from L Company and one platoon from K Company. Their task was to take four islands. All of these operations involved landing on islands where only a small number of Japanese soldiers were stationed—perhaps the crew of a radio station, a

Ennylabegan Island, Kwajalein Atoll, Marshall Islands, May 1944. This photograph of two sailboats beached on Ennylabegan shows the length, sail rigging, and outrigger typical of those that visited the island to trade with the natives.

weather station, or a lookout point. Sometimes the troops found nothing, not a living soul. I have to estimate because my data are not complete, but I think the Third Battalion probably took 15 islands in the mop-up operations.

One operation that was probably representative of many involved loading of troops into LCVPs, about a platoon in each. The transit to the island to be seized was never a problem, as the landing craft never left the lagoon. As the craft approached the island, they would line up in what amounted to a small "wave" and then head for the beach. The landing craft would go in as far as possible, then lower the front ramp, and the troops would splash ashore. They would spread out on the beach, set up a small communications center, then move inland. Any suspicious area was sprayed with rifle and BAR firepower. Sometimes nothing was there, and other times Japanese soldiers were killed. The patrols sometimes found them hidden in trees, and when shot, they would simply pitch out and fall to the ground or hang from a sling they had constructed in the tree. In most cases, the troops reported, they were forced to kill all the Japanese troops they encountered.

However, there were some exceptions. We did take a few prisoners in two or three instances, and on a couple of islands, the troops said that they found that the Japanese soldiers had all committed suicide. They did this by putting the barrel of the rifle in the mouth, putting the big toe on the trigger, then blowing off the back of the skull. Nobody from our aid-station detachment participated in these operations. They were handled strictly by the rifle companies and the aidmen assigned to those units.

These actions went on in April, May, and June of 1944. In every case the companies were successful in taking the island. Let me repeat: These were small mop-up operations only. Most of the time the troops went from Ennylabegan to the island they were assigned to assault on an LCI (Landing Craft Infantry). These useful craft were used extensively in our area as they were seaworthy, capable of carrying a couple of hundred troops, and able to run their bow right up on the beach so the troops could wade ashore.

In early June 1944, the task force that was destined to hit the Marianna Islands (Guam, Tinian, Saipan, and Rota) came through the South Pass at Kwajalein. It was a staggering collection of warships. There must have been three or four hundred ships of every description. There were aircraft carriers, destroyers, cruisers, troopships, LCIs (Landing Craft Infantry), LSTs (Landing Ship Tank), tankers — everything.

We went down to the end of the island to watch as they entered. It was truly an awesome sight. The overwhelming power of the U.S. fleet, with its support and transport ships, was encouraging. My experience on the *Mormacport*, when they used BAR men as part of the antiaircraft weapon, had left me in doubt about America as the arsenal of democracy. And my first few weeks on Makin Island, when we had only a few P-39s and P-40s as fighter planes, had reinforced that doubt. But six months made a difference, and with this gigantic task force laying off our island I believed, and I think everyone else believed, that nothing could stand up to the American war machine. The inability, the complete impotence, of the Japanese even to bomb the fleet while it lay motionless at anchor in the lagoon was all the proof needed to convince us that the war was going our way.

The task force gathered for about four or five days in early June and then one morning was gone. The battle was about to begin.

Air activity was at a very high level now. Virtually all the bombers taking off from Kwajalein were B-24 "Liberators." These airplanes have twin rudders and are easily distinguished from the B-17 (the "Flying Fortress"), which has only a single rudder. We did have a few B-17s operating out of Kwajalein, but as I said, most were B-24s. We also now had P-38 fighter planes at the base, and I suspect that most of their targets were in the Caroline Islands that lay to the west of the Marshalls and south of the Mariannas — particularly the big Japanese naval and air base at Truk. It was June 1944, and the third big offensive in the Central Pacific Area was about to begin in the Mariannas, the attacks on the Gilberts and Marshalls having taken place in late 1943 and early 1944.

By late July and early August, all our operations had ended. We collected shells, worked at a number of mundane jobs, went to church on Sundays, and did next to nothing. Doing nothing is tough. Being bored is worse. Along with almost everybody in the unit, I was getting weary and dissatisfied. We were active, we did things, but what we were doing seemed meaningless. On Makin (Butaritari) the action made each day something to remember. On Ennylabegan the inaction made the passage of time ponderous. We did little, yet we were fatigued. We read, swam, and shelled, and were weary and dissatisfied with it all.

We were getting "island-happy." It's a strange phenomenon — you can't escape an island. It's so patently true, it doesn't sink in for a while, but it's a reality. I did a lot of reading; mysteries and historical novels were my favorites.

We were saved from total boredom by two big USO shows, one by Bob Hope, the other by Jack Benny. They each brought a big band to accompany their respective troupe, so it was a thing to remember for me. There was always an LCT or LCVP going between Ennylabegan and Kwajalein, so on July 25, 1944, we hopped aboard one to take us to Kwajalein Island with its big Richardson Theatre where the show was to be held. Along with Hope were Jerry Colonna, Francis Langford, and Pat Thomas. Bob Hope's monologue was marvelous — many pointed jokes about local officers and military snafus. Jerry Colonna, old banjo-eyes, had a wild piercing voice, but he played great trombone. Francis Langford sang all the sentimental songs, and Pat Thomas danced. But it was the music of the big band — Les Brown, I believe — that I loved. It was a great show.

Then, on September 3, 1944, Jack Benny came to the Richardson Theatre, and we again went over to see the show. Benny brought Carole Landis, a movie sex symbol in those days; Martha Tilton, a fine jazz singer; Larry Adler, who did things on the harmonica that couldn't be done; and June Brunner, a dancer. Jack Benny put on a super show. At one point the band played some tunes like "String of Pearls," and soldiers and sailors went up and danced with the girls in the troupe. Everyone enjoyed it. It all ended too soon, but I've always had a soft spot in my heart for the performers who made the journey to these remote islands to entertain us.

Thinking back on those days on Ennylabegan and Butaritari, a strange paradox was at work: The normal became abnormal, and vice versa, in many aspects of life. Consider the following: Everyone was young, there were no "oldies," ours was only a "slice" of life, a virtual youth culture. We were at an age when female companionship was the rule, but there were no women; we lived a life of celibacy, an armed monistic order. The normal freedom to move, particularly the freedom to jump in your car and just go, is practically eliminated for soldiers on an island. The normal involvements in school, listening to pop music and just hearing the news, are a rare luxury overseas in these island paradises. Even the normal craving for some solitude is denied the soldier; one is constantly immersed in a sea of humanity where there is no escape, no privacy, no matter how high a priority one places on such a condition. Finally, there was no way to express yourself aesthetically in the military. To play music, to do something in music, had been important in my life, and now months and years would pass with no involvement. I could still listen. I couldn't play. There was nothing to buy; we saved, but for no purpose, and lost and won goodly sums gambling. Even cribbage became a game of chance. Life was definitely turned upside down.

We knew our stay on Ennylabegan was to end as late August arrived. It was, but it involved only a short transitional move to the main base on Kwajalein Island.

We moved from Ennylabegan to Kwajalein Island on August 25 and set up our tents across the street from the airfield on the ocean side of the island. We knew when we moved it was only for a few weeks, so we made little effort to fix up our company area. Air activity was intense on Kwajalein. We had 112 Corsairs come in on September 6. The next day, about 60 of them loaded up with 500-pound general-purpose (GP) bombs and took off to attack Truk. At least that was what we were told. Everything was now related to airplanes again—this time, all going out to bomb the Japanese.

In the evening, Survill and I would frequently hitch a ride to the Richardson Theatre or any unit that was having a movie we hadn't seen. This was our big night mission. I noted in my diary a few that we saw and list them here:

Presenting Lily Mars (musical with Judy Garland)
Lost Angel (drama)
Johnny Come Lately (with James Cagney)
Song of Bernadette (religious theme)
The Uninvited (horror show)
Broadway Rhythm (musical)
Up in Mabel's Room (comedy)
Four Jills in a Jeep (musical comedy)
Two Girls and a Gob (musical comedy)
Sweet and Low Down (Benny Goodman musical)

Our mail usually came once or twice a week and was always welcome. I loved getting letters from family and friends; they were like the bread of life to me.

Kwajalein was hot, in part because there were few trees left standing after the battle. Nature and thousands of human beings were destroyed in the fight. One mass grave for Japanese soldiers on the lagoon side of the island contained 1,200 bodies (or so the sign said), and there were a number of other hastily constructed common graves for the enemy soldiers killed in the island warfare. The largest common grave was located near the extremely long concrete dock that extended out from the island into the lagoon.

Near the end of September, we got news that we were to head back to Oahu for rest camp, so the last few days were spent in going to the dentist, visiting the pilots of the B-24s, listening to Tokyo Rose tell her version of the war in the Pacific, and packing up. We were on the move again.

We boarded our ship, the *General E. T. Collins*, on October 1, 1944, for the trip to Oahu. The ship was 522 feet long, 71.5 feet wide, an assault transport (AP-147). She was built in California and departed for the Pacific fighting area on August 14, 1944, so when we boarded her she was only six weeks old. Needless to say, the conditions were infinitely better than those on the *Mormacport* (I still cringe at the thought of that ship). There were only two large military groups on the ship, our Army battalion and a Marine battalion, so its wasn't too crowded.

We did little of interest on the ship—the usual gambling, practicing abandon-ship drill, staring at the ocean, and reading. I read. Everything was the same; meals, sleeping arrangements, the destroyer escorts; it was all becoming routine to us now. We had been at the front, or more accurately at the back of the front, for a year. Now we were heading to the rear. There was no pain associated with this departure, only anticipation of the pleasures that awaited us on our arrival in the Hawaiian Islands. We talked about the miserable food we had been eating for a year, food that often forced one to fast, and about the great steaks we would eat in Oahu. We talked about our protracted period of enforced sobriety and the exotic drinks we would buy when we got to Honolulu. All would be wonderful. Gluttony, girls, and good times dominated every conversation. Little else of moment occurred on the trip.

However, there is one story that warrants mention—the Japanese prisoners aboard the *Collins*. The trip from Kwajalein to Oahu took only five days because there were no intermediate stops and with the fighting moving ever westward toward Japan, the waters were becoming more secure for shipping. Thus, we didn't have to "zig and zag" so much. In any event, each day about 3:00 or 4:00 P.M. a group of about 35 or 40 Japanese prisoners would be brought up on the forward deck. They were a sorry-looking lot. Their heads had been shaved, they wore no clothing except for a white loin-cloth, and they seemed to have an unusual number of festering sores and wounds. They looked pale and wan, their faces and bodies with little color, at least compared with ours. We were all tanned and healthy looking. They looked thin and helpless, and I know they must have been frightened.

Up they came out of their iron "dungeon" each afternoon to be "hosed down." And that is exactly what happened. Two sailors hosed them down with water (I can't remember if it was fresh or salt) while they stood rather impassively in small groups, one minute bathed in sunshine, the next awash in water. They did try to clean themselves with soap, and the entire spectacle went on for about 15 minutes. During the hosing-down a few soldiers and Marines taunted these poor disheveled souls — I doubt they understood the ridicule — calling them names and threatening them with brutal and malevolent comments such as "How do you slants like this?" "We're going to hang you when we get to Hawaii," "You'll be sorry you were taken prisoner."

Nobody ever physically intervened to stop this behavior, but I believe that most aboard didn't like it. I know I didn't, and I'm still ashamed of the incident. It happened every single afternoon we were on the ship — always the hosing-down, always the same dullards taunting the prisoners, always the mass of us just watching, doing nothing. I wish I had spoken out.

Two other incidents associated with the prisoners come to mind. If you happened to eat right after they were fed, and they ate in the same place we did, there was never any ketchup — I think they drank it. Ketchup was a rare commodity overseas, but the Navy had it sometimes, and if the prisoners ate early, that was it, the ketchup quota for the day was fini.

The other incident occurred after we arrived in Oahu. I was "selected" for a work detail to unload the company gear. Thus, when we landed on Oahu on October 6, I stayed aboard for two days while the rest of my outfit went up to Schofield Barracks. Sometime in the afternoon of October 7, the Japanese prisoners were all marched off the ship to vans that would take them to a prisoner compound. This time they had clothes on, but it was clothing designed for American soldiers and sailors, blue fatigue clothes. Where they got these I shall never know because we always wore green. Perhaps it was old Navy gear. Anyway, the clothing was all much too large, so the prisoners had rolled up the sleeves and trouser legs. They each had on an absurd little blue overseas cap and huge beige GI shoes. What a sight! I didn't have a camera, but if I could have captured this on film, it would have been the picture of the year, showing total despair. If you didn't feel pity for those poor souls, you just had no heart. These were prisoners, helpless prisoners, not fighting soldiers and aviators. And our contact was personal, not detached. This was not one of our finest hours.

One last comment. The work detail turned out pretty well because there was a small kiosk on the dock. We all loaded ourselves up on milk, ice cream, sandwiches, Coke, and potato chips. And we had the entire hold of the ship to ourselves for sleeping. Not a bad deal.

On October 8, 1944, the work party unloading the boat finished up, and we were taken to Schofield Barracks by bus. But this time we went to "Hut City," the quarantine quarters associated with this huge base. Hut City was just that — scores of wooden huts, each holding six men, set in a lovely field of dust, red dust. It eventually covered everything.

We stayed in Hut City for about a week, catching up on mail, buying goodies at the huge PX, then headed out for "jungle training." We were really delighted to do this, especially after one solid year living in jungles. But the word *army* implies constant training, even in a noncombat zone. Actually, there is really nothing else to do—fight or train. We didn't need it. We didn't want it. But we had to do it.

So out we went to the training area located about 30 miles from Schofield Barracks. There we fired bazookas (antitank weapons), flamethrowers, and submachine guns, and even placed shape charges on pillboxes (shape charges are used to blow a hole through a pillbox into which grenades can then be tossed). During one of these exercises a member of one of our rifle companies was killed in an accident involving the placement of a shape charge on a bunker. In another incident, a trigger-happy soldier with a Thompson submachine gun inadvertently turned the weapon toward our group while demonstrating its correct use and loosed a burst of shots in our direction that missed us by inches. Only the grace of God saved us from some serious injury that day. It was hot and dirty and made no sense at all. In fact, it was nonsense. But it was something to do.

When we returned to Hut City, we found our camp inundated with Italian prisoners of war doing maintenance work. They had been captured in the North African campaign a year and a half ago and eventually sent to Oahu. They loved it. They had already learned some of the language because they had previously been in the Southwest before being moved to Hawaii. They didn't know why they had been moved, but they continually commented that they wouldn't trade places with us. They were all young, well tanned, seemingly in excellent physical condition, friendly, and big cigarette smokers. And believe it or not, the ones working on our hut all seemed to be competent carpenters. They didn't work too hard, but nobody cared — what was the point? Later we would see them on the base, and they always smiled, waved, and called out a friendly greeting. They also kept a close eye out for any attractive young women who might be going by, and she received whistles and comments (in Italian, of course) on her physical qualities. They were a wild bunch. I'll bet some are still there.

While we were in Hut City, our medical officer, Captain Dobbs, was sent to the First Battalion, and we got a real beauty—Captain Tankersley. Captain Dobbs had been with us a year, and he really never caused us any problem. He was there when needed, but that was it. He was soft-spoken, and competent as a physician from what I could see. His only distinguishing characteristic was his pure white legs. I know that's a rather strange thing to comment on, but he had no hair on his legs and almost always wore long khaki trousers, so on the rare occasions he wore shorts, as most of us did almost all the time, some guys would invariably give a wolf whistle as he crossed the volleyball court or mess area. Those chalky white legs did it. It never bothered him as far as I could tell. He took it with good humor.

Tankersley was another matter. He was big, overweight, balding, and had a big mouth. He was a sorry example of how to handle men, but his self-image was that of a great leader. He just didn't understand things, particularly that the sergeant ran things and he should deal with him. He was arrogant, lazy, and selfish; that is, he took care of himself at the expense of others. I didn't like him, and he knew I didn't like him, which was worse. Ours was not a creative relationship.

Near the end of October we were told that our battalion was to go to a rest camp on Kauai. That sounded good to us, and we started packing.

It may seem strange, but I never had any serious problems with loneliness or homesickness in the Army, and after a year overseas, what little I had experienced was about gone. As I said, I liked getting letters, but they didn't upset me, and they never affected me in any negative sense. I guess I had adjusted to Army life.

We boarded the USS *Hendry* on October 30, 1944, for the short trip to Kauai. The *Hendry* was 455 feet long, had a beam of 62 feet, and was a brand-new assault transport (APA-118) ("Following a rigorous shakedown cruise, *Hendry* sailed 23 October for Pearl Harbor, arriving 29 October"). We were the first troops to board the *Hendry*, and the trip to Kauai was almost a luxury cruise. The Navy did everything to make the trip pleasant. Pleasant, that is, until we dropped anchor off Hanapepe, Kauai, and prepared to disembark. It was October 31, Halloween, and what we did then could only have been arranged by witches (perhaps clowns would be a better metaphor).

Conditions were not too good; it was overcast, and a rolling sea was running. The swells were good sized. Apparently, the ship's captain (and our battalion commander went along with this), thought it would be a good time to practice an assault landing. So they unloaded all the LCVPs (Landing Craft Vehicle Personnel) and threw the landing nets over the side while the boat crews stationed themselves to take on the 1,200 troops of the Third Battalion.

The landing net was made up of manila line, two inches in diameter, and was approximately 15 feet wide and 30 to 35 feet long. The manila line was woven into 12- to 15-inch squares, which acted as a ladder for those climbing or descending the net. Though they work very well in calm waters, the nets were less than perfect in a rough sea, and the waters off Kauai that day were hardly placid.

Each one of us wore a life preserver, and most carried a rifle and canteen. We were ungainly to begin with. Three men went down each landing net at one time. This was adequate, but tricky on a day like this. The problem was to get from the deck to the LCVP without falling into the boat or getting crushed between the landing craft and the troopship. To compound the problem, the ship and the LCVP were going up and down in opposite directions. One minute you could almost step off the deck onto the LCVP; the next you could hardly see it far below. It was a delicate maneuver, dangerous and breathtaking at the same time.

It took quite a while to load all 1,200 troops because we were loading only three LCVPs at a time. I went down rather early, and our craft, along with a number of others, formed a large circle and followed one another around. This went on and on and on, for one and a half hours, until all the troops were in the boats and all the LCVPs had a chance to join one of the four or five circles of landing craft.

Many aboard, both soldiers and sailors, were getting seasick and vomiting. We cursed the boat crews, cursed the officers on deck, screamed at them to let us go ashore, but to no avail. This was to be a practice assault, and the captain was determined to do it correctly. Finally, after about two hours in the boats, we formed an assault line and ran for the shore. The boat crews ran us up on the beaches, and we all stumbled drunkenly out of the boats onto the sand. To say we didn't feel good was a gross understatement. We were on Kauai. This was our first moment of rest camp.

Kauai's climate is a paradox. Part of the island receives some of the heaviest rainfall in the world, and part is a virtual desert. Geologically and historically, Kauai is the oldest of the Hawaiian Islands. Waialeale Mountain, with its Kawaikini peak of 5,243 feet, is the wettest spot on earth with an average rainfall of over 400 inches of rain per year. The island also has a spectacular gorge, in the western half of the island, known as the Grand Canyon of the Pacific. This great gorge is over 3,500 feet deep, and its colors and beauty approach those of the Grand Canyon in Arizona. The western side of the island is called the Na Pali coast and is characterized by cliffs that rise straight out of the ocean 2,000 or 3,000 feet. It is a true island paradise. I had never seen such beauty. It has some similarities to Oahu, but Kauai's mountains, gorge, and desert are unique. We were stationed just at the foothills of Waialeale Mountain quite close to Kalaheo, a very wet

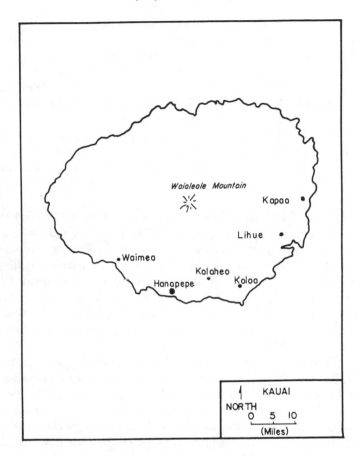

Kauai, Hawaiian Islands.

spot, and L Company was sent to a virtual desert, called Barking Sands, on the southwest coast of the island.

There was a great deal of intermarriage on the island, but the single largest ethnic group was the Japanese. There were much smaller groups of Portuguese, native Hawaiians and Americans on the island. Agriculture, papaya, taro, sugar cane, and pineapple dominated the economy in those days, with some cattle raising. Our battalion was spread all over the island. As I stated in my diary, "I Company is about 40 miles from us. L Company about 14, K about 6 and M Company is split up with their mortars and machine gun sections."

I was given a three-quarter-ton truck, a weapons carrier, and became a truck driver. Great! I had wheels and was for the most part free to roam all over the island — and I did, although most my expeditions were limited to the south and east coast of the island. Jim Nordale, Combs, and I were ordered to deliver B bags to the rifle companies, and we drove all over the island to do this. We particularly enjoyed Hanapepe and its large Portuguese community because of the pretty girls. We met a few. I remember one name only—Rose Vali, an attractive girl but one whose parents wouldn't let her leave the front porch. We quickly abandoned this lost cause and headed for Lihue. There we watched a football game between two high schools, Lihue and Kapaa. I remember only one thing about the game. All the players wore the regulation equipment except for one thing—no shoes. They ran, kicked, punted, did everything, but everyone was barefoot. I suspect that today this is not the case, but in October 1944 that was the practice.

Combs and I also spent some pleasant evenings at the USO club in Kalaheo. We usually would go down the hill from camp about twice a week to dance. The club was located close to the center of town and was managed, as far as we could determine, by just a few of the women from Kalaheo. One evening we met a young girl at the club, Betty Shimogawa. Bright, vivacious, and cheerful, she lived in Kalaheo with her mother, Mitsuyo Marugame Shimogawa. Mrs. Shimogawa was a kind, thoughtful, and hardworking person, one of the most active women involved in the day-to-day operation of the USO.

We danced, talked, had some soft drinks and food, and forgot the war. We three just had a good time. We did this again on two or three other occasions, and at one dance Betty introduced us to her mother. After we talked for a while, Mrs. Shimogawa invited Combs and me to her house for dinner. We instantly agreed on a date, and it turned out to be a special treat in what one might call civility and hospitality. We went to their house at the appointed hour, left our shoes at the door, and were invited to sit on mats placed on the floor. Betty's mother served us the best meal I had in my two and a half years in the Army. The food was excellent, and the way it was served was superb. She cooked everything right there on a small 12-inch-square hibachi. We laughed, talked, and forgot the Army. I never forgot that delightful evening or the kindness of Betty and Mrs. Shimogawa to two strangers. When we returned to camp, I wrote a letter to my parents and told them all about this very special day.

Large parts of the island were uninhabited when we were there, and once Survill, Nordale, Combs, and I took a hike through the hills. There were all kinds of plants, flowers and trees I could not identify, but we came upon a small waterfall (Kauai has some sharp, jagged mountains) tumbling down into a pool. It was something you might see in a movie. We all took off our clothes and dove into the pool. The water was fresh, clear, sparkling, probably safe to drink. It was refreshing. Even as I write this, I can't explain why we went on a voluntary hike because we *never* did such things. But

Kauai was a time when we had almost complete freedom to do as we pleased, and I suspect we may have become a bit bored with just reading and driving about the island and decided on a hike. In any event, it was a good decision.

It may have been Jim who suggested it. He was a big, tall, good-natured fellow from San Antonio. Actually, he was the living metaphor of the present TV image of a Texan. He was easygoing, smiled a lot, had a very good sense of humor, and loved all the girls he met. He did have a way with women. If anyone could get a girl to go out, it was Jim. They just liked him. I don't remember seeing him lose his temper in the two years we spent together. I can't think of a person in the entire outfit who didn't like him. You just seemed comfortable around him. He was, as they say, a nice guy.

It should be clear by now that jazz, the music of both combos and the big bands, was one of my passions. I was forever trying to get myself a better record player or a new record for the old recorder. On November 7, 1944, so my diary notes, "I got myself a recorder today—40 smackeroos, but it's really a nice job." By now I had a small collection of records that I would send with the company equipment, along with my record player, whenever we moved. It was easy to arrange as almost everyone else liked to listen to music, so my personal player and collection were always packed quite willingly by anyone in the detachment. Everyone knew about it. It was packed and shipped right along with all of our medical supplies, and probably with just as much care.

One day an officer stopped me and asked if I would bring my recorder and record collection up to the Officers Club and play for a dance they were planning. (Perhaps I should mention that in the late 1930s and early 1940s, it was very common in high school for social groups of all kinds to sponsor a dance with a big band or if money was tight, an individual playing records. Maybe it's still done—I don't go anymore—the music is too unfamiliar and too loud.) He said they would pay me five dollars and that food and drinks would be on the house. I agreed to do it. The evening of the party I went up to the Officers Club, set up my gear, turned the volume up to full since I had no way to amplify the sound, and started going through all my records. I enjoyed it. Everyone was dressed up, the women looked beautiful, the decorations were attractive, and the lights were turned low. They had a table with drinks and food, and it was a pleasant evening. As we neared the time for the end of the dance, a young woman from the Red Cross asked me to dance. I said sure. This was livin'—"A String of Pearls" by Glenn Miller, free beer, good music, and a pretty girl. Nothing better in Cleveland.

We spent almost six weeks on Kauai, the best six weeks I spent in the Army. But it came to an end as all things seem to do, and on December 13, 1944, we boarded an interisland ferry and left Kauai for Oahu.

We moved back into one of the quadrangles at Schofield Barracks. In a letter to my parents dated December 31, 1944, I wrote:

> Now don't get excited, and sit down because the age of miracles is not over, I know, because a bunch of us Pvts. have been promoted to the exalted rank of PFC. Just think, $4.80 a month more, the $.80 cents is overseas pay. I suppose you know that overseas pay is 20% of your base pay. I don't know whether or not I told you [this]. So now that this great and world important news has been relayed to you, you'll have to wait approximately one year and a half for another promotion.

The promotion was due to an act of the Congress of the United States, which stated that privates in the Army with one year or more overseas were, by law, promoted to Pfc. I was simply part of that illustrious group. I wish there were more to it, but in all honesty, that's the story.

Peter Lipson was one of the other privates promoted by that act of Congress in December 1944. Peter was from Perry, Georgia. He was about 6', slender, about 25 with hair starting to turn just a bit gray. He was fastidious in his hygiene and apparel, forever washing his hands, washing when they were hardly soiled. It was a strange compulsive behavior, and it brought him attention he didn't want or need. He was frequently teased, sometimes rather cruelly, because of this habit, and he was the butt of a lot of jokes. He was a harmless, soft-spoken "sad sack." He was weird, but he was ours, and although nobody ever physically hurt him we all teased him.

He had one more characteristic that brought him a great deal of unnecessary pain. He seemed to be terribly frightened all the time. There were certainly times when being scared was legitimate, but poor Peter lived in a state of constant fear and trembling. Rumors drove him mad. If there weren't any at the moment, we made them up. The rumors might be "There's a submarine alert," "We're going on a major invasion," "You're being transferred to L Company as an aidman." And so it went. Peter was childlike. I have grandchildren in their teens that have more common sense than Peter ever had. He was so pessimistic, so eager to hear good news, so infantile, he never should have been in the Army. How he got past the psychologist I shall never know. It is paradoxical but we liked and disliked him for his supersensitivity. Strange. And to this day, I don't understand the constant washing of one's hands.

As 1945 dawned, rumors of a move swept the quadrangle. We packed our gear yet again, my floating music department and all, went to the base theater and saw a live Betty Hutton show, and again took the miniature train to the docks. We were off on another adventure. Movement, constant motion, seems to me today to have been the mode of existence those two and one half years in the Army. But it was coming to an end, as we were to learn a little later.

"An Officer and a Gentleman" 8

Another Cruise, Patrols — Why Me?,
The Last Outpost, Koror: Why Us?,
Going Home, Change Is the Rule of Life

We trooped aboard the *USS Telfair* in Honolulu on January 15, 1945, on our way to the Palau Islands. Life aboard ship was "more of the same." The only interesting departure from other voyages was that this time we went in a convoy of six transports. The entire regiment went this time, two destroyers acting as escorts.

One unusual natural phenomenon occurred on the trip. We ran into a storm about a week out of Hawaii, and a number of waterspouts formed about three or four miles from the ship. They oscillated and moved, four or five of them together, and appeared as a tall column of water that ran from the ocean up to the overhanging low-scudding clouds. Perhaps they were the ocean variety of a tornado. I never found out. They soon disappeared and were forgotten.

We made two stops on the trip, one near Yap and another at Ulithi. At Ulithi there were 12 or 15 aircraft carriers, all lined up in a row. I thought at the time they looked very neat but also rather vulnerable to attack. There were a number of other ships lying at anchor, but the collection of carriers was somewhat unusual.

The convoy finally arrived off Peleliu, one of the southern islands of the Palaus, after a two-week trip, on February 1, 1945. We rounded up our gear, scrambled down the landing nets into the waiting LCVPs, and went ashore. "No messin' around."

The Japanese took the Palau Islands during World War I from the Germans. This seizure was legitimized by the League of Nations in 1920, and Japan controlled and fortified the islands until September–December 1944 when American Marines and Army forces captured the southern islands (see map). The Palaus are 4,000 miles west of Oahu but only 500 miles from the southern Philippines. The islands vary from flat coral atolls in the north

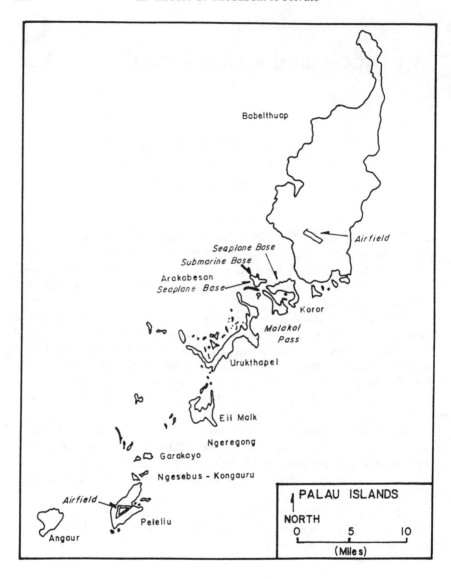

Palau Islands.

to rugged volcanic islands in the south. The natives are Micronesians and because of the islands' remoteness were some of the last to be discovered by the European adventurers.

Peleliu was invaded on September 15, 1944, by the First Marine Division. The island is about 12 square miles and was defended by 10,000 Japanese troops. It was not until early December that the island was declared secure. The United States had overwhelming air and naval superiority during the battle, but the Japanese had learned their lessons well in the Gilberts and Marshalls and were concealed and fortified in a series of caves along what was called Bloody-Nose Ridge. It was an extremely difficult campaign because of the terrain and the heat.

The military role of the 111th Infantry on Peleliu involved five activities: combat patrols through the hills and ridges on Peleliu, bombardment with 155-mm guns of the islands to the north of Garakayo still occupied by Japanese troops, outpost duty, setting ambushes, and taking the surrender and disarming of the Japanese troops on the northern islands. We had the usual tasks associated with food, clothing, shelter, fuel, and water, most importantly water. The necessities of life must be realized.

Our battalion area was located just north of the airfield. The medical detachment aid station was set up there, but we also operated a water station near the northern tip of Peleliu on Akarahoro Point. It was just a little south of the causeway that formerly connected Peleliu with the neighboring island of Ngesebus. Huge 155-mm cannon bombarded the Japanese on the northern islands, and they invariably began their shelling while we watched a movie. It was a shattering sight and sound. We would be watching, and WHAM, WHAM, WHAM, the guns let loose, and their shells rocketed over our heads on their way to harass the Japanese. Shelling didn't occur every night—it was tied to our movie schedule; it couldn't have been a coincidence. We had our own cannon company in the regiment, and I assume it was this group that did the firing.

The terrain of Peleliu Island was very rugged. Short, steep coral rock shot straight out of the ground. In many places these rocky hills went straight up. They were honeycombed with caves, and the fierce battle had turned a jungle into a tangled mass that made walking difficult. The hills were torn up—trees, coral rock, tons of old equipment, unexploded shells—a mess.

Getting into this difficult terrain with its openings, caves, and crevices and rooting out the remaining Japs was a responsibility of our unit. Virtually everyone went on patrols. There may have been some exceptions, but almost everybody participated. We conducted these patrols from the time we landed until we left the island. It was a daily exercise. Most of the patrol activity occurred on Peleliu and focused on the area called Bloody-Nose Ridge. The job of those on patrol was to kill or capture any Japanese soldiers encountered and look for evidence of soldiers. That was easy to do; we could leave some small piece of equipment or food and then check it a day or so later. Going on patrol was always a time of some anxiety, and it could be downright dangerous.

I must confess that I often wondered why we were going on patrols at all. It made little sense to me. The Japanese killed or captured were only

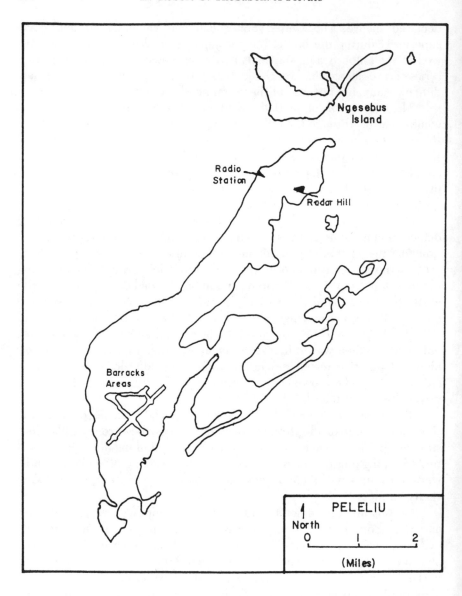

Peleliu, Palau Islands.

trying to hide. They may have stolen a little food or equipment but nothing of moment. They were certainly no threat. They could do nothing. But I suppose our officers feared the possible (a suicide attack) rather than the probable (merely a soldier trying to survive).

A typical patrol was manned by eight or ten soldiers from one of the "line" companies (I, L, K) and an aidman, and led by a sergeant or corporal. The line company would call the aid station, and Sergeant Neumann would assign one of us to go on the patrol.

Everybody—I repeat, everybody—took his turn, and you just didn't show up for sick call on the day you were supposed to act as the aidman for the patrol. There is a lot of "goofing off" (we called it goldbricking) in the military, but there are times when you take your turn. There was absolutely no pressure to volunteer for any patrol, however. There was an unsaid rule that you went when it was your turn to go and you were selected. There was never any trouble with this system. It worked. You never knew what line company you were going with or where they were going precisely. You just reported to their company headquarters and met the group you were going with.

Usually we were taken by truck up to the general area to be scouted. The rest of the patrol was then done on foot. The sergeant would explain our route and check our equipment. Everyone wore a green fatigue suit and helmet, and carried a rifle, BAR, or carbine. In my case I carried a carbine because it was lighter and I had to carry the extra gear contained in my medical kit. Nobody wore any indication of rank on his sleeve, and I never did have a red cross painted on my helmet. I thought then (and now) that such a practice was insane. It wasn't needed and was only a target. Nobody in my outfit ever wore insignia in the field.

The average patrol lasted for two or three hours, and we always walked single file, six or eight feet apart. Some patrols killed Japanese soldiers. A few captured soldiers. Still others found evidence of the enemy. And some had no contact whatsoever. We investigated caves, noted booby-trap wires, saw huge unexploded 16-inch naval shells, and were very alert and quiet, as inconspicuous and anonymous as possible.

On one patrol I remember going into a cave that had boards laid over the bodies of dead Japanese soldiers. Whether the cave was closed by bulldozers during the battle, suffocating those inside, or simply the last refuge of enemy troops, I don't know. I do know we went in, looked around, and left. Nobody took anything—it was a grisly scene.

I always liked walking in the fourth or fifth position. It seemed like a good (safe) spot. We would stop on occasion but never grouped up to smoke. When we finished the patrol, we were dismissed, our sergeant reported the results to the company commander, and we went back to our base camp and waited for the next assignment.

Though getting bombed can scare you, patrols seem more related to stress. Noise was the condition of the former; silence, of the latter. In bombing attacks you were motionless for the most part, scrunched into a corner. On patrol you were moving almost all the time. In bombing, you just took it. On some patrols, the troops could dish it out. The patrols were different, and the men who went as aidmen with the patrols were different. Edwin Oakley was a big friendly man who looked liked Charles Atlas. Leon Roberts was a not-so-gentle cynic from Brooklyn, New York, who always claimed he was going to picket our commanding officer's office after the war with a sign stating *Many soldiers died under his hands*. Mac McQuine seemed an awfully immature individual, but he had a good-natured approach to life. And Thomas Riller fit my stereotype of the typical southerner — slow moving and talking, not easily ruffled. We all went on patrol. When selected.

On April 3, 1945, John Survill and I celebrated our 21st birthdays together. At the time we were working together at the water station near the north end of the island. We drank all our beer, got a little high, and probably forgot to put the correct chemicals in the water we were responsible for purifying. It wasn't something we worried about very much. The water, or most of it, was sent to ships lying off shore.

In early April 1945, we heard the sad report that President Roosevelt had died. Everyone was sobered by the news, and all wondered how the new president, Harry Truman, would conduct the war. We knew it was almost over in Europe because our radio reports had American and Russian troops closing in on the last Nazi strongholds. Then, on May 8, 1945, two things happened, one momentous and one of little import. The war in Europe officially ended, and the Third Battalion moved again, this time to the northernmost island in the Palaus held by American troops, Garakayo.

By now I had been away from home almost two years and overseas about one and one half years. I remember thinking, "The war in the Pacific will never end. This is how my life will be led. I shall be in the Army forever." These thoughts didn't really dismay me. I was not homesick at all. I hadn't forgotten my family and friends at home; I was just resigned to living the way I was, as a soldier. I know this may sound strange, but I clearly remember thinking, "This is how life is." It must have been resignation or adjustment, I really don't know. I know it was a fact.

On May 8, 1945, we arrived on Garakayo, about five miles north of Peleliu. The battalion with its aid station was established in the south-central part of the island, and I was sent to act as an aidman for M Company's machine-gun outpost on the northwest part of the island (see map of Garakayo). There was also a major dock installation on Garakayo.

A water-purification facility was established at the point, and because of my great experience on Peleliu, I worked on this project also. It was a good deal. I was completely on my own, away from every last vestige of authority except for the sergeant who ran the machine-gun outpost. There were about 15 men assigned to the outpost since it had to be manned all night, every night.

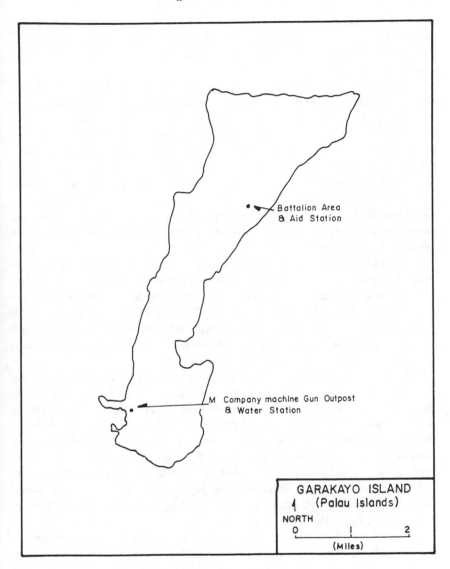

Battalion Area
& Aid Station

M Company machine Gun Outpost
& Water Station

GARAKAYO ISLAND
(Palau Islands)
NORTH
0   1   2
(Miles)

Garakayo, Palau Islands.

The problem was that some of the more tenacious and "intense" Japanese soldiers on the northern islands had in the past built rafts, floated down to the islands captured by the Americans, and then tried to cause as much mayhem as they could. The outpost's task was to shoot them out of the water. I slept in a pyramidal tent about 50 yards from the outpost. Back at battalion headquarters, some engineers put up a quonset hut, a real luxury, but I would never have traded my deal for their fancy tin shack. I told everybody it was terrible out in the boonies, hoping to keep the outpost assignment. I did. I stayed there the entire four months we spent on the island.

I never saw a movie on Garakayo; they were all shown at battalion headquarters. I didn't care; I liked the freedom on outpost duty. There was another "perk" with this assignment. Three times a day a truck drove out from Headquarters with food for all of us, just like pizza delivery today. We played cribbage, went swimming, talked to sailors put ashore on our dock for a beer party, watched the water purifier, and scanned the ocean at night for rafts. Tough duty. It was the best four months I spent in the Army. I read at least a hundred books, and I became a cribbage expert. All I really had to do was to make sure that any injury to the 15 men on the machine-gun crew was promptly treated. Believe me, I tried to take good care of them because I wanted to keep the job.

To add to my good fortune, I received a ten-dollar-a-month raise in June. The rifle companies in our battalion were awarded the Combat Infantryman's Badge, and we were given the Combat Medic's Badge. So each one of us got a badge and a noticeable raise. Our contribution, compared with that of the divisions that frontally assaulted Butaritari, Kwajalein, and Peleliu, was minor. But we took the badge and the money and told ourselves that our efforts were probably worth something.

In early August 1945, atom bombs were dropped on Hiroshima and Nagasaki. In my small unit, there was no question that Truman had made the correct decision. Nobody knew what the atom bomb was, and nobody really cared. It had killed a lot of Japanese, and we hoped it would force them to surrender. That was what concerned us. I don't remember a single person raising the fundamental moral issue of killing innocent people. Perhaps we should have, but we didn't. It's a contradiction I cannot explain. We knew very well that an invasion of Japan was coming, that we would probably be part of that effort, and that the assault would mean millions of casualties. I think the same way today.

Now events began to occur in rapid order, sparked by the near drowning of a sailor. Let me explain. From time to time the Navy would put ashore 40 or 50 sailors on our dock so they could swim, sun, and drink beer. Most of them invariably got falling down drunk. Also, after a few beers, one or two of them would leave our area and go back in the jungle looking for souvenirs. They cared nothing about the dangers lurking there. They were fortified on beer, and after weeks and months at sea, nothing could stop them. We *never* did this. A few of them *always* did this.

On one such day I was in my tent when Sergeant Brady called me to report that a sailor had just been pulled, half drowned, from the water. I ran the 50 yards to the beach and found a sailor who had begun to turn blue.

I began giving him artificial respiration, and after 10 minutes or so he seemed to be breathing OK. Since the wind was blowing very hard that day, I asked a couple of sailors to help me carry him to the nearest tent so I could continue my efforts in a more protected spot.

We picked him up and started down the path to the tent, but he began to turn blue again, so we dropped him in the sand, and I began applying artificial respiration again. I could see that my technique was rubbing all the skin off his back in the area of his kidneys because the sand was blowing all over us. But I kept it up. He was *not* going to turn blue on me again. It was a bizarre scene—the patient's coloring alternating between chalky white, blue, and a reddish flush; the sand whipping and stinging our bare skin; everyone offering advice in a chorus that made no sense at all; surrounded by sailors and soldiers just standing and watching while they smoked and drank more beer.

I asked somebody to call the battalion aid station for help. He reported in a minute or so that they would send a truck. I kept up the only primitive technique I knew for about another 10 or 15 minutes. Somehow, I think with God's help, he was still breathing when the truck arrived. The men from the aid station took him on a stretcher to the truck and drove away. I learned later he survived. I bet he didn't drink a lot of beer on a dock after that.

While the "drowning" saga was going on, a couple of Navy souvenir hunters and explorers went into the jungle. I had just returned to my tent when they came running and screaming out of the jungle. "We saw one, we saw one. We ran into a Jap." Sergeant Brady and I talked to them, asked them where, when, and what they had seen and told them to get down to the dock and get off the island. They did.

Brady decided that it might be smart to set up an ambush and get the Jap if we could. He asked me if I would join him in his little exercise, and I agreed. Why not? I liked Brady, and he rarely asked anybody to do anything. After dinner we grabbed our rifles and worked our way back in the jungle to a point about 100 or 150 yards from our area, near the spot the sailors had said they saw the Jap soldier. We huddled down and started looking.

Night fell, and we had been on the ambush only about two or three hours when we heard a call from my tent, the one near the water station and closest to the jungle: "The war's over! The war's over. Hey, you guys, the war's over!" Brady and I looked at each other, shrugged our shoulders, and said in unison, "Let's go!" We got up and walked out of the jungle for the last time.

In my next several letters to my parents, I served as a reporter and analyst on the great news from the Pacific. (Notice the vocabulary, the penetrating analysis, the brilliant use of metaphor. Surely this must have helped my parents better understand the conflict.) On August 11, I reported:

The biggest news we had last night was that the Japs had accepted the ultimatum. And I mean everybody here really went wild. We broke out our last remaining beers and then got news reports from the other outposts.

A few days later, on August 16, 1945, I offered the startling insight that the Japanese had surrendered because we had hit them with an atom bomb:

Out here everybody thinks it was the atomic bomb that finally wised them [the Japanese] up.

Soon I predicted, on August 22, 1945, success for MacArthur in ruling the Japanese:

The last few days on the news it sounds as if MacArthur is going to sign the peace terms right in Tokyo. He's a good man to run that lousy country. He'll rule them the way they should be ruled. Maybe now they'll wise up.

Finally, I gave a distinctive American touch to the reports on our soldiers and Marines setting foot on Japanese soil:

We were all over at the other outpost the other day listening to the radio broadcast of the Allied landing in Japan. The way they announced it, it sounded like a baseball game.

On September 11, 1945 the Third Battalion left Garakayo and went back to Peleliu. We were to move again.

We had no sooner arrived on Peleliu than we were informed that we would leave the next day for Koror. Our battalion was given the "honor" of accepting the surrender and disarming of the Japanese troops, all 35,000 of them, in the northern islands. "Why us?" we cried. "Give this glorious honor to the First or Second Battalion. What if they don't know the war is over?" We tried everything, but to no avail. We were picked, and we boarded an LCI the next day. The LCI is a versatile craft, perfect for the waters surrounding the Palau Islands. They are armed, have a rather "boxy" profile, and they can carry 300 or 400 troops easily. We had three LCIs for our battalion as we left Peleliu.

We threaded our way through many of the Palaus' 200 volcanic and limestone islands as we moved north on our 20- to 25-mile trip from Peleliu to Koror. Only a few of the islands are inhabited. Most are rocky and jut sharply out of the water. All are totally covered by dense vegetation. Sometimes our transit between islands was so tight you could almost touch the vegetation on the island. As we approached the island of Koror, the

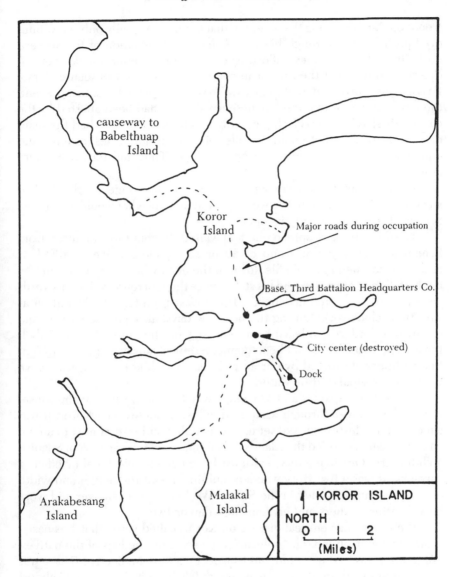

The following labels appear on the map: causeway to Babelthuap Island; Koror Island; Major roads during occupation; Base, Third Battalion Headquarters Co.; City center (destroyed); Dock; Arakabesang Island; Malakal Island; KOROR ISLAND; NORTH; 0 1 2 (Miles)

Koror, Palau Islands.

capital of the Republic of Palau today, there was vivid evidence of the naval air attacks and their effectiveness in the scores of sunken ships half in and out of the water.

It was a strange, ghostly sight, especially the barges lying half submerged or run aground. These had been used by the Japanese general commanding Babelthuap to send down reinforcements to his beleaguered troops on Peleliu during the height of that conflict. Actually only a few hundred probably got through because American domination of the air seriously limited the Japanese effort. Another reason the air attacks were so determined was that the American commanders wanted to secure Kossol Passage, just north of Babelthuap, as a PBM patrol-plane base. In any event, there was no doubt that the Japanese naval effort had been aborted by the carrier air strikes. It was a ship graveyard. Our ship approached the main dock on Koror, and we could see piles of ammunition, rifles, cannon, and equipment of all kinds piled up on the dock. Tons and tons of military equipment.

But no Japanese. Not a living soul. We were encouraged by the stacked weapons and ammunition. We were apprehensive of what would occur next because there was nobody in sight.

We disembarked, spread out, and waited. In about five minutes, from behind a small ridge, a group of 20 or so Japanese officers with their orderlies marched in single file down to the dock where they were met by our battalion commander and his staff. There they surrendered their swords and other weapons to our officers. There wasn't a hitch. It all went off as smooth as clockwork. During the next few days, all Japanese officers and troops were ordered to leave Koror and stay on the huge island of Babelthuap. The two islands had been connected by a causeway (see map), but that had been destroyed by our air attacks, and while I was on Koror, we were always separated by water.

The rifle companies and M Company set up outposts near the causeway, and we moved through what used to be a small town on Koror. It was almost totally destroyed. We set up our battalion aid station next to an old church. Spain had ruled the islands at one time, and it had a look of Spanish architecture. Our living quarters must have been an old hotel or officers' barracks. It was a two-story wooden building, about the length and width of an army barracks back in the States. We built a little shower and were busy treating soldiers and civilians in a day or two.

We ran into a venereal disease on Koror, called yaws, that was nasty. It manifested itself in large "volcano"-type sores on the legs of the natives. We treated it as best we could, but I suspect we were ineffective. There was no penicillin in those days; at least we didn't have it. We "cured" almost everything with sulpha powder. In fact, nothing healed in that moist, humid climate. But that didn't stop some of the more virile troops from engaging in sexual activity with some of the native women and with a few Japanese prostitutes left behind when the troops were forced to evacuate Koror and go to Babelthuap. In the evening it was not unusual to see a soldier going through the rigors associated with an Army prophylactic treatment. These measures to preserve the health of the troops were offered, and given, without question by the medics on technician duty. Sometimes there were

Koror Island in the Palau Islands, September 1945. This photograph, taken one week after their surrender, shows Japanese soldiers from Babelthuap marching to their gardens on Koror to work in the fields.

as many as four or five undergoing the treatment. It takes some time, is rather gross and unseemly, particularly since it was done in full view of any casual walker passing by. All of this was, of course, raw and graceless. And all involved swore never, never to engage in such activity again.

Cigarettes were the medium of exchange with the local people and the Japanese soldiers. Our battalion commander usually let 100 or 200 come from Babelthuap to Koror each day to do agricultural work since most of the gardens were located on our island. The Japanese who came over quickly learned that they could trade equipment for cigarettes. We wanted the souvenirs. They wanted the cigarettes. We had cartons and cartons — they sold for only 50 cents each. The causeway, or what was left of it, became the trading center. In two days I was able to trade a few packs of cigarettes for a Japanese flag, and one day I traded two cartons of cigarettes, one dollar, for an officer's samurai sword. (It's hanging on my gun rack as I write these memoirs.) I could have quickly sold it for 200 or 300 dollars at the time.

It was just a lucky trade. I was there at the right moment. The Japanese officer was leading a group of about 100 soldiers from Babelthuap to work. I went up to him, he bowed (they all did), and I pointed to the sword he carried and held out the two cartons of cigarettes. He simply unbuckled the sword and held it out to me, and we exchanged the cigarettes for the sword right then and there. It all took about 30 seconds.

I also had a Japanese carbine. Everyone in our battalion had a rifle or carbine. The battalion commander had sent out an order that all Japanese weapons and ammunition were to be dumped in the ocean and that anyone who wanted a rifle was welcome to come and pick one out. We all did. That was the extent of my trading.

About this time our unit began to break up. Men were being sent home based on points. As I remember it, we were accorded one point for every month of active service, one extra point for every month of foreign service, and five points for every campaign star awarded. I had three stars, one each for the Gilberts, Marshalls, and Palaus; two years overseas; and two and a half years of service. It added up to 65 or 70 points. The old-timers in our outfit like Sergeant Neumann, Oakley, Roberts, McQuine, and Riller were the first to go. I was glad to see them go because I knew our turn would come all the sooner.

Sergeant Neumann turned a problem (his terrible seasickness) into a benefit. It was approximately a three-week trip by ship from Peleliu to the States, and he would never have survived a voyage so long because he became so ill. So the military authorities decided to fly him home—the only soldier in the entire regiment. Mercy does exist.

Sometime in early October, about the fourth or fifth, I received a telephone call, my first in two and a half years. The voice on the other end of the phone said, "Hey, Thob, how about picking me up? I'm down here at the dock on Koror." I had no idea who it was. And the use of my nickname, Thob, was something I hadn't heard for over two years. It was Jack Foley, an old high school friend from Shaker Heights. I leapt into an old Japanese car—we had a number of these as well as bicycles that were left by the Japanese when they moved to Babelthuap—and drove like a fury over the two miles or so to the dock.

My God—there he was, a Marine officer. I've never experienced anything like it since. Somehow I was home. The two years were over. He looked and talked the same. I couldn't believe what was happening. We embraced, shook hands, and embraced again. I just couldn't believe it. Jack said he had talked to my mother just before leaving the States and knew exactly where I was located, so when he arrived on Guam, he hitched a ride on a plane to Peleliu, found I was on Koror, and then hopped on one of the LCIs that plied between the two islands and came up to Koror. It was possible to do things like this at that time. There were few rules, guards, inspections. Nobody cared. If you broke a rule, where could they send you? But a flight from Guam, hundreds of miles away, was something extraordinary.

We talked excitedly for a few minutes, and then, as best I can remember,

Jack opened the conversation: "Listen, I can only stay overnight. I have to go back to Guam tomorrow. How about going down to Peleliu with me? We'll have a nice dinner and drinks at the transit officers' barracks, spend the night there, and then tomorrow I'll hop a plane back to Guam and you can come back to Koror." I didn't know what to say for a minute. Then I blurted out, "Jack, maybe you haven't noticed — I'm a private. Privates aren't really welcome at the officers' club." Without a moment's hesitation he said, "That's no problem. I've got an extra shirt and overseas cap with gold bars you can put on when we're aboard the ship on the trip to Peleliu. You can do it, Thob. Let's go." I didn't know what to say. I wanted to go, but the consequences worried me. I said, "Jack, I think it's against Army regulations — impersonation of an officer is a federal offense. People go to prison for doing such things." "Who'll know?" he said. "The transit officers' barracks is like a floating crap game — it changes every day. Nobody knows anybody."

After a few moments' thought about what he had gone through to get here, I agreed in an immortal phrase: "What the hell, I'll do it. But first I have to get permission. Don't worry about that. I don't think that'll be a problem." We hopped in the car and drove back to the aid station. I introduced Jack to our warrant officer, John Rollins, a new member of our unit, and in two minutes had his approval. Off we went to grab the LCI to Peleliu.

Before going on with this story, I want to say something about Jack and our relationship. We were friends throughout high school. We played ice hockey together, dated the two Harper sisters for a year or so during high school, loved music and dancing, and belonged to the same high school and college fraternities. We were good friends. Jack was 6', about 185 pounds, had a reddish blond tinge of color in his hair and sharp-chiseled features (somewhat like Kirk Douglas's). He played hockey and football, but his real forte was theater. He was a first-rate actor. As I said, during our senior year at Shaker Heights High School, we put on the play *Hamlet*. Jack played Hamlet, and if you know the play, that is an extremely complex and challenging role to fill. He was super. I was Guildenstern, probably the smallest part in the play.

Jack liked all the girls, and my impression was that they all loved him. He was a complete extrovert, an "operator" with women, always ready to have a party. He was Irish through and through, always a leader. He led by the force of his personality and his powers to persuade. He never forced things. He didn't have to. He spent a year or so at Carnegie Tech before joining the Marines. After the war he began making and selling TV commercial spots. He eventually married, had seven children, and lived for years in California until his death in the fall of 1990.

But back to the story. Near the end of the two-and-a-half-hour trip to Peleliu I put on the shirt and cap and became a Marine officer, gold bars and all. Fortuantely, there was no saluting; we had given that up almost two years ago. We walked over toward the officers' barracks first because I had to register for a room that night. We decided that since I had no official I.D., I should register as Lt. Richard Black. We picked this name in honor of a mutual friend from our high school days—Dick Black. Black was an agreeable guy and would certainly have approved of our plan. As you can see, real planning was involved in this operation.

I walked in to face the sergeant on duty at the desk, tried to act nonchalant, introduced myself to the sergeant as Lt. Richard Black, and stated that I wanted to sign up for a room for the night. He looked at me, a bit too closely as far as I was concerned, and then pushed the registration form in my direction and went on about his other tasks. I filled out the form, was assigned a room and given a key, and we left. I took a *very* deep breath as I walked out. We went to our rooms (by now I was really beginning to get into this officer act), cleaned up a bit, and headed for the bar and dining room.

We sat down at a table and ordered some drinks from some poor enlisted man. After I had fortified myself with two or three mixed drinks, I called out to the waiter in much the same tone the others did for more drinks. I don't know how many we had—way too many. I do remember singing old college fraternity songs with gay abandon: "Delta Tau Delta, Delta—you are my safest shelter" et al. We were in superb voice. We forgot everybody else in the room, and there were some from Australia and England. We got louder and better as time and drinks blurred our minds but not our spirits.

Later, much later, we were told that we had better eat if we wanted any food because the kitchen was going to close. We ordered steaks and ate like kings. About 11:00P.M. we wove our way back to the officers' barracks—full of booze, food, and goodwill. It had been a night to remember.

The next morning, I dressed and shaved, and Jack and I had breakfast at the Officers Club. Then I checked out, and we walked over to the airport. On the way I gave him back the official trappings of a Marine officer. He arranged a ride to Guam, and I watched the plane take off into the morning sun. It was one of the great days of my life. I had been an "officer and a gentleman" for 24 hours. And I spent that 24 hours with a friend I shall never forget.

With the plane out of sight, I walked back to the dock, grabbed the first LCI going to Koror, left my life of illusion, and returned to reality. I'll take illusion.

Back on Koror, as the month of October wore on, I lost my wristwatch. My parents had given it to me for graduation from high school, and it had my name engraved on the back. I was getting ready to take a shower one day and tossed the watch in the top of the mosquito bar over my cot while I went to the shower. When I returned, it was gone. To have something stolen was very unusual; we rarely had problems with theft. All of my imaginative detective work designed to recover the watch was in vain, and I gave it up for lost.

As the end of October drew near, John Survill and I finally had the requisite number of points to go home. On October 28 we said goodbye to our friends, left Koror, and went back to Peleliu to get the ship that would take us back to the States.

The ship to take us home, the *Custer*, lay at anchor off Peleliu, and we spent October 29 and 30 turning in all our gear. It was a confusing and chaotic two days. One afternoon I got in a poker game — a rare thing for me to do as I didn't have the stomach for gambling. One of the soldiers playing in the game, I didn't know him at all, ran out of money and offered a watch for sale that he had acquired in another game. The watch was passed around, and when it came to me, I recognized it as the one stolen from my mosquito bar. I pointed to the name, showed him my dog tags, and claimed the watch. He protested and said he had bought it in good faith. The situation became a bit tense, but I offered him five dollars, which he accepted, and I had my watch back. Strange!

On October 31 we were ordered to report to the local aid station to get a flu shot. News had recently arrived announcing a big flu epidemic in the States, and the Army didn't want us to succumb to disease just as we returned home. We all took the shots. In the middle of the night I awoke feeling very sick. I was terrified. If I was really ill, and I was, I knew I would be sent to the base hospital until I was cured. "My God," I thought, "that could be weeks."

I decided to say absolutely nothing. I was determined to get on that ship. That was *my* ship. I was going home on it come hell or high water. I got up off my cot to get a drink of water and noticed a number of other soldiers who looked a lot like me — terrible. We talked a bit and decided that we had the flu. Halloween must not be my day. Halloween 1944 was the day the Navy made us all sick by circling the LCVPs for hours off Kauai. Now on Halloween 1945 it was the Army's turn. They gave us the flu. But not one soldier said one word. Not one soldier went on sick call. Not one soldier even asked for an aspirin. We were going to get on that ship, ironically, with "the rising sun in the Pacific."

On November 1, 1945, we boarded our ship for the trip to the States, and we left Peleliu that day heading east. I lashed my Japanese carbine to my bunk belowdecks, but I carried the samurai sword and flag with me at all times. To put it down for an instant would have meant the end. To make it easier, I wrapped the sword in some old fatigues and carried it slung over my back. When I wanted to sit down, I could just move it to my shoulder. It was no big problem.

At night the ship was brightly illuminated. No more blackouts. We had movies on the afterdeck every night, and I remember well climbing and straddling a boom on the ship and riding it like a horse on the large Pacific Ocean swells as I watched the movie. It was beautiful: millions of stars, the sparkling phosphorescent bow waves, the moon — and we were going home. Any time we made any departure, no matter how slight, from our eastward course, a cry of woe went up, and once or twice the officer of the deck felt compelled to come on the public address system to explain the deviation. It was a long trip, but in two weeks we arrived at Oahu. Nobody wanted to stop, but we needed provisions. We got them and headed east again.

The sailors on board did what sailors always do — scrape and paint. They were going to be aboard a long time. We were going to get off. They carried on with normal routines. Some of the troops started throwing clothing off the ship. I don't know why. Perhaps it was just an act that helped them demonstrate that their days in the service were drawing to a close.

On November 21, 1945, we sighted the United States. To say it was exciting is not enough. For me, there was a rush of emotion, tears welled in my eyes. I remember running and pushing to the front of the ship, the side of the ship, anyplace to get a better look. We were heading for San Pedro in southern California. We pulled in at a dock to the sound of music from a band playing patriotic and popular tunes.

It was unbelievable. We were home. We waved, screamed, cried, almost ran around in circles. We were *home*. It was a fantastic moment — kind of like one's wedding night. It happens once in a lifetime.

The public address ordered "All troops prepare to disembark." I ran to get my gear from the bunk, but I couldn't get the damn rifle untied. I had lashed it to the bunk so tight that I couldn't loosen the knots. "The hell with it," I thought. I left it there for some sailor with more patience than I had at the moment and moved to the gangway. A few minutes later I was on American soil. It had been two years and fourteen days. As the popular song of the day said, "It's Been a Long, Long Time."

We went directly to Camp Anza, located near San Pedro harbor in California where I sent Barbara and my folks a telegram saying I had arrived safely. There was a "shuttle" flight between the East and West coasts for soldiers who lived in those areas. November 22, 1945, was the last time I ever saw John Survill. He was from New Jersey and left that day. There was no big goodbye, just a handshake, a word wishing him well and a pat on the shoulder. We had seen and said everything we had to say over the past two and a half years. Those of us who lived someplace in the vast area between California and the East Coast boarded a troop train that headed east through the southwestern states toward Camp Atterbury, Indiana. I remember passing through an area in Arizona, between two ranges of hills, that was filled with thousands and thousands of airplanes. It was a military airplane graveyard, kind of an eerie sight. We talked, slept as we could, and on November 26 we arrived at Camp Atterbury.

On November 27 we were issued ODs and given the ribbons, stars, and insignia we had earned. The next morning, November 28, 1945, I went through a little ceremony in which I received my Honorable Discharge from the U.S. Army. We went directly from the ceremony to a bus that was to take us to the train. Just before the bus that was to take us to the train, they had a card table set up, and as I passed, the sergeant in charge asked if I would like to join the Army Reserves. He said, "It's a chance to keep your rank." It took only a moment to say, "No thanks" before I boarded the bus.

The train ride from Camp Atterbury to Cleveland was slow as there were many stops to drop off soldiers. We finally arrived at the terminal in Cleveland where I was met by my mother, father, sister, her new baby, grandmother, and girlfriend, Barbara Harper. It was over. My dad drove us all home, and there we talked, had refreshments, and talked some more. My dad finally said he was going to bed and that I could use his car to take Barbara home. That was the first time in my life I had ever driven my dad's car. Perhaps change really is the rule of life.

Epilogue

It has been 50 years since I signed up for the draft, half a century. That's a lot of time. In that time I met, married, and lived with my wife, Janet, for over 45 years; helped raise two boys; earned a doctorate at the University of Cincinnati in political science; and worked full-time at two careers—one in the oil industry for a few years, which I disliked, and one as a university professor for many years, which I love. I have traveled and camped throughout the United States and made many trips to Europe, both East and West, that included stays as long as six and nine months. But never have I lived life in such a constant, protracted state of motion, new experiences, and intensity as the days I spent in the Army. There are months, perhaps years, I can't even remember when I worked in the oil industry. This was definitely not so in my career as a university professor. I wouldn't trade this lifestyle for anything. It has always been intellectually stimulating and personally rewarding to me and, I hope, to my students, wife, and all my family. But for sheer motion, experiences, and intensity of living over a protracted period, for living life where minutes not months are remembered, my life in the Army during World War II prevails over the other periods.

Shortly after my discharge in December 1945, my father invited me to attend a meeting of the American Legion. I went to the dinner meeting with him and my uncle, Harold Van Schoor. That was the one and only contact I ever had with a veterans' group. I have absolutely nothing against them. I recognize the social benefits of membership, the political power they wield, and the good they do for veterans and their families, but I've never been a joiner, and I dislike meetings—all kinds.

Furthermore, I have never established or maintained any postwar ties with anyone from my training battalion or my regular outfit. I think this rather strange. Frankly, I did feel some bonding with the men in the training battalion, but I never felt or thought of our medical detachment as a cohesive unit. My only effort to contact anyone was prompted by these memoirs. On December 19, 1988, a few days after I finished the first draft of this book, I called John Survill in New Jersey, 43 years after I last saw him in California on November 21, 1945. He sounded the same on the telephone, and he said I did also. Perhaps it was a combination of finishing the writing, Christmas, and the desire or need to hear a voice from the past. We had a nice conversation.

Military life was a learning experience for me. I learned something about the world we live in, its geography, people, and cultures. I learned something about human nature and psychology and in so doing learned something about myself as an individual and the values, beliefs, and attitudes that shape my behavior.

And I learned some things about human relationships — about power, authority, freedom, and equality. I also learned a few "lessons for life" in the Army that have helped me throughout my life, lessons such as the importance of *time* as a precious commodity (it's so easy to waste); the importance of not taking life too seriously (I have to keep relearning this); the importance of self-discipline and accepting responsibility for one's actions (it's all too easy to blame one's misfortunes on external circumstances); and the importance of being a part of a group — a family, church, university, social club — anything.

Military life was a passage for me, a turning point in my life and in some sense a transition period. It changed me psychologically and socially. I learned the meaning and the value of freedom, of control over my own life when I had little. And my trip on the *Mormacport* taught me the value of fundamental human equality through gross privilege and inequality for some at the expense of others. Further, my involvement in some meaningless activities in the Army sensitized me to the possibilities that might exist in meaningful work. Finally, I saw little of heroism or cowardice in the Army. What I saw was men doing their duty, simply acting in a responsible manner, sometimes in difficult circumstances. Soldiers put up with a lot just to "get along" with the other men in their outfit. If I have a "clearer perception and livelier impression" of these values today (freedom, human equality, the importance of work, and duty or responsible conduct), then part of the credit rightfully belongs to my experience in the Army.

In August 1990, my wife, Janet, and I went back to Kauai. It was my first visit to the island since the fall of 1944. We went up to Kalaheo so I could show her the town and the area where we were based while in rest camp. We stopped in the Community Center, and I asked one of the older citizens where the former USO was located. The women pointed across the street and said, "Right over there." I asked if she knew Betty Shimogawa. She said she did, but that Betty's married name was Ihara and that she managed the appliance business now located in the old USO building.

The next day, Janet and I went to the shop, walked in, and saw a woman sitting at the desk. I said, "I'm looking for Betty Shimogawa." She said, "That's me. How do you know my maiden name?" That was it. We began talking and didn't stop for three hours. She took us out for lunch and later invited us to join her at a big Hawaiian wedding and luau held at a resort near the Fern Grotto on the Wailua River. Janet and I had expected to spend an hour or so with Betty. Instead, we spent the day and found a new friend. It was the high point of the trip — all due to the kindness and hospitality one woman, Mrs. Mitsuyo Shimogawa, extended to a lonely soldier almost a half century ago.

So I bring these memoirs to a close. It has been a marvelous therapy for me, and my good wife need never again listen to any "war stories." But I think that there is one circumstance where the old war stories will reappear for a few more years.

Let me explain. Each winter Janet and I go to Florida, Anna Maria Island. There we have a circle of friends, all "aged" — 65 and over. We have frequent little parties from 5:00P.M. to 6:30P.M. to talk and socialize, but sometimes the men end up on one side of the room and the women on the other. When this happens, often the talk turns, somehow, to a story about World War II. Then, as in Shakespeare's *Henry the Fifth*, when the king spoke to his troops on the eve of the battle of Agincourt, all listen as the storyteller for the evening recalls a particular incident in his military life and "what feats he did that day."

Appendixes

Appendix C: Registration Certificate and Notice of Classification

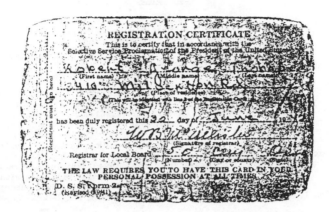

NOTICE TO RECRUITING SERVICES

Local Board No. 50
Cuyahoga County

NOV 20 1942
(Local Board Stamp)
City Hall—Shaker Heights
Cleveland, Ohio

53
035
050

This is to certify that:

Robert George Thobaben
(First Name)   (Middle Name)   (Last Name)

3413 Wilverton Rd Shaker Hts Cuyahoga Co Ohio
(Place of residence as shown on line 2 of his Registration Card Form 1)

has been classified by this local board in accordance with Selective Service Regulations but without physical examination and has been placed in Class 1-A, available for general military service, and will not be ordered to report for induction for a period of 1 week from date hereof.

David Andrew, Chairman

By W B McCallister
(Signature)-in-fact   (Title)

Note to Recruiting Officers: This form must be attached to Enlistment Record.

DSS Form 190.

Appendix D: Orders to Report for Active Duty

RESTRICTED

WAR DEPARTMENT
Army Service Forces
Headquarters, Fifth Service Command
Fort Hayes, Columbus, Ohio

13 May 1943

Special Orders
No. 113   E X T R A C T

100. Each of the following named Privates, members of the ERC Unasgd, is ordered to active duty. Each will proceed at his own expense from his home to Armed Force Induction Station, 1250 Ontario Street, Cleveland, Ohio, to arrive thereat not later than 31 May 1943, reporting upon arrival to the CO for physical examination and under the provisions of paragraph 53, AR 150-5, 30 September 1931 be reimbursed at the rate of 5¢ per mile. Upon completion of physical examination each will be included in the daily shipment to the Reception Center for processing and assignment to an appropriate Replacement Training Center of the Army Ground Forces or Army Service Forces. Each reservist will take with him to the Reception Center a transcript of his college academic and ROTC records for presentation to the Classification Officer. TDN. FD 31 P 431-02 A 0425-23.

Thomas J Ansbro, 15131333, 18871 Naumann Ave, Euclid, Ohio.
Warren H Corrigan, 15133099, 3924 Riveredge Rd, SW, Cleveland, Ohio.
Herbert W Hanousek, 15359056, 3541 Pennington Rd, Shaker Hts, Ohio.
William R Mapes, 12214497, 3275 Glencairn Rd, Cleveland, Ohio.
Carmelo F Nicolosi, 15358905, 3312 E 145th St, Cleveland, Ohio.
Robert N Pritchard, 15358925, 1842 Beersford, E Cleveland, Ohio.
Herbert F Ross, 15358774, 4073 Conover Rd, University Hts, Ohio.
David Spoar, 15132890, 957 Linn Dr, Cleveland, Ohio.
Charles C Svec, Jr, 15358718, 5111 Anthony St, Maple Hts, Ohio.
Leonard R Szymanski, 15133038, 278 E Lucius Ave, Youngstown, Ohio.
Marvin S Terlitz, 15133014, 12699 Cedar Rd, Cleveland Hts, Ohio.
Robert G Thobaben, 15311634, 3413 Milverton Rd, Shaker Hts, Ohio.
Kingsley P Thompson, 15358854, 1780 Delmont Ave, E Cleveland, Ohio.
Walter W Urnetz, Jr, 15358850, 6131 Stanbury, Parma, Ohio.
William B Ward, 15358849, 2288 Westminster Rd, Cleveland, Ohio.
Nicholas J Zuzolo, 15132242, 617 Spring St, Niles, Ohio.
   (Auth: WD Memo No. W150-1-43, dated 1/27/43.)

101. Each of the following named Privates, members of the ERC Unasgd, is ordered to active duty. Each will proceed at his own expense from his home to Armed Force Induction Station, 424 East Fourth Street, Cincinnati, Ohio, to arrive thereat not later than 31 May 1943, reporting upon arrival to the CO for physical examination and under the provisions of paragraph 53, AR 150-5, 30 September 1931. be reimbursed at the rate of 5¢ per mile. Upon completion of physical examination each will be included in the daily shipment to the Reception Center for processing and assignment to an appropriate Replacement Training Center of the Army Ground Forces or Army Service Forces. Each reservist will take with him to the Reception Center a transcript of his college academic and ROTC records for presentation to the Classification Officer. TDN. FD 31 P 431-02 A 0425-23.

Thomas R Allgeyer, 15399027, 530 Church St, Ludlow, Ky.
John R Beck, 15317275, 658 Nelson Pl, Newport, Ky.
Herbert T Behlen, 15317203, 3851 St Lawrence Ave, Cincinnati, Ohio.
Carl F Brock, 15317084, 579 Carlisle St, Cincinnati, Ohio.
John W Cappel, 15317330, 4525 Floral Ave, Norwood, Ohio.
Lucien Farley, 15317064, 1120 Jefferson Ave, Glendale, Ohio.

RESTRICTED

HEADQUARTERS FIFTH SERVICE COMMAND
Army Service Forces
Fort Hayes, Columbus, Ohio

MEMORANDUM: Instructions for Enlisted Reservists called to active duty.

1. It is essential that you bring with you all copies of these orders when reporting for active duty.

2. Attached hereto are orders calling you to active duty with the Army of the United States and directing that you report to the Commanding Officer at the Reception Center indicated on the date designated.

3. TRANSPORTATION

You will be reimbursed for travel from your home to the Reception Center at the rate of five cents per mile upon reporting at Reception Center.

4. CLOTHING

If you are being called directly from civilian life without prior service, it is advised that you take only sufficient civilian clothing necessary for the trip inasmuch as all civilian clothing will be returned to your home upon issuance of uniform.

If you were formerly in the service and are being recalled to active duty, all articles of clothing retained by you upon your release from active duty now in your possession will be taken with you to the Reception Center.

5. It is highly inadvisable to travel by automobile, because it may be necessary to abandon your automobile upon change of station, due to the difficulties of obtaining tire repairs and additional gasoline rations.

N O T I C E

ARRANGE TO LEAVE YOUR HOME AT SUCH TIME TO ENABLE YOU TO REPORT AT RECEPTION CENTER INDICATED BY 12 O'CLOCK NOON ON EFFECTIVE DATE OF YOUR ORDERS.

HEADQUARTERS FIFTH SERVICE COMMAND
ARMY SERVICE FORCES
FORT HAYES, COLUMBUS, OHIO

ERC, Unasgd
SPKER 201- Thobaben, Robert G.   May 18, 1943

Subject: Change of Active Duty Reporting Date.

To   :   Robert G. Thobaben,
            3413 Milverton Road,
            Shaker Heights, Ohio.

        1. Special Orders issued by this headquarters, ordering
you to report for active duty on May 31, 1943, are being, or have
been mailed to you. These orders direct you to report to an Armed
Force Induction Station, specified in the orders, on May 31, 1943.

        2. These orders are being amended to change the report-
ing date to June 1, 1943.

        3. You are, therefore, directed to report to the Armed
Force Induction Station named in your orders on June 1, 1943 instead of May 31, 1943. All other directions in the orders apply
except for the above change in reporting date.

            By command of Major .General WALLACE:

                              N. H. SHORTRIDGE,
                              Captain, F. A.,
                              Asst. to C. of Mil. Pers. Br.

Appendix E: Berthing Space and Troop Mess Ticket (West Point)

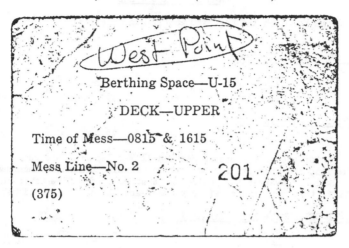

Berthing Space—U-15

DECK—UPPER

Time of Mess—0815 & 1615

Mess Line—No. 2

(375)   201

1		3		5	6	7
1	2	3		5	6	7
1	2	3		5	6	7

	9	10	11	12	13	14
8	9	10	11	12	13	14
8	9	10	11	12	13	14

TROOP MESS TICKET

Robert C. Thebaben   Pvt   15 311634   9433

(Name)   (Rate)   (Serial No.)   (Unit)

No meals served without this card. Use of card issued to another will result in disciplinary action.

Robert C. Thebaben   111th Inf. Hq. Co.

(Holder's Signature)   (CO of Troops)

15	16	17	18	19	20	21
15	16	17	18	19	20	21
15	16	17	18	19	20	21

22	23	24	25	26	27	28
22	23	24	25	26	27	28
22	23	24	25	26	27	28

Appendix F: Award of Medical Badge

<u>R E S T R I C T E D</u>

(Par 1 GO 17 Hq 111th Inf Regt APO 265 12 Jun 45 contd)

<u>IN COMPANY L 111TH INFANTRY</u>

RANK	NAME	ASN	EFF DATE
Pvt	Bernard C Keeley	39 711 121	9 May 45

<u>IN COMPANY M 111TH INFANTRY</u>

Pfc	Raymond Cuesta	32 240 482	9 May 45

2. Under the provisions of Section II War Department Circular 66,
1 March 1945, and upon the recommendation of unit commander concerned, the
Medical Badge is awarded the following personnel, effective dates indicated,
for satisfactory performance of duty under actual combat conditions:

<u>IN MEDICAL DETACHMENT 111TH INFANTRY</u>

RANK	NAME	ASN	EFF DATE
CAPT	JULES J HOROWITZ	O 471 901	5 Feb 44
CAPT	VINCENT R SCHETTINI	O 305 504	26 Mar 45
CAPT	ROBERT A DEMO	O 422 816	18 Dec 43
CAPT	IRVING W KRAMER	O1 689 774	18 Dec 43
1ST LT	DAVID T DRESDALE	O 474 656	5 Feb 44
2D LT	CLINTON L GAMMON	O2 047 323	8 May 45
S Sgt	Robert M Peters	20 308 292	5 Feb 44
S Sgt	Arthur A Neumann	36 028 538	18 Dec 43
Tec 3	James E MacDonald	20 307 620	5 Feb 44
Tec 3	John J Puhy	20 318 752	5 Feb 44
Tec 3	John F Ryan	20 307 600	8 May 45
Tec 3	John E Henrickson	36 028 530	18 Dec 43
Tec 3	Leslie A Waeltz	36 077 134	18 Dec 43
Tec 4	William J Calbreath	36 077 091	31 Jan 44
Tec 4	John N Stevenson	36 027 911	5 Feb 44
Tec 4	Leon Zibelman	20 307 629	5 Feb 44
Tec 4	Robert E Jones	35 575 493	8 May 45
Tec 4	Henry E Weber	33 022 441	8 May 45
Tec 4	Charles L Lott	33 023 621	18 Dec 43
Tec 4	Maxwell R McClain	33 016 321	18 Dec 43
Tec 4	Edwin Olejniczak	36 014 916	18 Dec 43
Cpl	John D Clifford	36 077 058	31 Jan 44
Cpl	Sidney Williamson	33 016 316	8 May 45
Cpl	Sam J Petrone	36 014 905	18 Dec 43
Tec 5	Willie F Ham	35 459 660	31 Jan 44
Tec 5	Carl W Barg	36 077 072	31 Jan 44
Tec 5	John C Lauersdorf	35 526 679	5 Feb 44
Tec 5	Edward Solovitz	20 307 603	1 Feb 44
Tec 5	Edward J Tierney	20 307 641	1 Feb 44
Tec 5	Daniel B Waltz	33 011 623	2 Feb 44
Tec 5	Samuel R Buchanan	20 319 030	26 Mar 45
Tec 5	William J Schwankoff	36 023 059	8 May 45

R E S T R I C T E D

(Par 2 GO 17 Hq 111th Inf Regt APO 265 12 Jun 45 contd)

IN MEDICAL DETACHMENT 111TH INFANTRY (CONTD)

RANK	NAME	ASN	EFF DATE
Pvt	Henry J Frey	13 058 113	18 Dec 43
Pvt	Paul E Hauessler	31 167 987	18 Dec 43
Pvt	Robert K Leonard	12 127 927	18 Dec 43
Pvt	James C Owens	38 283 605	18 Dec 43
Pvt	Julian A Roebuck	34 002 944	18 Dec 43
Pvt	Wilbur E Schafer	33 033 968	18 Dec 43
Pvt	John J Survill	32 922 999	18 Dec 43
Pvt	Robert G Thobaben	15 311 634	18 Dec 43

BY ORDER OF LT COLONEL KEMP:

O F F I C I A L:

J F MOWERY
1st Lt 111th Inf
Adj

J F MOWERY
1st Lt 111th Inf
Adj

DISTRIBUTION:
B
Plus 3— TAG
Awards & Decoration Br

R E S T R I C T E D

—4—

Appendix G: Letter from Colonel Ayers, 111th Infantry

HEADQUARTERS 111th INFANTRY REGIMENT
ABOARD USS OSMER APA 40

17 November 1945

TO: The Members of the 111th Infantry, 48th Coast Artillery
      Battalion, 819th Tank Destroyer Battalion, and Attached
      Troops of the 1111th Army Garrison Force, APO 265

We are now approaching the shores of the Continental United States. The
Regiment is designated for inactivation. Before we are dispersed to separation
centers I feel that I should extend to you men who have been serving in, and in
close association with, the Regiment during the period we have spent in the
Palaus, my heartfelt appreciation for the fine work you have done there. Every
job that you have been given has been performed in a superior manner. This
could not have been accomplished without the highest degree of loyalty and co-
operation on the parts of all of you, both commissioned and enlisted. We landed on a recently secured island, where conditions of sanitation, shelter, and
security left much to be desired and stupendous tasks to be performed. When we
left the Islands, after a period of nine months occupancy, the living conditions
which we had established were, in my opinion, superior to those to be found on
any other islands in the Pacific Combat Areas. Through unceasing effort you had
erected Quonset housing and mess facilities, policed all areas, established Headquarters, aid stations, supply and sanitation facilities; all this while engaged
concurrently on reconnaissance, combat patrol, island sweeps, and security missions. In the latter two months the Third Battalion of the Regiment was engaged
in occupation and disarming operations in the recently surrendered, formerly
Japanese-held, islands in the Northern Palaus. Your performance of duty in all
phases rates the highest commendation. I hereby express that commendation.

On arrival in the States you will be scattered to the four winds. You
will return to your homes and loved ones as veterans of the Pacific War. You
will again take your places as civilian citizens of the greatest Nation in the
World. You will find some conditions not entirely to your liking. I adjure
you to maintain that same fixed purpose; to make the Nation the place you en-
vision it, to establish the better life we have fought for, and to win the
peace, that you have evidenced in winning the war.

I give you my best wishes for happiness and success in whatever endeavors
you may essay. Your actions, aspirations, and accomplishments in the years to
come will reflect as great credit on you as your determination and will-to-do
may warrant. Set your goal high, and hold as your slogan the old cry of the
Infantry, "Follow Me".

Sincerely,

R G AYERS
Colonel, 111th Infantry
Commanding

Appendix H: Honorable Discharge and Enlisted Record

Army of the United States

VOL 55 PAGE 718

RECEIVED FOR RECORD
DEC 5 - 1945
DONALD F. ....ER
COUNTY RECORDER
CUYAHOGA COUNTY, OHIO

Honorable Discharge

This is to certify that

ROBERT G THOBABEN   15 311 634   Private First Class

111th Infantry Medical Detachment

Army of the United States

is hereby Honorably Discharged from the military service of the United States of America.

This certificate is awarded as a testimonial of Honest and Faithful Service to this country.

Given at   Separation Center
Camp Atterbury Indiana

Date   28 November 1945

F. A. SCHLEUDER
MAJOR   C E

1. LAST NAME - FIRST NAME - MIDDLE INITIAL	2. ARMY SERIAL NO.	3. GRADE	4. ARM OR SERVICE	5. COMPONENT
Thobaben Robert G	15 311 634	Pfc	INF	ERC

6. ORGANIZATION	7. DATE OF SEPARATION	8. PLACE OF SEPARATION
111th Inf Med Dth	28 Nov 45	Sep. Center, Camp Atterbury, Ind.

9. PERMANENT ADDRESS FOR MAILING PURPOSES	10. DATE OF BIRTH	11. PLACE OF BIRTH
3413 Milverton Rd Shaker Hgts Cuyahoga Ohio	3 Apr 24	Cleveland Ohio

12. ADDRESS FROM WHICH EMPLOYMENT WILL BE SOUGHT	13. COLOR EYES	14. COLOR HAIR	15. HEIGHT	16. WEIGHT	17. NO. DEPEND.
See 9	hazel	brown	5' 10"	135 lbs.	None

18. RACE	19. MARITAL STATUS	20. U.S. CITIZEN	21. CIVILIAN OCCUPATION AND NO.
WHITE X NEGRO OTHER (specify)	SINGLE X MARRIED OTHER (specify)	YES X NO	Student College X-02

MILITARY HISTORY

22. DATE OF INDUCTION	23. DATE OF ENLISTMENT	24. DATE OF ENTRY INTO ACTIVE SERVICE	25. PLACE OF ENTRY INTO SERVICE
	12 Dec 42	1 June 43	Athens Ohio

SELECTIVE SERVICE DATA	26. REGISTERED YES / NO X	27. LOCAL S.S. BOARD NO.	28. COUNTY AND STATE	29. HOME ADDRESS AT TIME OF ENTRY INTO SERVICE
				See # 9

30. MILITARY OCCUPATIONAL SPECIALTY AND NO.	31. MILITARY QUALIFICATION AND DATE (i.e., infantry, aviation and marksmanship badges, etc.)
Litter Bearer 657	Combat Medical Badge

32. BATTLES AND CAMPAIGNS
Central Pacific   Eastern Mandates   Western Pacific

33. DECORATIONS AND CITATIONS
Asiatic-Pacific Theater Ribbon w/3 Bronze Stars   Good Conduct Ribbon World War II Victory Medal

34. WOUNDS RECEIVED IN ACTION
None

35. LATEST IMMUNIZATION DATES				36. SERVICE OUTSIDE CONTINENTAL U. S. AND RETURN			
SMALLPOX	TYPHOID	TETANUS	OTHER (specify)	DATE OF DEPARTURE	DESTINATION	DATE OF ARRIVAL	
2Jan45	14 Nov44	15Dec44	YF 16 Nov 43	8 Nov 43	Asiatic-Pacific	12 Nov43	
				14 Nov 45	USA	21 Nov 45	

37. TOTAL LENGTH OF SERVICE		CONTINENTAL SERVICE		FOREIGN SERVICE		38. HIGHEST GRADE HELD
YEARS	MONTHS	DAYS	YEARS	MONTHS	DAYS	
0	5	14	2	0	14	Pfc

FOR CONVENIENCE, A CERTIFICATE OF ELIGIBILITY NO. 74 05 8 [?] ISSUED BY [?] ADMINISTRATION TO BE USED FOR THE RIGHTS PROVIDED ANY ANNUITY OR INSURANCE BENEFIT UNDER TITLE III OF THE SERVICEMEN'S READJUSTMENT ACT OF 1944, AS AMENDED, THAT MAY BE AVAILABLE TO THE BEARER TO WHOM THIS SEPARATION PAPER WAS ISSUED.

39. PRIOR SERVICE
None

40. REASON AND AUTHORITY FOR SEPARATION
AR 615-365 Convn of Govt RR 1-1 Demobilization 15 Dec 44

41. SERVICE SCHOOLS ATTENDED	42. EDUCATION (Years)		
None	Grammar 8	High School 4	College 1

PAY DATA   You 8350

43. LONGEVITY FOR PAY PURPOSES			44. MUSTERING OUT PAY		45. SOLDIER DEPOSIT	46. TRAVEL PAY	47. TOTAL AMOUNT, NAME OF DISBURSING OFFICER
YEARS	MONTHS	DAYS	TOTAL	THIS PAYMENT			
2	11	17	$300	$100	None	$16.25	147.04 H.F. GILLIE, CAPT. F.D.

INSURANCE NOTICE

IMPORTANT   IF PREMIUM IS NOT PAID WHEN DUE OR WITHIN THIRTY-ONE DAYS THEREAFTER, INSURANCE WILL LAPSE. MAKE CHECKS OR MONEY ORDERS PAYABLE TO THE TREASURER OF THE U. S. AND FORWARD TO COLLECTIONS SUBDIVISION, VETERANS ADMINISTRATION, WASHINGTON 25, D. C.

48. KIND OF INSURANCE	49. HOW PAID	50. Effective Date of Allotment Discontinuance	51. Date of Next Premium Due (One month after 50)	52. PREMIUM DUE EACH MONTH	53. INTENTION OF VETERAN TO
Nat. Serv. X U.S. Govt. None	Allotment Direct to V.A. X	30 Nov 45	31 Dec 45	$6.50	Continue X Continue Only Discontinue

54.	55. REMARKS (This space for completion of above items or entry of other items specified in W. D. Directives)
RIGHT THUMB PRINT	No DAYS LOST UNDER AW .107 ASR SCORE 2 SEPT 45 64 LAPEL BUTTON ISSUED Inactive Serive in ERC from 12 Dec 42 Thru 31 May 43

56. SIGNATURE OF PERSON BEING SEPARATED	57. PERSONNEL OFFICER (Type name, grade and organization / signature)
Robert G. Thobaben	L M REDDING 1st Lt AC

WD AGO FORM 53 55
1 November 1944

This form supersedes all previous editions of WD AGO Forms 53 and 55 for enlisted persons entitled to an Honorable Discharge, which will not be used after receipt of this revision

OHIO WORLD WAR II   CLAIM   336171
COMPENSATION APPLIED FOR   NO.

Sources

Four sources provide the data for this memoir: letters mailed home, a diary, photographs, and my memory. From June 1, 1943, to November 28, 1945, I wrote 191 letters to my parents and my sister. Though I didn't know it, my mother saved them all, even numbered them for me. The diary runs from November 7, 1943, to November 8, 1944. I started it the day we left the United States and quit a year later. It had simply become too tiresome to keep it up. (Now, of course, I wish I had been more diligent.) My camera took 127 film, which produced very small prints by today's standards. But I sent these photographs home in my letters from time to time, and again my mother saved them for me. She even put each one in a photo album and labeled most of them. Finally, I have relied on my own memory of events during this two-and-a-half-year period.

Forty-seven years have passed since my discharge. In that time my marriage, foreign travel, education, and career (a university professor of political science) have affected my understanding of World War II and my role in that conflict. This is not an apology. It is a fact. One stage of my life ended in November of 1945, but another began.

The solitary goal of this story is to relate, with as much honesty as I can muster, the rites of passage, psychological and social, of a young soldier. It was a time when I lived life at a high level of intensity, the turning point in my life. I remember many specific days, hours, and even minutes during this period. Then there are times when only the letters, pictures, and diary provide continuity. It was exciting. It was a transition. I did and saw a thousand things—all telescoped into one short period (although it seemed very long at the time). I wouldn't want to do it again. I wouldn't give up the experience for anything.

Index